# THE ANARCHIST PAPERS

# THE ANARCHIST PAPERS

Dimitrios Roussopoulos, editor

BLACK
ROSE
BOOKS

Montréal/New York/London

Black Rose Books No. EE302
Hardcover ISBN: 1-55164-181-X (bound)
Paperback ISBN: 1-55164-180-1 (pbk.)

Canadian Cataloguing in Publication Data
Main entry under title:
The Anarchist papers
Rev. ed.

Includes bibliographical references.
Hardcover ISBN: 1-55164-181-X (bound)
Paperback ISBN: 1-55164-180-1 (pbk.)

1. Anarchism.  I. Roussopoulos, Dimitrios I.

HX833.A53 2001     320.5'7     C00-901405-5

C.P. 1258
Succ. Place du Parc
Montréal, H2W 2R3
Canada

2250 Military Road
Tonawanda, NY
14150
USA

99 Wallis Road
London, E9 5LN
England
UK

To order books:

In Canada: (phone) 1-800-565-9523 (fax) 1-800-221-9985
email: utpbooks@utpress.utoronto.ca

In United States: (phone) 1-800-283-3572  (fax)  1-651-917-6406

In the UK & Europe: (phone) London 44 (0)20 8986-4854 (fax) 44 (0)20 8533-5821
email: order@centralbooks.com

Our Web Site address: http://www.web.net/blackrosebooks

A publication of the Institute of Policy Alternatives of Montréal (IPAM)

Printed in Canada

The Canada Council | Le Conseil des Arts
for the Arts | du Canada

# CONTENTS

We know that in politics there is no useful and honest practice possible without a theory and a clearly determined goal. Otherwise, inspired as we are with the largest and most liberal feelings, we might end up with a reality diametrically opposite to those feelings: we might begin with convictions that are republican, democratic, and socialist — and finish as Bismarckians or as Bonapartists.

*—Michael Bakunin*
*Federalism, Socialism, and Anti-Theologism, 1867*

# INTRODUCTION
## Dimitrios Roussopoulos

All the essays included in this book were published in the journal *Our Generation**(1961–1994) except for the material on the "Showdown in Seattle: A Renewal?" which took place in the fall of 1999. This event brought wide-spread attention to a new generation picking up the fruit from the field the previous generation had sown. A thirty-year cycle is once more repeating itself. The militant social, political, economic, and cultural activism of the late 1920s and 1930s was re-born in the late 1950s and 1960s. And now again, in the late 1990s and into the 2000s a new thirty year cycle of radical activism is upon us.

Do these cycles have an accumulative effect? Can one generation learn deeply enough from the previous generations of radicals to not only avoid the mistakes but also build solidly on the concrete experiences of the past? Given the volume of recorded material on past experiences it is certainly more likely that this cycle will go further. As history is being made again we have to also continue to evaluate what has already been accomplished. To this end, this book is a contribution.

### *Our Generation's* Place in History
When *Our Generation* was founded in the fall of 1961 it was a journal devoted to the research, theory and review of the all important question of world peace, presenting alternative solutions to human conflict, eliminating war as a way of life. In our statement of purpose we quoted William James: "What we now need to discover in the social realm is the moral equivalent to war; something heroic that will speak to men as universally as war does, and yet will be compatible with their spiritual selves as war has proven itself to be incompatible." The statement went on to add, "This must be the ethic of our generation, the goal, if our lives are to be meaningful. To this direction our journal is dedicated. It

*See listings of *Our Generation* on the website www.web.net/blackrosebooks. Some back issues are still available. The first edition of *The Anarchist Papers* sold out and was followed by *The Anarchist Papers 2*, and, *The Anarchist Papers 3*. Included in this series are *The Radical Papers* (see end of this book for details). All contain some of the best articles published in *Our Generation*.

requires a re-examination of our present social structure, our thoughts, our economic interaction, our ethics." For the next several years we published informative and analytical material that aimed to generate and enrich the *politics of protest.*

By 1963, we noted that the new peace movement had exhausted traditional means of protest, and so we began publishing material that both reflected and encouraged the *politics of resistance.* The movement was analyzed as a social movement in the tradition of previous movements. How its goals were to be achieved became as important to *Our Generation* as the objectives themselves. During that year the editors clearly questioned classical insurrectionary change and determined that it appeared to be excluded from our type of society. What was needed was a majoritarian and horizontal social transformation that minimized violence. Two issues of the journal were thus devoted to a study of revolutionary non-violence as a philosophy of change and the building of a type of movement in which it would be assured that power rests at the base.

By 1966, the journal turned its attention to the *politics of institutional change.* Social change was put on the agenda by the student new left. Called participatory democracy, the kind of social change advocated questioned traditional class analysis and opened a new investigation of how we were to move toward a classless and warless world in a society of advanced capitalism. Of continued interest for us was the ongoing assessment of 'the new movement and its theory of organization' — as a supplement in a 1968 issue was called in response to C. George Benello's important study of a libertarian sociology of organization, *Wasteland Culture: Notes on Structure, Restructuring and Strategy for Social Change.*

In the spring of 1969, the journal published a substantial critique of social democracy and offered as an alternative perspective the concept of an extra-parliamentary opposition as a congruence for movements for radical social change. The fall 1971 issue saw the publication of various articles on the city and urbanization which attempted to place the new politics within a meaningful geo-political space. In the same issue we published Murray Bookchin's seminal piece *Toward a Liberatory Technology,* which gave a real grounding to calls for decentralization in highly industrialized societies.

In the years that followed, an ongoing analysis of structural and material trends in our society were studied and the results published alongside a critical assessment of new social movements such as women's liberation and the ecology movement. During this entire history our underlying motive was that of trying to ascertain how humanity could avoid international conflict, especially a third world war.

The readership of *Our Generation* changed through the years, although there was a steady group who supported its evolution of ideas. Those who hold State power over us also took note of this development.

On June 15, 1971, the Solicitor-General of Canada, Jean-Pierre Goyer, wrote a worried letter to his Cabinet colleagues referring to a report from the 'Security Service' warning about the dangers of an extraparliamentary opposition which seeks the "creation of counter or parallel institutions within society but opposed to it and to the electoral process." The letter noted that the theoretical reference for this extra-parliamentary opposition was the journal *Our Generation*.

What this politician and State official was worried about was the existence of social movements that were not only critical of representative or parliamentary democracy and political parties, but that offered a different notion of society that was authentic: local, decentralized and participatory. This kind of social and political arrangement would not only challenge the centralization of political and economic power but would encourage popular intervention in areas considered the exclusive prerogative of the State on an ongoing basis.

Every social and political revolution since that of 1789 had both a democratic and libertarian dynamic at its heart. Pushing up from below were social movements not satisfied with 'representation only' and periodic elections to gain consent and give the State legitimacy. These social forces sought direct involvement in the decision-making process. They sought to control the politics of daily life through communal and workplace self-management. In a word, they sought direct democracy, not one mediated through representatives. This kind of power by people has always worried not only liberals like Mr. Goyer but also those to his political right and left.

The 1960s was a decade which also reflected this "democratic" vs. libertarian dynamic. This reflection began for some of us when we sought to directly participate in questions of foreign and defence policy, two of the most restricted and closely guarded domains of the central State. During the early part of this decade this reflection was further refined by such political philosophers as Hannah Arendt, author of the important study *On Revolution*. In this work she suggested that the natural outgrowth of revolutions has been the localist council system of self-government as the most authentic expression of popular objectives; that these communal forms may provide the pattern for a new kind of politics based on the power of cooperation between local units, and so ensures political freedom. Hannah Arendt, who had become well-known for her studies of totalitarianism, pointed out that the council, the organ of participation, has been totally neglected by the political party, the organ of representation, which developed at the same time. *On Revolution* developed a theory of a radical alternative to existing parliamentary politics: direct democracy at the local level, and federation at the regional and national levels.

For us this also meant that a country's external relations with other countries were no mere reflection of a declared public philosophy but rather reflected the prevailing values of dominant institutions. These promoted a formal, consenting and passive form of democracy. A democracy of participation, on the other hand, sought new social forms of local or community control through which the powerless can act. Unconsciously, the generation of the 1960s, as well as that of the 1970s, picked up the longstanding libertarian dynamic that Arendt, Bookchin, Goodman, Woodcock and others had detected in the historical upheavals of the past.

This cry for democratization and participation had wide repercussions. In May 1975, the Trilateral Commission's *Report of the Trilateral Task Force on the Governability of Democracies* was made public. Several features of the original unpublished version of this Report are noteworthy. Pessimism and authoritarianism pervade the document, specifically Prof. Samuel P. Huntington's section on America, called "The democratic surge of the 1960s: a challenge to all existing authority systems." As more people became involved in public affairs, according to Huntington, their disappointment was inevitable, given the unresponsiveness of certain political institutions.

The result was a rapid decline in the belief that the State and its supporting agencies were neutral. There was also an accompanying disenchantment with political parties. The Report concluded that if the system was to correct itself, this "excess of democracy" must be reduced. It argued for an emphasis on the fact that the "arenas where democratic procedures are appropriate are limited." Since the functioning of the system requires "some measure of apathy and noninvolvement" active citizens and groups should be cooled out.

The recommendations included: more economic planning because an increase in average income encourages political apathy; stronger political leadership (read centralization of political power); government aid to political parties and financing of elections; restrictions on the freedom of the press, e.g., "...there is also the need to assure to the government the right and the ability to withhold information at the source"; cutbacks in education because the democratization of education has raised expectations; alienation attacked at its roots, therefore "a more active intervention in the area of work." Experiences in the co-management of the workplace are rejected in favour of State aid for experimentation with new forms of work organization.

During the decade of the 1970s, notwithstanding the attempt of the mass media to convince us that the movement was dead, feminists founded the women's liberation movement, environmentalists founded the ecology movement, and citizen groups sprang up in various urban centres to fight not only for better housing and green spaces, but also for community control. Among the more radical of these movements the question of social change, decentralization and participation surfaced, spilling over into an ongoing debate and experimentation.

The early 1980s witnessed a renewed and much more powerful peace movement. June 1982 witnessed one million demonstrators in the streets of New York City. Initiated by the *politics of protest*, it moved into the *politics of resistance* in several countries, notably Britain and West Germany. Once again, this social movement (often a point of convergence for the movements of the 1960s and 1970s facing the inflexibility of the nuclear State), begun not only to question the legitimacy of the system but also to act outside the parliamentary order through the use of civil disobedience.

It was no mere coincidence that in Britain, the birthplace of parliamentary democracy, we saw civil disobedience through peace camps, largely organized by women, using this new method of resistance. Alongside this campaign we also saw a consciousness moving towards the *politics of institutional change* in the form of *local socialism* — that is, a form of socialism favouring a re-definition of the role of the municipality and all major questions facing citizens, including ecology, war and peace. It was, as well, no mere coincidence that in West Germany, a society with a highly authoritarian past, the massive anti-nuclear power movement of the 1970s which began in the countryside and which stressed the importance of regionalization and decentralization, moved from the politics of protest and resistance to that of institutional change as embodied by the Greens, who combine ecology, feminism and pacifism. In these situations and others, class-based insurrectionalism, led by vanguard political parties, had been shunned.

Almost all of these and related ideas are in substance part of the libertarian socialist and anarchist tradition. It was the purpose of *Our Generation* to help make this movement *self-conscious* of its theoretical and practical past, present and potential future.

We had planned that the March 1984 issue would be our last. Some of us had become dissatisfied with the journal's content and orientation. Others wanted to undertake new work. Our managing editor felt no longer able to undertake a role she had shouldered as a volunteer for many years. And, as always, financing was precarious. But when rumours started to circulate that *Our Generation* had 'folded,' people were 'shocked' and 'disappointed.' We faced an international situation at an all-time low, with the emergence of an organized and ideological Right-wing in the United States, Canada and Britain, on the one hand, and a disquieting confusion in the anti-authoritarian/libertarian movement, on the other. An urgent need to help clarify the perspectives of the new social movements of the 1980s was evident. Our readers wanted the journal to continue. We agreed to do so, but in a renewed form, and for the next ten years, we published a journal with an international focus, and circulation, within an explicitly libertarian socialist and anarchist framework.

The winter of 1994, saw the last issue of *Our Generation*. Having founded the journal in 1961 and having worked continuously at publishing it for thirty-three years, it was time to adapt to new conditions. The era of journals with influence was coming to an end. Intellectual action was to be found more in the field of books and on the Internet. So with Volume 24, Number 2, we ceased to publish. At the time of the last issue the editorial board consisted of Martha Ackelsberg, C.George Benello (1927-1987), Martin Blatt, L.Susan Brown, Noam Chomsky, John P.Clark, Yolande Cohen, Claire Culhane, Jean-Pierre Deslauriers, David G. Gil, David Goodway, J.Frank Harrison, Lucia Kowaluk, Nicole Laurin-Frenette, Myrna Margulies Brietbart, Robert Mayo, Pat Murtagh, Graeme Nicholson, Carlos P.Otero, Alan Ritter, George Salzman, Stephen Schecter, Thomas W. Simon, Joel Spring, A.Gary Webster, George Woodcock, and myself, Dimitrios Roussopoulos, as general editor.

### The Present Volume

The essays in this volume by Murray Bookchin, Chris Southcott and Jorgen Pedersen, Frank Harrison, George Woodcock, and Cornelius Castoriadis all appeared in *Our Generation*, Volume 16, Numbers 3, and 4, published during the Spring/Summer of 1985.

It is appropriate, therefore, to begin with an essay by Murray Bookchin. What was being called for was the *creation of politics*. The communitarian emphasis of anarchism had been pushed aside by anarcho-syndicalism. If a perspective that takes into account the true nature of contemporary capitalism can help attain fundamental and qualitative social change, then a libertarian politics in the classical meaning of the word 'politics' had to be placed on the agenda. Politics in this sense is defined not as parliamentarism or Statecraft or party 'politics,' but the management of our affairs as citizens in communities, in the city. After several decades of writing critical studies of historical and contemporary issues, Bookchin initiated this long-awaited and much needed movement-building perspective.

Chris Southcott and Jorgen Pedersen assess the Greens. Much had appeared in the liberal and Left-wing press that attempted to dismiss *Die Gruen* as a temporary aberration or a throw-back to the past. The authors clarified an important aspect of the critique against the Greens. No other political organization had a programme for change which attempted such a bold synthesis of important social issues. The Greens were in many ways a convergence of the new social movements of the 1960s to the 1980s.

To understand different kinds of human domination we must be able to assess how power functions in different societies. Frank Harrison shows that opinion in Canadian society, for instance — one of the most liberal democracies — was kept within the relatively narrow confines of the freedom to consent. Harrison warned us to be alert to the machinations of the State, which nibble away at civil liberties. Anarchism is suggested as a multifaceted critique of all forms of repression.

What is progress to liberals and socialists is not progress to anarchists. This distinction is made by George Woodcock in his examination of Paul Goodman. Woodcock's, and Goodman's, view of anarchism is traditional in that it seeks to preserve the best of the past, and aristocratic, in that quality is sought. This perspective enriches everyday life, nourishing what is left of the natural in human living.

Cornelius Castoriadis was part of a generation of intellectuals who left Marxism to become a libertarian socialist. *The Fate of Marxism* is an example of a relentless and rigorous logic taken to its logical consequence. Castoriadis undertook an exhaustive study of the Russian revolution, rejecting Leninism or Bolshevism, but the process of critique did not end there, he went on to reject Marxism as such. What many still hold onto, however, is the Marxist 'method,' and here Castoriadis is at his most insightful.

The essays by Noam Chomsky, Graham Baugh, Thomas W. Simon, Alice Wexler, and Marsha Hewitt all appeared in *Our Generation*, Volume 17, Number 1, published during the Fall/Winter of 1985-86.

In one of Noam Chomsky's classic essays, he analyzes the contractions underlining the American annual celebration of 'Columbus Day,' where Columbus is honoured without recalling the slaughtered, decimated and dispersed indigenous people and culture upon which the USA was built. The estimates, at the time of the writing of this essay, suggested that some 20 million indigenous people were killed in Latin America and some 12-15 million north of the Rio Grande. Written during the Reagan years in the White House, it sweeps through a number of other contradictions that had been kept away from the public view.

In a seminal and lucid critique, Graham Baugh reviewed the influential book by Robert Paul Wolff, *In Defense of Anarchism*. In the essay, Baugh comes to grips with Wolff's ethical theory upon which his book is based. Originally published in 1970, the book introduced many readers to an anarchist consideration.

Thomas W. Simon, in an essay with much panache, defends utopian dreaming by crisscrossing the lines between environmentalism, feminism, and anarchism. More specifically Simon writes about 'eutopian' writing as in the works of Callenbach, Piercy, and LeGruin.

Alice Wexler was a pioneer among a new generation of scholars and writers that gave serious contemporary attention to Emma Goldman. Her work entitled *Emma Goldman: An Intimate Life* was based on new research materials that added new dimensions to the life and influence of the famous anarchist. Marsha Hewitt confronts the question of feminist separatism, and in doing so draws on the insights of Emma Goldman and what she attempted to do while building an emancipatory movement where women's rights were to be central.

The section entitled 'Showdown in Seattle' is published here, in a book, for the first time. It was an event that witnessed the public emergence of a new mass movement of protest. The streets of Seattle were a human mixture of all sort of political colours. But among these were anarchists who were very important in the organization of the mass action before and during the heady Seattle days. These anarchists worked to bring large numbers of people together organizationally: by training them in non-violent civil disobedience, and, in coordinating the thousand and one logistical details using new ingenious means of independent communication world-wide. There were also some street fighters and commercial property smashers; they also called themselves anarchists. These experiences have earned a place in this volume.

From the *Non-Violent Activist*, published by the War Resisters League during January/February 2000, we publish "Democracy in Seattle's Streets" by Chris Ney. This article reflects the fruit of months of careful planning, wide-ranging community outreach and the extraordinary (if uneasy) coalition that occupied the streets of central Seattle. Also reflected is the effectiveness of militant, mature, disciplined, non-violent direct action or civil disobedience.

Through an interview conducted by David Barsamian, Noam Chomsky puts the new movement in context, thereby showing that there is some continuity with the previous generation of radicals.

The "Black Block Interview" was first published in the February/March 2000 issue of *Active Transformation*. The person interviewed is anonymous for obvious reasons, and is published here to fill in a perspective from this end of the political spectrum. Based on a series of small groups influenced by the 'Autonomen' in Germany, the Black Block have used a 'hit and run' strategy in various mass demonstrations. It is not possible to determined if this interview is representative of Black Block activists as a whole.

In the August 2001 issue of *Le Monde Diplomatique*, Susan George, who is a regular contributor and vice-chair of Attac France, states, with reference to the Genoa demonstrations in July 2001:

> There is some evidence of complicity between the authorities and gangs of Black Block agents provocateurs that damaged parts of the city.

In a footnote George adds:

> A member of the clergy, Don Vitallano Della Salo, has reported having seen Black Block group members emerging from a police van in Genoa, and there have been reports that some of the group actually acted as agents provocateurs under police instruction, (*La Repubblica*, 22 July 2001, *Le Monde*, 24 July 2001).

There have been several other similar reports from reliable sources including from anti-globalisation activists with the Genoa Social Forum, the principal organizing coalition against the G8 July meeting.

Finally, in the "Open Letter to the Seattle Trashers, the Unions, the Peaceful Protesters and the Non-Violent Resisters" by Scott Weinstein, Phillipe Duhamel and Jim Campbell, we have the analysis of three libertarian veterans of the new generation of radicals. The perspective advanced here has contributed to a large scale debate in the new movement with an international resonance.

The questions which have yet to be fully debated and answered include: Is fundamental social change possible in the developed countries of the northern hemisphere in the 21st century? Whatever the answer, it has to be fully fleshed out. What can be included in radical protests and be considered effective? Effectiveness must be first and foremost defined as those actions that build the base of the new movement, and which prepare it for the long haul.

# THESES ON
# LIBERTARIAN MUNICIPALISM
*Murray Bookchin*

Historically, radical social theory and practice have focused on two arenas of human societal activity: the workplace and the community. Beginning with the rise of the Nation-State and with the Industrial Revolution, the economy has acquired a predominant position over the community — not only in capitalist ideology but in the various socialisms, libertarian and authoritarian, that emerged early in the last century. The shift from an ethical emphasis on socialism to an economic one is a problem of far-reaching proportions that has been widely discussed. What is relevant to the immediate issue at hand is that the socialisms themselves early acquired disquieting bourgeois attributes of their own, a development most markedly revealed by the Marxian vision of attaining human emancipation by the domination of nature, a historic project that presumably entailed the 'domination of man by man,' the Marxian and bourgeois rationale for the emergence of class society as a 'pre-condition' for human emancipation.

Unfortunately, the libertarian wing of socialism — the anarchist — did not consistently advance the primacy of ethics over the economistic. Perhaps understandably so, with the rise of the factory system, the *locus classicus* of capitalist exploitation, and the emergence of the industrial proletariat as the 'bearer' of a new society. For all its moral fervour, the syndicalist adaptation to industrial society and its image of the libertarian trade union as the infrastructure of a liberated world marked

*Murray Bookchin has been a major spokesperson for more than twenty years for the ecology, appropriate technology and anti-nuclear movements. He is the author of seven books, including* Our Synthetic Environment, Post-Scarcity Anarchism, The Limits of the City, Toward An Ecological Society *and* The Ecology of Freedom. *He lives in Vermont and is Director Emeritus of the Social Ecology Institute.*

a disturbing shift in emphasis from communitarianism to industrialism, from communal values to factory values.* Certain works which acquired an almost doxagraphic sanctity in syndicalism were to heighten the significance of the factory and, more generally, the workplace in radical theory, not to speak of the messianic role of the 'Proletariat.' The limits of this analysis, too, need not be examined here. Superficially, they seemed to be justified by the events of the First World War era and the 1930s. Today, the situation is otherwise; and the fact that we can criticize them with the sophistication provided by decades of hindsight hardly allows us the right to patronizingly dismiss proletarian socialism for its lack of foresight.

But the point must be made: the factory, and for much of history the workplace, has actually been the primary arena not only of exploitation but of hierarchy — this together with the patriarchal family. It has served not to 'discipline,' 'unite,' and 'organize' the proletariat for revolutionary change, but to school it in the habits of subordination, obedience, and mindless drudgery. The proletariat, as do all oppressed sectors of society, comes to life when it sheds its industrial habits in the free and spontaneous activity of *communizing* — the living process that gives meaning to the word 'community.' Here, workers shed their strictly class nature, their status as the counterpart of the bourgeoisie, and reveal their human nature. The anarchic ideal of decentralized, stateless, collectively managed, and directly democratic communities — of confederated municipalities or 'communes' — speaks almost intuitively, and in the best works of Proudhon and Kropotkin, consciously, to the transforming role of libertarian municipalism as the framework of a liberatory society, rooted in the nonhierarchical ethics of a unity of diversity, self-formation and self-management, complementarity, and mutual aid.

The Commune, *qua* municipality or city, must be singled out from its purely functional role as an economic realm, where human beings acquire the opportunity to perform nonagricultural tasks, or as the 'imploded centre' (to use Lewis Mumford's language) of heightened

---

* For a particularly disturbing example, one has only to read Abad de Santillian's *El Organismo Economico de la Revolucion* (Barcelona, 1936), translated into English under the title *After the Revolution*, a work that exercised immense influence on the CNT-FAI.

intercourse and propinquity to illuminate its historic function in transforming the quasi-tribal folk united by blood ties and custom into a
body politic of citizens united by ethical values based on reason.

This vast transforming function brought the 'stranger' or 'outsider'
into a common bond with the traditional *genoi* and created a new
sphere of interrelationships: the realm of *polissonomos* — literally, the
managing of a *polis* or city. It is from this conjunction of *nomos* and
*polis* that the abbreviated word 'politics' derives, a term that has been
denatured into mere statecraft, just as the word *polis* has been mistranslated
as 'State.' These distinctions are not etymological niceties. They reflect
a very real degradation of *concepts*, each of immense importance in
itself, to suit ideological ends. Anti-authoritarians are repelled by the
degradation of the term 'society' into 'State,' and with good reason.
The State, as we know, is a distinct artifact of ruling classes, a professionalized monopoly of violence to assure the subjugation and exploitation of human by human. Anthropology and social theory have
shown how it began to slowly emerge from the broader background
of hierarchical relationships, its varying forms and degrees of development, its full contours in the modern Nation-State, and possibly
its future, most complete form in the totalitarian State. So, too, anti-
authoritarians know that the family, workplace, cultural forms of
association in the fullest, anthropological sense of the word 'cultural,'
personal inter-relationships, and generally the private sphere of life,
are uniquely *social* and intrinsically distinguishable from statist. That
the social and the statist can infiltrate each other such that archaic
despotisms were examples of the patriarchal *oikos* writ large and the
modern totalitarian State's absorption of the social reflects the expanded
meaning of the word 'bureaucracy' (the psychotherapeutic and educational
realms as well as the traditional administrative) are evidence of the
impurities that exist in all modes of societal organization.

The emergence of the city opens to us in varying degrees of development not only the new domain of universal *humanitas* as distinguished
from the parochial folk, of the free space of an innovative civicism as
distinguished from tradition-bound, biocentric *gemeinschaften*; it also
opens to us the realm of *polissonomos*, the management of the *polis* by
a body politic of free citizens, in short, of *politics* as distinguished from
the strictly social and statist. History affords us no 'pure' category of
the political realm any more than it offers us any image beyond the
band and village level of non-hierarchical social relationships — and,

until recent times, of pure statist institutions. 'Purity' is a word that can be introduced into social theory only at the expense of any contact with reality as we have known it in history. But approximations of a politics, invariably civic in character, do exist that are not primarily social or statist: the Athenian democracy, New England town meetings, the sectional assemblies and Paris Commune of 1793, to cite the most noteworthy examples. Fairly permanent in some cases, ephemeral in others, and admittedly greatly flawed by so many of the oppressive features that marked all the societal relationships of the eras in which they existed, they can nevertheless be collected in their small fragments and large pieces to provide an image of a political realm that is neither parliamentary nor bureaucratic, centralized nor professionalized, social nor statist, but rather civic in its recognition of the city's role of transforming a folk or a monadic agglomeration of individuals into a citizenry based on ethical and rational modes of association.

To define the social, political, and statist in their categorical specificity and to see the city in its historical evolution as the arena within which the political emerges *apart* from the social and the statist is to open areas of investigation whose programmatic importance is enormous. The modern era is defined 'civically' by urbanization, a malignant perversion of citification that threatens to engulf both town and country, and render their historic dialectic almost unintelligible in modern eyes. The confusion between urbanization and citification is as obscurantist today as the confusion between society and State, collectivization and nationalization, or, for that matter, politics and parliamentarism. The *urbs* in Roman usage were the physical facts of the city, its buildings, squares, streets, as distinguished from the *civitas*, the union of citizens or body politic. That the two words were not interchangeable until late imperial times when the very concept of 'citizenship' had declined, indeed, to be replaced by caste-oriented names and subjects of the Roman imperium, tells us a very poignant and highly relevant fact. The Gracchi had tried to turn the *urbs* into a *civitas*, to recreate the Athenian *ekklesia* at the expense of the Roman Senate. They failed, and the *urbs* devoured the *civitas* in the form of the Empire. Conceivably, the yeoman-citizens who formed the backbone of the Republic could have turned it into a democracy, but once they 'came down from the Seven Hills' on which Rome was founded, they became 'small,' to use Heine's words. The 'idea of Rome' as an ethical heritage diminished in direct proportion to the growth of the city. Hence, "The greater Rome grew, the more this idea dilated; the individual lost himself in it: the great men who remain eminent are borne up by this idea, and it makes the littleness of the little men even more pronounced."

There is a lesson, here, to be learned on the perils of hierarchy and 'greatness,' but also an intuitive sense of the distinction between urbanization and citification, the growth of the *urbs* at the expense of the *civitas*. But still another question arises: is the *civitas* or body politic meaningful unless it is literally, indeed, protoplasmically, *embodied*? Rousseau reminds us that "houses make a town, but [only] citizens make a city." Conceived as merely an 'electorate' or a 'constituency,' or, to use the most degraded word the State has applied to them, 'taxpayers' — a term that is virtually a euphemism for a 'subject' — the inhabitants of the *urbs* became abstractions and, hence, mere 'creatures of the State,' to use American juridical language in regard to the legal status of a municipal entity today. A people whose sole 'political' function is to vote for delegates is no people at all; it is a 'mass,' an agglomeration of monads. Politics, as distinguished from the social and statist, involves the re-embodiment of masses into richly articulated assemblies, the formation of a body politic in an arena of discourse, shared rationality, free expression, and radically democratic modes of decision-making.

The process is interactive and self-formative. One may choose to agree with Marx that 'men' form themselves as producers of material things; with Fichte, as ethically motivated individuals; with Aristotle, as dwellers in a *polis*; with Bakunin, as seekers of freedom. But in the absence of self-management in all these spheres of life — economic, ethical, political, and libertarian — the character formation which transforms 'men' from passive objects into active subjects is painfully lacking. Selfhood is as much a function of 'managing,' or, preferably, communizing, as managing is a function of selfhood. Both belong to the formative process the Germans call *bildung* and the Greeks *paidaia*. The civic arena, whether as *polis*, town, or neighbourhood, is literally the cradle for civilizing human beings beyond the socializing process provided by the family. And to put matters bluntly, civic 'civilizing' is merely another expression for *politicizing* and rendering a mass into a deliberative, rational, ethical body politic. To achieve this concept of *civitas* presupposes that human beings can assemble as more than isolated monads, discourse directly with modes of expression that go 'beyond words,' reason in a direct, face-to-face manner, and arrive peacefully at a commonality of views that renders decisions possible and their implementation consistent with democratic principles. In forming and functioning in such assemblies, citizens are also forming themselves, for politics is nothing if it is not educational and if its innovative openness does not promote character formation.

Hence the municipality is not merely a 'place' in which one lives, an 'investment' into a home, sanitary, health, and security services, a job, library, and cultural amenities. Citification historically formed a sweeping transition of humanity from tribal into civil modes of life that was as revolutionary as the transition from hunting-gathering to food cultivation, and from food cultivation into manufacturing. Despite the absorptive powers of the State, a later development, to meld civicism with nationalism and politics with statecraft, the 'Urban Revolution,' as V. Gordon Childe was to call it, was no less sweeping than the Agricultural Revolution and the Industrial Revolution. Moreover, like all its predecessors, the Nation-State still contains this past in its belly and has not fully digested it. Urbanization may well complete what the Roman Caesars, the Absolute monarchies, and the bourgeois republics failed to do — obliterate even the heritage of the Urban Revolution — but this has not yet been accomplished.

Before turning to the revolutionary implications of a libertarian municipal approach and the libertarian politics it yields, it is necessary to deal with one more theoretical problem: policy-making as distinguished from mere administration. On this score, Marx, in his analysis of the Paris Commune of 1871, has done radical social theory a considerable disservice. The Commune's combination of delegated policy-making with the execution of police by its own administrators, a feature of the Commune which Marx celebrated, is a major failing of that body. Rousseau quite rightly emphasized that popular power cannot be delegated without being destroyed. One either has a fully empowered popular assembly or power belongs to the State. The flaw of delegated power completely tainted the council system (soviets, *Raten*), the Commune of 1871, and, of course, republican systems generally, whether municipal or national. The words 'representative democracy' are a contradiction in terms. A people cannot engage in *polissonomos* by placing *nomos*-making, legislation, or *nomothesia* in surrogate bodies that exclude it from the discourse, reasoning, and deciding that gives politics its very identity. No less significantly, it cannot deliver to administration — the mere execution of policy — the power to formulate what must be administered without laying the groundwork for the State.

The supremacy of the assembly as a formulator of policy over that of any administrative agency is the only guarantor, to the extent that one exists, of the supremacy of politics over statecraft. This unblemished degree of supremacy is all the more crucial in a society that is entangled with experts and executors for the operations of its highly specialized social machinery, and the problem of maintaining popular-assembly supremacy is only heightened during any period of transition from an administratively centralized society to a decentralized one. Only if assemblies of the people, from city neighbourhoods to small towns, maintain the most demanding vigilance and scrutiny over any coordinating confederal bodies is a libertarian democracy conceivable. Structurally, this issue poses no problems. Communities have relied on experts and administrators without losing their freedom from time immemorial. The destruction of these communities has usually been a statist act, not an administrative one as such. Priestly corporations and chiefdoms have relied on ideology and, very significantly, on public naïveté, not primarily on force, to attenuate popular power and ultimately eliminate it.

The State has never absorbed the totality of life in the past, a fact which Kropotkin implicitly indicated in *Mutual Aid* when he described the richly textured civic life that existed even in oligarchic medieval communes. Indeed, the city has commonly been the principal countervailing force to imperial and National-States from ancient times to the recent present. Augustus and his heirs made the suppression of municipal autonomy a centrepiece of Roman imperial administration as did the Absolute monarchs of the Reformation era. To 'tear down the city walls' was a fixed policy of Louis XIII and Richelieu, a policy that was to surface later when the Robespierrist Committee of Public Safety moved ruthlessly to restrict the powers of the Commune in 1793-94. The 'Urban Revolution,' in effect, has haunted the State as an irrepressible *dual power*, a potential challenge to centralized power throughout much of history. This tension exists to the present day, as witness the conflicts between the centralized State and the municipality in America and England. Here, in the most immediate environment of the individual — the community, the neighbourhood, the town, or the village — where private life slowly begins to phase into public life, the authentic locus for functioning on a base level exists insofar as urbanization has not totally destroyed it. When urbanization will have effaced city life so completely the city no longer has its own identity, culture, and spaces for consociation, the bases for democracy — in whatever way the word is defined — will have disappeared and the question of revolutionary forms will be a shadow game of abstractions.

By the same token, no radical outlook based on libertarian forms and their possibilities is meaningful in the absence of the radical consciousness that will give these forms content and a sense of direction. Let there be no mistake about the fact that all democratic and libertarian forms can be turned against the achievement of freedom if they are conceived schematically, as abstract ends that lack that ideological substance and organicity from which every form draws its liberatory meaning. Moreover, it would be naïve to believe that forms like neighbourhood, town, and popular communal assemblies could rise to the level of a libertarian public life or give rise to a libertarian body politic without a highly conscious, well-organized, and programmatically coherent libertarian movement. It would be equally naïve to believe that such a libertarian movement could emerge without that indispensable radical *intelligentsia* whose medium is its own intensely vibrant community life (one is reminded here of the French intelligentsia of the Enlightenment and the tradition it established in the quartiers and cafés of Paris), not the assortment of anemic *intellectuals* who staff the academies and institutes of western society.* Unless anarchists develop this waning stratum of thinkers who live a vital public life in a searching communication with their social environment, they will be faced with the very real danger of turning ideas into dogmas and becoming the self-righteous surrogates of once-living movements and people who belong to another historical era.

---

* For all its shortcomings and failings, it was this radical intelligentsia that provided the cutting edge of every revolutionary project in history — and, in fact, literally *projected* the very ideas of social change from which the people drew their social insights. Perikles was to exemplify them in the ancient world, a John Ball or a Thomas Munzer in the medieval and Reformation eras, a Denis Diderot during the Enlightenment, an Emile Zola and Jean-Paul Sartre in relatively recent times. The academic *intellectual* is a fairly recent phenomenon: a bookish, cloistered, incestuous, and career-oriented creature who lacks life experience and practice.

It is undeniably true that one can play fast-and-loose with words like 'municipality' and 'community,' 'assemblies' and 'direct democracy,' overlooking the class, ethnic, and gender differences that have made words like 'the People' into meaningless, even obscurantistic, abstractions. The sectional assemblies of 1793 were not only forced into conflict with the more bourgeois Paris Commune and the National Convention; they were battlegrounds in their own right between propertied and propertyless strata, royalists and democrats, moderates and radicals. To anchor these strata in exclusively economic interests can be as misleading as to ignore class differences entirely and speak of 'fraternity' or 'liberty' and 'equality' as though these words were often little more than rhetoric. Enough has been written, however, to thoroughly demystify the humanistic slogans of the great 'bourgeois' revolutions; indeed, so much has been done to reduce them to mere reflexes of narrow bourgeois self-interest that we now risk the possibility of losing all sight of their populist *utopian* dimension. After so much has been said about the economic conflicts that divided the English, American, and French revolutions, future histories of these great dramas would now serve us best if they revealed the bourgeoisie's fear of *all* revolutions, its innate conservatism and proclivity for compromising with the established order. They would also serve us best if they revealed how the oppressed strata of the revolutionary era pushed the 'bourgeois' revolutions beyond the narrow confines the bourgeoisie itself established into remarkable areas of democratic principles with which the bourgeoisie has always lived in an uneasy and suspicious accommodation. The various 'rights' these revolutions formulated were achieved not because of the bourgeoisie but in spite of it by the American yeoman farmers in the 1770s and the *sans culottes* of the 1790s — and their future becomes increasingly questionable in a growing corporate and cybernetic world.

But this very future and recent trends — technological, societal, and cultural which shake up and threaten to decompose the traditional class structure produced by the Industrial Revolution — raise the prospect that a general interest can emerge out of the particular class interests created by the past two centuries. The word 'people' may well return to the radical vocabulary — not as an obscurantist abstraction but as a highly meaningful expression of increasingly rootless, fluid, and technologically displaced strata which can no longer be integrated into a cybernetic and highly mechanized society. To the technologically displaced strata we can add the elderly and the young who face a dubious future in a world that can no longer define the roles people play in its economy and culture. These strata no longer fit elegantly into a simplistic division of class conflicts that radical theory structured around 'wage labour' and 'capital.'

The 'people' may return to this era in still another sense: notably as a 'general interest' that is formed out of public concern over ecological, community, moral, gender, and cultural issues. It would be unwise to downplay the crucial role of these seemingly marginal 'ideological' concerns. As Franz Borkenau emphasized nearly fifty years ago, the history of the past century tells us only too clearly that the proletariat can become more enamoured of nationalism than socialism and be guided more by a 'patriotic' interest than a 'class' interest, as any one who visits the United States today would quickly learn. Quite aside from the historic influence such ideological movements as Christianity and Islam have exercised, both of which *still* reveal the power of ideology to rise above material interest, we are also faced with the power of ideology to work in a socially progressive direction — notably ecological, feminist, ethnic, moral, and countercultural ideologies within which one encounters pacifist and utopistic anarchist components that await integration into a coherent outlook. In any case, new social movements are developing around us which cross traditional class lines. From this ferment, a general interest may yet be formed which is larger in its scope, novelty, and creativity than the economically oriented particular interests of the past. And it is from this ferment that a 'people' can emerge and sort itself out into assemblies and like forms, a 'people' that transcends particularistic interests and gives a heightened relevance to a libertarian municipal orientation.

At a time when Orwell's image of 1984 can be clearly translated into the 'megalopolis' of a highly centralized State and a highly corporatized society, we must explore the possibility of counterposing to these statist and social developments a third realm of human practice: the political realm created by the municipality, a historic development of the Urban Revolution itself that has not been fully digested by the State. Revolution always translates itself into dual power: the industrial union, soviet or council, and the Commune, all oriented against the State. A thorough examination of history will show that the factory, a creature of bourgeois rationalization, has never been the locus of revolution; the most explicitly revolutionary workers (the Spanish, Russian, French, and Italian) have mainly been transitional classes, indeed traditional decomposing agrarian strata which were subject to the discordant and ultimately corrosive impact of an industrial culture that is itself already becoming a traditional one. Today, in fact, where workers are still in motion, their battle is largely defensive (ironically, a battle to maintain an industrial system that is faced with displacement by a capital-intensive, increasingly cybernetic technology) and reflect the last stirrings of a waning economy.

The city, too, is dying — but in a very different sense from the factory. The factory was never the realm of freedom. It was always the realm of survival, of 'necessity,' which disempowered and desiccated the human world around it. Its emergence was bitterly resisted by craftspeople, agrarian communities, and a more humanly scaled and communalistic world. Only the naïveté of a Marx and Engels who fostered the myth that the factory serves to 'discipline,' 'unite,' and 'organize' the proletariet could oblige radicals, mystified in their own right by the ideal of a 'scientific socialism,' to ignore its authoritarian and hierarchical role. The abolition of the factory by an ecotechnics, creative work, and, yes, by cybernetic devices designed to meet human needs, is a desideratum of socialism in its libertarian and utopian forms, indeed, a moral precondition for freedom.

By contrast, the Urban Revolution played a very different role. It essentially created the idea of a universal *humanitas* and the communalizing of that humanity along rational and ethical lines. It raised the limits to human development imposed by the kinship tie, the parochialism of the folk world, and the suffocating effects of custom. The dissolution of genuine municipalities by urbanization would mark a grave regression for societal life: a destruction of the uniquely human dimension of consociation, of the civil life that justifies any use of the word 'civilization' and the body politic that gives meaning and identity to the word 'politics.' Here, if theory and reality enter into conflict with each other, one is justified in invoking Georg Lukacs' famous remark: "So much the worse for the facts." Politics, so easily degraded by 'politicians' into statecraft, must be rehabilitated by anarchism in its original meaning as a form of civic participation and administration that stands in counterposition to the State and extends beyond those basic aspects

of human intercourse we appropriately call social.* In a very radical
sense, we must go back to the roots of the word in the *polis* and the
unconscious stirrings of the people to create a domain for rational,
ethical, and public intercourse which, in turn, gave rise to the ideal
of the Commune and the popular assemblies of the revolutionary era.

Anarchism has always stressed the need for moral regeneration and
for a counter-culture (to use this word in its best sense) against the
prevailing culture. Hence its emphasis on ethics, its concern for a
coherence of means and ends, its defence of human rights as well as
civil rights, notably in its concern for oppression in every aspect of
life. Its image of counter-*institutions* has been more problematic. It
would be well to remember that there has always been a *communalist*
tendency in anarchism, not only a syndicalist and an individualist
one. Moreover, this communalist tendency has always had a strong
municipalist orientation, one which can be gleaned from the writings
of Proudhon and Kropotkin. What has been lacking is a searching
examination of the political core of this orientation: the distinction
between a realm of discourse, decision-making, and institutional development that is neither social nor statist. Civic politics is not intrinsically
parliamentary politics; indeed, if we restore the authentic historic
meaning of the word 'politics' to its rightful place in the radical
vocabulary, it is redolent of the Athenian citizens' assembly and its
more egalitarian heir, the sectional assemblies of Paris. To reach back
into these historic institutions, to enrich their content with our libertarian
traditions and critical analyses, and to bring them to the surface of
an ideologically confused world is to bring the past to the service of
the present in a creative and innovative way. Every radical tendency
is burdened by a certain measure of intellectual inertia, the anarchist
no less than the socialist. The security of tradition can be so comforting
that it ends all possible innovation, even among anti-authoritarians.

Anarchism is beleaguered by its concern over parliamentarism and
statism. This concern has been amply justified by history, but it can
also lead to a siege mentality that is no less dogmatic in theory than

---

* Before concluding these remarks, it is worth noting that the distinction between the social
and the political has a long pedigree, one which goes back to Aristotle and was to surface
continually over the history of social theory, most recently in the works of Hannah Arendt.
What both thinkers lacked was a theory of the State, hence the absence of a tripartite
distinction in their writings.

an electoral radicalism is corrupt in practice. Yet if libertarian municipalism is construed as an *organic* politics, a politics that *emerges*
from the base level of human consocation into the fullness of a genuine
body politic and participatory forms of citizenship, it may well be the
last redoubt for a socialism oriented toward decentralized popular
institutions. A major feature of a libertarian municipalist approach is
that it can evoke lived traditions to legitimate its claims, traditions
which, however fragmentary and tattered, still offer the potential for
a participatory politics of challenging dimensions to the State. The
Commune still lies buried in the city council; the sections still lie
buried in the neighbourhood; the town meeting still lies buried in
the township; confederal forms of municipal association still lie buried
in regional networks of towns and cities. To recover a past that can
live and be reworked to suit liberatory ends is not to be captive to
tradition; it is to ferret out uniquely human goals of association that
have abiding qualities in the human spirit — *the need for community as
such* — and which have welled up repeatedly over the past. They linger
in the present as stillborn hopes which people find within themselves
at all times and which come to the surface of history in inspired
moments of action and release.

These theses advance the view that a libertarian municipalism is
possible and a new civic politics is definable as a dual power that can
counterpose assembly and confederal forms to the centralized State.
As matters now stand in the Orwellian world of the 1980s, this
perspective of dual power may well be one of the most important ones,
doubtless among others, that libertarians can hope to develop without
compromising their anti-authoritarian principles. Further: these theses
advance the view that an organic politics based on such radical participatory forms of civic association does not exclude the right of
anarchists to alter city and town charters such that they validate the
existence of directly democratic institutions. And if this kind of activity
brings anarchists into city councils, there is no reason why such a
politics should be construed as parliamentary, particularly if it is
confined to the civic level and is consciously posed against the State.*

---

\* One would hope that the ghost of Paul Brousse is not invoked against this thesis. Brousse
used the libertarian municipalism of the Commune, so deeply ingrained in the Parisian people
of his time, against that very communalist tradition — that is, to practise a purely bourgeois
form of parliamentarism, not to bring Paris and French municipalities into opposition to the

It is curious that many anarchists who celebrate the existence of a 'collectivized' industrial enterprise, here and there, with considerable enthusiasm despite its emergence within a thoroughly bourgeois economic framework can view a municipal politics that entails 'elections' of any kind with repugnance, even if such a politics is structured around neighbourhood assemblies, recallable deputies, radically democratic forms of accountability, and deeply rooted localist networks.

The city is not congruent with the State. The two have very different origins and have played very different roles historically. That the State penetrates *every* aspect of life today, from the family to the factory, from the union to the city, does not mean that one self-righteously withdraws from every form of organized human interrelationships, indeed from one's own skin, to an empyrean realm of purity and abstraction, one that would validate Adorno's description of anarchism as a 'ghost.' If there are any ghosts that haunt us, they take the form of a dogmatism and ritualistic rigidity so inflexible that one slips into an intellectual *rigor mortis* no different in kind from that which settles over a corpse frozen in the eternity of death. The power of authority to command the individual physically will have then achieved a conquest more complete than the imperatives produced by mere coercion. It will have laid its hand on the human spirit itself — its freedom to think creatively and resist with ideas, even if its capacity to act is blocked for a time by events.

centralized State, as the Commune of 1793 tried to do. There was nothing organic about his views of municipalism and nothing revolutionary about his intentions. Everyone has used the image of the Commune for different purposes: Marx to anchor his theory of the 'proletarian dictatorship' in historic precedent; Lenin to legitimate a totally Jacobin 'politics,' and anarchists, more critically, for communalism.

# THE GREENS: NATIONALISM OR ANTI-NATIONALISM
*Chris Southcott and Jorgen Pedersen*

The Green Party[1] of the Federal Republic of Germany is one of the best examples in the world today of an attempt to put forward alternative solutions to contemporary social problems. Using neither traditional liberal ideas nor an ideology based on historical materialism or State socialism, the Greens have managed to present a coherent framework of action which has allowed them to become a major force in West German society.

Despite the obvious importance of the movement, the Greens have received little serious attention outside West Germany. The information available seems to be limited to sketchy and sometimes contradictory press reports. Many of these reports show a perverse pleasure in identifying the Greens according to traditional ideological conceptualizations. Although it may facilitate the work of the writer to be able to drop new social movements into preconceived classifications such as 'left', 'right', 'progressive', 'reactionary', 'nationalist', 'communist infiltrated', 'pacifist',or 'dangerous militants', the result for the reader is miscomprehension.

The object of this article is to provide a better understanding of the Greens by attempting to describe them according to their own particular social context rather than engaging in a fetishism of words. The authors believe that this type of analysis is important in order to allow alternative movements in other countries to learn from the experience in West Germany. It is not, however, our intention to outline a 'German model' which can be copied by other movements. Our purpose is rather to point out some of the social conditions which

[1] The term 'movement' instead of 'party' would be considered more appropriate by many supporters of the group.

*Chris Southcott is the principal author of this article. He and Jorgen Pedersen are doctoral students at l'Ecole des Hautes Etudes (Paris).*

exist in West Germany today and which facilitated the formation of such a movement.

We will proceed by first discussing some of the analyses of the Greens presented in the press and elsewhere. While not dismissing the value of these commentaries, we will point out some of the weaknesses they show in attempting to grasp the reality of the movement. This will lead us into the final section in which we will suggest reasons for the relative success of the Greens in West Germany, in comparison with other countries. Here we shall place special emphasis on the influence of nationalism.

In discussing the presentation of the Greens in the written media outside West Germany, it seems appropriate to start with that accusation pinned on many western alternative movements: of being 'communist-inspired' or controlled. This idea is most evident in the French press. In an article in the French weekly *Paris-Match*, we see the Greens referred to as "wolves of the Kremlin disguised in green wool."[2] Not to be outdone, but perhaps more reserved, another French weekly, *Le Point*, refers to the recent social movements in West Germany as a time "when green turns to red."[3] The North American press, following its tradition of declared objectivity, is less prepared to comment on any hypothetical link between the communists and the Greens. This does not exclude, however, references to certain leaders of the Greens as "erstwhile marxist-leninists."[4]

The first question one must ask is whether these accusations carry a measure of truth. To what extent are the Greens supporting the 'communist cause'? If one looks at the situation with the view that 'if they aren't with us, they are against us,' the response coming from one side of the Atlantic would have to be 'yes'. Of course, using this same logic, the response to a question such as 'Are the Greens capitalist reactionaries?' coming from somewhere on the banks of the Volga, would also have to be 'yes'. Use of this logic in attempting to understand Die Grünen has, obviously, little value.

It would be ridiculous to deny that the existence of an alternative movement such as the Greens weakens the 'American hand' in West

---

[2] *Paris-Match*, Oct. 15, 1982, p. 69.
[3] *Le Point*, Apr. 19, 1982, p. 81.
[4] *New York Times*, Sept. 18, 1982, p. 5:3.

Germany; that is, if we refer to the traditional post-war dominance by American military and political interests. But to carry the argument further and to imply that this presence strengthens the 'Russian hand' requires justification by a narrow-minded military logic which places little value on the power of the democratic spirit. The idea that the only way to defend Western democracy against a totalitarian-militaristic regime is by getting the people to stop expressing those beliefs which oppose a constant, incessant military build-up seems, according to this logic, to make perfect sense. Perhaps it would not have made sense to Benjamin Franklin, Thomas Jefferson, or Thomas Paine, all critics of militarism, but then again, how big were their budgets?

The belief that development of democratic values, independent of military power, is essential to the defence against totalitarianism may not be very popular right now,[5] but it is with this view that one must try to understand the Greens. What ,they are attempting to establish is a pluralistic and democratic discourse in a country whose experience in this area is, as shall be discussed later, very limited.

It was with this idea, for example, that during the formation of the party a proposal to exclude members of the West German Communist Party was narrowly defeated.[6] It was felt that to live up to its democratic ideals the party should be open to all.

The entering of the Greens into the Bundestag proves, at least symbolically, that a German State can tolerate a plurality of opinions. Using a logic which places some value on the 'power' of liberal democratic values, it is reassuring that the society sitting on the 'frontline' of eventual military hostility has learned to experience and appreciate democracy rather than showing itself to be unsure of its ability to live with a plurality of opinions.

Another explanation which seems to get a great deal of attention is the idea that the Green movement was made possible by a new 'successor generation'. It is quite common to hear the remark that the youth of West Germany no longer share their parents' memories and lessons of the last war. There is, however, quite a dispute over whether this

---

[5] Witness the hostility in certain sectors of the Western press towards certain demands by the Greens for democratic reforms instead of military build-up.
[6] *New York Times*, Nov. 7, 1979, p. 9.

is because the young are more conscious of the horrors of the last war or because they are less so.

James M. Markham, writing for the *New York Times*, states that "a new generation, no longer burdened by guilt for Hitler's crimes, is coming into the corridors of power in West Germany."[7] He continues by stating that these youth have largely "broken with their parents' view of themselves and of the world." He reasons that for these youths "spotty instruction in school about the Nazi period... and the passing of years has made the war remote." These views are also shared by such people as former West German defence minister Hans Apel, who believes "the younger people in our country and in Europe have to some extent never learned the lessons of history. They don't know anything about Hitler."[8]

Whatever the validity of their judgement, the point to remember about these statements is that ignorance of the National-Socialist period of German history has allowed the establishment, by young people, of a movement based on profound anti-militarism, the importance of the quality of life, and grass-roots democracy.

For those who may have a little trouble understanding this sort of logic, there is relief to be found in the existence of an alternative view of the 'generation gap of guilt'. This other view sees that the youth in West Germany are, in fact, all too aware of the horrors of the last war; that whereas their parents were able to 'bracket' or put away their feelings of guilt in order to get on with the task of reconstruction, the youth of today are now forced to face up to it. Manfred Rommel, Christian Democratic mayor of Stuttgart and son of the infamous Field Marshal Rommel, has stated that "the history of the Third Reich remains undigested in many stomachs... the younger generation is even more critical than the older one."[9] Rommel goes on to state that the "fixation" of the young people on the Hitler era has forced them to learn the "wrong lessons. They look at their parents' mistake in accepting Hitler's authority and they conclude that they should not accept any authority at all."

---

[7] *Ibid.*, Aug. 17, 1983, p. 1.
[8] Quoted in Seyla Benhabib, "The West German Peace Movement and Its Critics," in *Telos*, no. 51, Spring 1982, p. 153.
[9] *New York Times*, Oct. 3, 1982, Section IV, p. 2.

In analyzing these opposing perspectives, the second seems to make more sense. It would, of course, be foolish to state that all the young people who participate in the Green movement are experts on the history of National-Socialism in Germany, and, as a result, share a personal feeling of guilt. But on the other hand it is not rare to find in the sentiments expressed by many of the Green supporters a justification of the movement as an attempt to make amends for 'crimes of the past'.

As for the contention that West German youth have not received much instruction in the history of the Third Reich, it is interesting to note that it was not until the 1960's that schools in West Germany started to treat National-Socialism seriously. It was only in 1962 that the ten state ministers of education issued uniform directives stating that the Third Reich was "to be observed in the context of German history so that the seductive appeal of a synthesis of nationalism and socialism can be comprehended, a synthesis that was then revealed to be void of all human and social content." [10] According to historian Gordon Craig, it was in fact the parents of today's youth who received little instruction about this era. [11] This is mainly due to the fact that during the 40's and 50's the teachers and curriculum were little changed from the rosters of prewar days.

Another element of the Green movement which receives a great deal of attention is their position on reunification of the two Germanies. Much of the discussion is based on the writings of Peter Brandt and Herbert Ammon who see the role of the West German peace movement as setting the foundations for the reunification of East and West Germany. Brandt and Ammon state that "the 'national task' of Germans in both East and West Germany is thus not the imprisonment in the alliances prescribed to them, but a thorough overcoming of the status quo." [12]

It is important to state, first of all, that the link between Brandt and Ammon and the Greens is tenuous. The position of the former has not played a very important role in the formation of the Greens' policies. In discussions with members of the Green Party, the issue

---

[10] Gordon A. Craig, *The Germans*. New York: G. P. Putnam's Sons, 1982, p. 75.
[11] *Ibid.*
[12] Herbert Ammon and Peter Brandt, "The German Question," in *Telos*, no. 51, Spring 1982, p. 33.

was not perceived to be very serious.[13] This seems to be the case for the peace movement in general. In the words of Seyla Benhabib, "the Ammon and Brandt position is not widely shared, possibly because it assumes all too naïvely that there is a compatibility, if not collusion, between the interests of other European nations in peace and the reunification of the two Germanies — under whatever political form."[14]

The youth of West Germany seem to have come to accept the existence of two German States. Some see the existence of East Germany as not that different from the existence of Austria.[15] This is reflected in a poll conducted in 1983, wherein 43% of the young West Germans polled — compared to 20% for the overall population — regard East Germany as "a foreign country."[16]

The idea of reunification is almost non-existent in the programme of the Green Party. Their *Bundesprogramm* compiled for the 1983 federal election contained only one line which could be interpreted as a reference to this position. In their 'Policy of European Peace,' they call for the dissolution of military blocs such as NATO and the Warsaw Pact. "In this way," states the policy, "the ground-work would be laid for a solution to the division of Europe and Germany."[17] It is perhaps not without symbolic importance that the party apparently places the problem of 'the division of Europe' in importance before that of 'the division of Germany.'

Another position which seems to be frequently associated with the Greens is that of anti-Americanism. John Vinocur, in an article in the *New York Times*, refers to the Greens as that force in West German politics most overtly anti-American.[18] According to Vinocur, the Greens believe the U.S., the symbol of industrialism, can only be the ultimate aggressor. This anti-Americanism is also noted by the Greens themselves; witness the recent resignation from the party of one of its founders, Gerd Bastian. According to Bastian, since 1982 the party has become much too preoccupied with protesting American policies as opposed to Soviet policies.[19]

---

[13] Interview with Albert Sellner and Daniel Cohn-Bendit, Frankfurt, May 3, 1984.
[14] Benhabib, *op. cit.*, p. 153.
[15] Interview with Albert Sellner, Frankfurt, May 3, 1984.
[16] *New York Times*, Aug. 14, 1983, p. 10.
[17] Die Grünen, *The Program of the Green Party of the Federal Republic of Germany*, Bonn, p. 19.
[18] *New York Times*, July 5, 1981, Section IV, p. 3.
[19] *Grünes Bulletin*, Jan. 1984, p. 4.

It is difficult to deny the existence of this anti-Americanism. An analysis of the language employed by movement members shows that considerable time is spent pointing out the negative aspects of American society, while little time is spent on the positive aspects. In the words of Gerhard Armanski, American society is "seen in terms of clichés of the Wild West and Indians, slavery, immigration, unlimited expansion, growing military strength and a ubiquitous imperial presence."[20] In this sense, the Greens have fallen into the trap set for most new social movements: in order to mobilize people it is easier to be against something than for something.

The Greens do not deny this anti-Americanism. They justify it by stating that these negative feelings are directed towards "the American government (especially the Reagan administration) and not the people of America."[21] Daniel Cohn-Bendit, veteran of the Paris student insurrection in 1968 and candidate for the Greens in Frankfurt, points out that many of the visions and cultural manifestations of the movement are in fact borrowed from American culture of the 1960's.[22]

In an interview published in *The Nation*, Rudolf Bahro, former East German dissident and now one of the intellectual 'gurus' of the Greens, stated that it is only 'surface anti-Americanism'.[23] He insists that the movement is against the power structure in both the East and the West. When he lived in East Germany he fought for unilateral disarmament in the East. Because the Greens live in the West, Bahro suggests, they must fight for disarmament against the Western power structure, dominated by the United States. "If you live in the West you fight against the Western dragon."[24]

An interesting aspect of the attempts to describe and understand the phenomenon of the Greens is a resurgence of a 'German soul'. In an article published in 1981, Vinocur seems to agree with Bahro's idea of 'surface anti-Americanism'. He refers to this anti-Americanism as a "reversion to anti-Western and anti-modernistic currents traditional

---

[20] Gerhard Armanski, "Anti-Americanism in the Peace Movement," in *Telos*, no. 52, Summer 1982, p. 191.
[21] Interview with Heidi Dann, spokesperson for the Greens, Bonn, May 5, 1984.
[22] Interview with Daniel Cohn-Bendit, Frankfurt, May 3, 1984.
[23] *The Nation*, Oct. 8, 1983, p. 296.
[24] *Ibid*.

in German society."[25] He cites as an example of this tradition Max Weber's distrust for "anglo-saxon materialism." According to Vinocur, "the notion that Germany is a special entity between East and West has been more of a constant in German thought of the past 150 years than any special admiration for or spiritual relationship with the U.S."[26] In a different article Vinocur reasserts the resurgence of the "traditional notion of a German middle way between the West, often denounced as mercantile and empire, and Eastern Europe, seen as more romantic and less corrupt."[27] This view seems to be shared by Stanley Hoffman, who also links current anti-Americanism to "an expression of nostalgia for German purity, culture, and distinctiveness."[28]

The historian Craig reaches back into the past and cites the importance of the "failure of the Enlightenment" in Germany. He refers to German romanticism as the inevitable result of the inability of the empirical rationality of the *Aufklärung* to establish itself in German society. He cites the German sociologist Ernst Troeltsch who contends that German philosophical thought rejected "the universal egalitarian ethic... the whole of the mathematico-mechanical spirit of science of Western Europe [and] a conception of Natural Law that sought to blend utility with morality."[29]

It is also in reference to this historical tradition that the historian Fritz Stern has postulated that the Greens "marked the return of cultural despair and the re-emergence in politics of the German soul."[30] He refers to the fact that the adherents to this new movement "prided themselves on their anti-political nature, on their anti-party purity. They revelled in tumultuous irresponsibility." For Stern this German soul, the force behind the *Sturm und Drang*, the pre-Hitler youth movement of the 20's and 30's, has "re-emerged in politics in a greenish-reddish tinge."[31]

Understandably, it is very hard to measure the effect of this ideological tradition on the movement today. If it does play an important role,

[25] *New York Times*, July 5, 1981, Section IV, p. 3.
[26] *Ibid.*
[27] *New York Times*, Nov. 15, 1981, Section VI, p. 117.
[28] Stanley Hoffman, "American Liberals and Europe's Anti-Nuclear Movement," in *Dissent*, Spring 1982, p. 150.
[29] Craig, *op. cit.*, p. 33.
[30] *New York Times*, Oct. 13, 1982, p. 31:1.
[31] *Ibid.*

its influence is so ingrained in the subjectivity of its participants that it is impossible to isolate. Certainly many of the Greens' objections to current society can be linked to that vast philosophical tradition described as 'German romanticism'. This is the case whether it be Kantian metaphysics, Nietzschian fatalism, Husserlian or Heideggerian phenomenologism, or even the lament for *Gemeinschaft* expressed by neo-Kantian sociologists such as Tönnies, Weber, and Simmel. Add to these, of course, the monuments of German 'romantic' writing such as Schelling, Goethe, and Fichte.

It is important to point out, however, that the expression of such ideas in recent times has not been limited to Germany. They were also current among youth in the United States and France in the 1960's and 1970's. In fact, the influence of American social movements and their respective writers appears so great that in discussing the re-emergence of the 'German soul' one could contend that the basis for this re-emergence occurred first in the United States and was then, like many aspects of American culture, transferred to Germany.

One thing is certain, however; the Greens themselves never refer to their beliefs as the result of a resurgence of traditional Germanic ideological currents. This is at least partially because of their full awareness of the consequences of being linked to such movements as *Sturm und Drang*. They avoid like a plague any reference to a former Germanic, non-materialistic 'purity'.

It is important to realize that most of the elements discussed above — reunification, anti-Americanism, German romanticism — can be linked in one way or another to a contention that at times seems to dominate the debate: that the Greens represent a resurgence of German nationalism. What is evident and most striking concerning this aspect is not the importance of the influence of nationalism, but a total confusion as to what is nationalism. There is no agreement as to what constitutes nationalism and therefore there is no agreement as to its role. This will be discussed further in the conclusion of this article but for the time being we can mention some of the basic opinions put forward.

Writing in an article in *Telos*, Russell Berman describes the 'central motor' of the peace movement as "less survival and arms limitation than the vision of national autonomy."[32] He also describes it as an economic nationalism in that "to the extent that the peace movement can be characterized as anti-American, it is so as a manifestation of an awakened nationalism and as a reflection of the objective economic importance of West Germany's successful Ostpolitik."[33]

Josef Joffe, an editor of the West German daily *Die Zeit*, writing in the *New Republic*, uses the idea of nationalism but takes care to differentiate between "aggressive nationalism" and "pacifist nationalism." Whereas "aggressive nationalism" was the glue of the European fascism of the 20's and 30's, "pacifist nationalism is perhaps the only common tie that binds the shaky coalition commonly labelled as the peace movement."[34] He continues by stating that "unlike its bloody-minded forebearers, the new German nationalism is Candide-like, inward-bound, almost escapist. Its message is not Deutschland über alles but Leave us alone... It is nationalism but it is parochial...."

The view that the peace movement, and by inference the Greens, is a nationalist phenomenon is rejected by the German sociologist Joachim Hirsch: "What argues against all this — at least on the European level — is its internationalist direction, its overall rather leftist orientation, its anti-statism and its distrust of any form of super-power policy."[35] Hirsch suggests that "What might develop in the peace movement is something like a new patriotism, a feeling of common vulnerability, solidarity and responsibility for the future of society."

In fact, upon closer investigation, Hirsch's 'new patriotism' closely resembles the 'pacifist nationalism' of Joffe. Hirsch refuses to call it nationalism in order to avoid any comparison of today's movement with the German nationalist movements of the past. "Insofar as [the peace movement] is based on the ideas of a peaceful coexistence of peoples, of liberty, equality and tolerance, there is here a clear difference from what nationalism has until recently meant in this country."[36]

[32] Russell Berman, "Opposition to Rearmament and West German Culture," in *Telos*, no. 52, Summer 1982, p. 141.
[33] *Ibid.*, p. 142.
[34] *New Republic*, Feb. 14, 1983, p. 20.
[35] Joachim Hirsch, "The West German Peace Movements," in *Telos*, no. 51, Spring 1982, p. 139.
[36] *Ibid.*

The very vagueness and uncertainty which surrounds the concept of 'nationalism' prohibits anyone from stating with any degree of assurance whether the Greens represent a nationalist movement. What is certain, however, is that the Greens, in their official statements, go to great lengths to avoid mentioning the term 'German nation'. When they refer to the need for autonomy from the two super-powers, it is almost always in reference to European autonomy. It is not without symbolic importance that in their publications they prefer to use phrases such as 'the people living in the Federal Republic' rather than 'we Germans'. The Greens try as much as possible to avoid the overt nationalism demonstrated in peace movements such as that of Canada.

In trying to evaluate the many reasons for the popularity of the Greens in West Germany, it should be noted that the importance of their particular beliefs is not limited to West Germany. Throughout the West, and even to a certain extent in the East, alternative movements seem to be regaining an importance lost in the 1970's. The peace movement, the most vivid example, is prominent not only in West Germany but in the Nordic countries, Italy, Great Britain, Japan, Australia, New Zealand, the United States and Canada. These movements all share a call for the shifting of attention "from problems of distribution to grammar of forms of life," to quote Habermas. [37]

It is hard to deny, however, that in West German society these ideas have gained special prominence. Not to be ignored is that in addition to this popularity, the movements in West Germany have shown a remarkable tendency for collective action — a tendency which is somewhat lacking in other countries. It is this desire, shared among various movements, to cooperate in collective action, which has made possible the formation and success of the Green Party. Any discussion centring on the success of the Greens must deal not only with the popularity of alternative movements, but with the social and historical conditions which have created a desire for collective action.

Our own evaluation will be divided into what may be called objective and subjective reasons. In discussing the first of the objective reasons, one must point to the strategic position of West Germany. In regard to the East-West conflict it is a 'frontline State'. In any such conflict West Germany would be one of the first countries affected. The decline

[37] Quoted in Benhabib, *op. cit.*, p. 155.

of détente during the last year of the Carter administration obviously caused West Germans to worry. Because of the potential threat posed by any East-West military conflict, many citizens of the Federal Republic viewed their security as dependent upon *Ostpolitik* as opposed to military strength. One can easily imagine the effect of public announcements in America concerning the possibility of 'limiting nuclear war to Europe'. Once again, the geo-political situation of Germany calls for a new logic of defence.

One must add the fact that of all Western countries, West Germany is the most militarized. In addition to having the largest national army of the European NATO countries, it serves as host and training field to 200,000 American soldiers, not to mention the extensive British, French and Canadian presence. It is almost impossible to travel in the country without being confronted by miles and miles of fences which surround military installations. What other Western country has special traffic lanes and indications for tanks and other military vehicles along its major highways? In addition to the psychological effect of this visible military presence, we must take into account the restrictions on liberties which this necessitates. Not only is much of the country 'off-limits' to Germans, but the people must also submit to more extreme security regulations than in other countries.

It is essential to understand also the desperate ecological situation which exists in the Federal Republic. The country has been exposed, for going on a century, to an enormously high degree of urban concentration and industrialization. Much of the natural open space which does exist is used for military manoeuvres. These impingements have caused extensive damage to the natural environment.

In discussing the subjective factors behind the Greens' success, it is essential to return to the question of 'nationalism'. We repeat the difficulty in using the term 'nationalism' because of the ambiguities of the word. To call the Greens a nationalist movement would mean relating them to other nationalist movements such as the German youth movements of the 20's or the independence movement in Québec in the 60's and 70's. Despite its calls for the right of self-determination with respect to foreign powers, the Greens share little with these other movements. The central theme of these former movements was the defence and glorification of specific historical and cultural traditions which must be guarded against 'outside' influences through the existence of a strong and effective national State. The Greens, on the other hand

— anti-Americanism aside — exhibit no desire to defend past historical and cultural traditions. In fact, we postulate that it is precisely this lack of national sentiment which has allowed the growth of an alternative movement such as the Greens.

Returning to the article by Josef Joffe: he remarks that the current situation in West Germany may be the result of "truncated nation-building,"[38] stating that "the Federal Republic evolved as a country without continuity, as a fragment floating in the here and now, cut off from its roots yet tied to the Nazi past by guilt, shame, and remorse."

This situation poses tremendous problems for the West German State which, because of the heritage of National Socialism, cannot insist on the protection of a common cultural patrimony in order to evoke sympathy towards it. Joffe explains,

> Given the catastrophic end of the ultra-nationalist orgy of the Third Reich, the Federal Republic became a half nation without national symbols — bereft of identity, patriotism, or any other underpinning of legitimacy. Its main source of legitimacy was economic performance. And the remains of nationhood were submerged in Europe and the Atlantic Alliance...[39]

Joffe notes that while this may have been enough for "shell-shocked parents," the situation with the new generation is no longer the same.

The absence of any sense of national identity in West Germany was also pointed out by Volker Gransow and Clauss Offe in an article entitled "Political Culture and the Politics of Social Democratic Government."[40] Because of "racist and chauvinist perversions" of the concept of the nation under National Socialism, it can no longer provide Germans with a sense of shared past and common future.

The State in West Germany is seen, therefore, as lacking the 'patriotic strength' of other States. While the East German State can be linked to the past through its pretentions of a communist 'struggle against fascism', this is not the case in the West. In the words of Lewis Edinger, the State in West Germany is not regarded by most Germans as a reflection of *Volkswille* but as a "great impersonal corporation with

[38] *New Republic*, Feb. 14, 1983, p. 20.
[39] *Ibid.*
[40] Volker Gransow and Clauss Offe, "Politische Kultur und sozialdemokratische Regierung-spolitik," in *Das Argument*, 23:128, p. 551.

its managers (government), supervisory board of directors (parliament) and administrative staff (civil service)."[41]

Although this condition may seem a problem for the establishment of respect for the State, it seems to have allowed an enormous degree of creative freedom for alternative movements. Whereas in most countries the State can use the power of national consensus to discourage challenges to its essential role and structure, this is not the case in West Germany. Whereas the strength of traditional State logic, and the view of impossibility of change which usually accompanies this force, discourages alternative movements in most countries, the weakness of the State in the Federal Republic, brought on by its inability to evoke a historically based 'national' sympathy among its citizens, increases the chances of success and therefore the popularity of the movement. West German journalist Albert Sellner has referred to the vision in the country as a "new political culture."[42] The weakness of the West German leaders has made possible the dream of a new society.

Using this perspective we can now see how it is not the presence of national sentiment which has made possible the success of the Greens, but rather its absence. Although the logic of State capitalism which exists in West Germany is very similar to that of other Western countries, the lack of an historically and culturally based national consensus allows hope for the founding of a new logic; one that places greater emphasis on the environment, decentralization, democracy, and a new quality of life.

[41] Quoted in Craig, *op. cit.*, p. 49.
[42] Interview with Albert Sellner, Frankfurt, May 3, 1984.

# CULTURE AND COERCION
## J. Frank Harrison

Recently, I was presiding over a public meeting at which two Soviet academics were presenting their views on the question of nuclear disarmament. They presented their arguments — which specifically supported official Soviet foreign policy — in the face of an obvious undercurrent of anti-Sovietism. Everything from the Hungarian invasion of 1956 to the downing of the Korean airliner in 1983, everything from the GULAG to Sakharov's exile in Gorky, was presented as a self-evident demonstration of Soviet nastiness and deceit.

To criticize the excesses of the Marxist-Leninist superpower is indeed legitimate. However, there is always a tendency for the kind of anti-Sovietism described here to form part of an uncritical acceptance of Western international and domestic politics. As has so often been the case during the Cold War of the last forty years, criticism of the communists has been combined with an uncritical affirmation of the liberal (and therefore capitalist) democracies. It is a view which springs from a Manichean approach to politics, which divides the world into either good or bad States, condemning the latter. It is also a view that is especially useful for the powerholders in society, whoever they may be, and over whatever kind of system they may exert their power. The vision of 'external enemies' has always unified societies, generating conformist obedience, the uncritical and voluntary acceptance of the *status quo*.

Enthusiastic and non-reflective criticism of communist abuses of political power must be regarded as one of the means whereby political unity is maintained in modern States. In the hatred of the objective

*J. Frank Harrison is the author of* The Modern State: An anarchist analysis *and has edited* Statism and Anarchy *by M. A. Bakunin. Dr. Harrison is currently chairperson of the Department of Political Science at St. Francis Xavier University in Nova Scotia.*

enemy, personified in the form of the USSR, individuals affirm their support of their own society. For those of us who have been re-reading George Orwell's *1984*, we might recall the hate campaigns described as part of his anti-utopia, Oceania, where group and national unity are affirmed in the passionate and mindless hatred of the 'other.' It also has the advantage of dehumanizing the entire population of the enemy State, so that should a hot war break out, you can liquidate them without offending moral principles. So, during the Vietnam War, Americans were quite content to kill the 'gooks'; and during the Falklands War, the British were permitted to kill 'Argies' without any threat to their moral sentiments.

As a result of the character and content of our knowledge about politics (political culture), our political vocabulary has a strong normative element. We have 'hurrah' words like democracy, and 'boo' words like socialism. Party politics takes place within extremely limited boundaries of competition. Defeated Liberals and NDP candidates do not hesitate to congratulate their rivals, affirming the system and its actions as fundamentally satisfactory, even in their own defeat. There is an inability to step beyond the boundaries of the limited political vocabulary and political imagination which confirms established power structures in society and in the State. And at times, when hysteria is whipped up by the press, the public gives a predictably Pavlovian response to the linguistic bells of control.

This is not to say that communism is not worth criticizing. Marxism-Leninism is a thoroughly unattractive form of politics both ideologically and structurally. However, to confine one's criticism to a pro-capitalist polemic, to remain within the unacknowledged yet distinctive parameters of liberalism, is to accept self-censorship and subordination to another kind of domination; that is, subordination to the hierarchies of capitalism and the modern bureaucratic State.

To assess political power — or power and hierarchy in any form (patriarchal, economic, political, cultural or religious) — it is necessary to step back from the world, to be sceptical of all values, to refuse to nail one's colours to any of the symbols of authority which we find in the world. This does not mean that we should become simple scientists, chasing after the impossible goal of value-freedom. Like Nietzsche, I would say that value-free science plays into the hands of those who possess power, and is therefore a mechanism of domination. Those who work in either the physical or the social sciences ought to make judgements about the practical consequences of their work. They should provide more than what the Frankfurt School called 'technical' reason, which is a narrow empiricism incapable of a critical orientation (see Habermas and Marcuse for the development of this theme).

To assess power as it exists in various societies is to consider and question types of human domination. I would suggest that an appropriate critical position for this task might be summarized by the term 'anarchist.' The popular image of the anarchist, and the one which is promoted by the media, is that of a dark-cloaked bomb thrower whose only concern is violent disruption. And certainly some anarchists are advocates of violence for various reasons which I will not go into here. However, in itself, anarchism simply means the rejection of rulers as unnecessary. It frequently has at its root the same image of humanity as does classical liberalism; and that is the rational individual who is capable of making all decisions concerning his/her own life. However, more consistent than liberal thought, the anarchist position unequivocally rejects political, economic, cultural, sexist and other forms of domination — the interlinked hierarchies which confine our lives and perpetrate the established order. It is, therefore, consistently critical, avoiding elegant authoritarian myths which are the substance of so much political thought from Plato to the present, including that of the Marxists of various shades.

It also avoids the predisposition of social scientists to assume the 'necessity' of structured systems of authority in human affairs, proclaimed as the 'iron law of oligarchy' by Robert Michels after he had studied the highly oligarchic German Social Democrats at the end of the last century. Raymond Aron more recently presented it as follows:

> The order of industrial society, then, assumes forms both oligarchical and hierarchical. In one, leaders of the multiple hierarchies are engaged in constant dialogue and the political subsystem is relatively separate from other subsystems. In the other, the political subsystem, organized as a single party, imposes a supreme, temporal, and spiritual authority over all the leaders of all other hierarchies; all of society thereby becomes political since administration, government, society, and the state are merged. [1]

No wonder the French students in 1968 proclaimed, "Better wrong with Sartre than right with Aron." Such frozen formulae contradict the basic intellectual requirement that, like Socrates, we question everything — a requirement which to my mind makes political enquiry a necessarily radical activity.

A recent collection of anarchist studies entitled *1984 and After* [2] takes major themes of Orwell's novel (*1984*) and explains how North American society and politics continues to reflect his totalitarian imagery. My purpose here is to supplement those arguments by considering, i) cultural, and ii) police powers that manipulate our ideas and actions in the liberal and capitalist Canadian State.

Of course, Orwell's hypothetical anti-utopia is dominated entirely by a political élite whose motivation is the self-subsistent narcotic of bureaucratic State power. In his *1984* all forms of repression are drawn into the singular vortex of the State. Our own real world is not so simple, and economic structures exist with their own kind of influence and power. Partially in consequence of this the novel is usually regarded as a vicious satire against the Soviet State; and there is nothing wrong with that, unless we fall into a justification of the liberal State as well. Jean Ellezam correctly argues,

> Liberalism seizes on *Nineteen Eighty-Four* for justification. However, opposition to totalitarianism does not in any sense imply unconditional

[1] Raymond Aron, *Progress and Disillusion*, Mentor, 1969, pp. 58-59. A *Britannica Perspective* on the 200th anniversary of the *Encyclopaedia Britannica* (1968).
[2] Marsha Hewitt and Dimitri I. Roussopoulos (eds.), *1984 and After*. Montréal: Black Rose Books, 1984.

acceptance of the bourgeois world. There are other dualities besides capitalism *versus* socialism in the ideological spectrum; Manicheism is a poor model...

Criticism of the bourgeois system is evident, explicit or implicit, in all of Orwell's writing. ...This is why his popular image as a liberal is paradoxical.[3]

With this in mind we must turn to our own society with a more jaundiced eye, and consider the extent to which our Canadian culture generates an inability to think critically, turning to police coercion where informal methods fail.

Opinion in liberal society is kept within relatively narrow parameters. Freedom of expression thereby becomes for the vast majority of the population freedom of conformity. Dissident voices are thus deprived of a share in the common sense of the society, no matter how rational may be the criticism. Any language of politics that does not partake of political parties, Parliament and politicians, is meaningless to the population at large. Further, it is extremely unlikely that they will ever hear that language. The increasing centralization of communications creates a veritable monopoly of language and information. Anyone who has tried to produce a newspaper or journal 'against the current' will realize the massive difficulties of financing and marketing alternative ideas. It becomes very difficult to suggest to any wide audience that there is a causal relationship between private property and unemployment, between public appointments and party affiliation, between wealth and influence, between law and oppression. We are told that there are no 'classes' in the USA and Canada, that liberal democracy gives everyone a voice in politics, that we are freer and richer and generally better-off than anyone else in the world.

Meanwhile it remains a truism that there is very little difference between political parties in this Canadian system of 'brokerage politics'. Each party tries to appeal to as broad a spectrum of the population as possible, its leaders and candidates saying anything that might prove appealing. In consequence, everyone ends up saying the same thing, no-one takes election promises seriously, and the suggestion that elections

---

[3] Jean Ellezam, "Critical Dimensions of Orwell's Thought," *Ibid.*, p. 130.

might give a 'mandate' to anyone to pursue a specific line of policy becomes ridiculous. [4]

The Premier of Nova Scotia, John Buchanan, who has been known to say that metric measures have a flavour of communism about them, made another telling statement during last Fall's provincial election campaign. He stated quite clearly that there were no issues in the election. And he was right.   Image, not issues, is the stuff of our

[4] Concerning the existence of a 'mandate', a recent study of Canadian politics concludes that "Elections may focus the attention of public and politicians alike on important problems and reflect or even generate conflicts, but their ability to produce policy mandates is doubtful... Elections decide who shall govern, but not the substance of policy." Harold D. Clarke, Jane Jenson, *et al.*, *The Politics of Discontent in Canada.* Toronto: Gage, 1984, p. 172. Moreover, the authors add that "the patterns of choice on issues combine to thwart a *policy* mandate, especially on any policy representing long-term planning or fundamental restructuring of the economy or the society." *Ibid.*, p. 182.

Nonetheless, we find that President Reagan, who received the support of about 30% of the electorate, claimed that "the people of this country made it very plain that they approved what we've been doing." (William Johns reporting in *The Globe and Mail*, Nov. 8, 1984: "Reagan sees win as new mandate for policies")

Similarly, when introducing economic legislation into the House of Commons on November 8, 1984, the Finance Minister of the federal government, Michael Wilson, referred frequently to 'our mandate.' The new Tory government of Canada was seen as having been given democratic permission to change radically the Canadian economy: "For too long, government has tried to substitute the judgements of politicians and regulators for the judgements of those in the marketplace, through excessive regulation and by trying to buy its way with borrowed money out of each new problem that arises... We have suffered for too long from the growing gap between the rhetoric of reliance on the private sector and the reality of increasing government intervention." (*Chronicle-Herald*, Halifax, Nov. 9, 1984) This mythical maximization of economic activity in a situation of free market capitalism can have horrendous results in practice — as Thatcher's U.K. demonstrates; and Canadians certainly did not vote for it.

politics. Politics for the public becomes entirely a question of *style without content*.

This has best been seen in the USA, where an apparently senile actor, who has increased poverty at home and the possibility of nuclear war abroad, is enthusiastically elected to a second term as the country's President. His electoral road-show had little to do with issues. His rallies have been described as 'politics as Hollywood.'

> Every event is scripted and rehearsed and every camera angle and lighting arrangement practised with the kind of Bergmanesque detail seen in *Fanny and Alexander*.
>
> The audiences on these occasions are the equivalent of film extras. In the hour or two before a Reagan rally begins they are vigorously taken through their paces. The carefully selected warm-up person, often a broadcasting personality brought in especially from California, takes them through a chorus of 'four more years', a round of banner-waving, and also leads the band in several pieces of patriotic music. The crowd are warned not to use too much energy during the rehearsal, but to save their full blast for the arrival of the superstar of the show.
>
> ...In this world of Hollywood fantasy the blemishes which the real life world of the presidency offers are blotted out. The principal actor never appears in public, except on stage; that way he is never associated with all the real world events which might impinge on the screen image.... All then that remains is the script. The key is to avoid any substance about the future and to string together a series of Bob Hope-style one-liners about the opponent.[5]

Given this, it is not surprising that the existence of thirty-five million Americans living in poverty, Reagan's inability to stay awake during important meetings, a growth in the national debt to $1.57 trillion, an accelerated arms race, and a reduction in government financed social services — it is not surprising that this goes unnoticed. We are faced with the strange phenomenon of Reagan supporters amongst the un-employed in soup kitchens in Michigan, where thousands had been laid off from automobile plants. Why would 70% of these people

---

[5] Alex Brummer, "Ronald Reagan's Script Leaves Reality Behind," *Manchester Guardian Weekly*, Nov. 4, 1984.

support Reagan? Because this is the politics of style without content, with a modicum of what George Orwell called Doublethink.[6]

And lest my fellow Canadians slip too easily into self-congratulation, it should be remembered that the new Prime Minister was conspicuous in his failure to make policy statements during the last election campaign. Moreover, if the American election had been held in Canada, all the indications are that Reagan would have been elected here too.[7]

The politics of conformity, it seems, are very much with us. And how could this not be the case given the control of information. Noam Chomsky has called it 'brainwashing under freedom'. Here criticism is permitted, even encouraged, but only as long as it operates within the boundaries of accepted opinion. Chomsky stresses "the utility for propaganda of a critical stance that incorporates the basic assumptions of official doctrine and thereby marginalizes authentic and rational critical discussion."[8] Moreover, when it becomes a choice of facts that are to be presented to the public, let us remember that some things are reported, and others are not. When Soviet fighters downed the Korean airplane in 1983, the *New York Times* devoted seven pages to the event. Very good. However, what about the downing of an Angolan plane shortly thereafter by the American and South African-backed UNITA terrorists, killing 126 people? That got 100 words in the *New York Times*, with no comment. And ten years earlier when Israel downed a civilian plane that had strayed over the Suez Canal during a sandstorm, killing 110 people, the *Times* argued that "no useful

---

[6] Patrick Martin, "Voting Reveals Picture of Two U.S. Societies," *The Globe and Mail*, Nov. 7, 1984.

[7] See James Rusk, "Reagan Tops Poll in Canada," *The Globe and Mail*, Nov. 2, 1984:

"If Canadians were electing the president of the United States, President Ronald Reagan and running mate George Bush probably would clobber their Democratic opponents, Walter Mondale and Geraldine Ferraro, according to a current poll.

The Reagan-Bush ticket is almost 19 percentage points ahead of the Democrats, according to a national poll of more than 1,000 Canadians over the age of 18 conducted earlier this week by Winnipeg-based Angus Reid and Associates.

The telephone survey of 1,063 Canadians found that the Reagan-Bush ticket would win the votes of 47.1 per cent of those surveyed if they had a vote in next Tuesday week's U.S. election, while the Mondale-Ferraro ticket would get the vote of 28.5 per cent, and 24.4 per cent did not know how they would vote."

[8] Noam Chomsky, "1984: Orwell's and Ours," in Hewitt and Roussopoulos, *op. cit.*, p. 70.

purpose is served by an acrimonious debate over the assignment of blame."

"In such ways," argues Chomsky, "history is shaped in the interests of those in power."[9] And Canadian newspapers play the same game. Open your local newspaper on any day, and you will find stories such as the one printed by my local rag, the *Chronicle-Herald* of Halifax. We are told that the Soviet Union has not been invited to celebrate the Canadian Navy's seventy-fifth anniversary because of the 1979 invasion of Afghanistan and the 1983 downing of the KAL flight 007.[10] No mention is made of American activities in Latin America, or of the invasion of Grenada (which even Britain's right-wing government condemned).

As in Orwell's Oceania, we have to have our hatreds and our preferences in the proper perspective. In consequence we have media-generated selectivity, distortion, and the encouragement of political narrowness (if not downright ignorance). Moreover, to the extent that electoral politics are trivialized by both political parties and the media, the singular act of political participation to which most of us ever aspire (i.e., voting) becomes a simple affirmation of the *status quo*.

On the other hand, it is not all self-repression based upon an uncritical mentality bred of the brainwashing called education, information and the news. Most citizens of Canada would even admit that their own personal 1985 is not entirely dependent upon techniques of persuasion. Even though it is true that "the broad normative tolerance of individuals in the modern capitalist state stifles any passionate rebellion,"[11] the police still play a significant political role. Who could ever deny this after the revelations of the McDonald Commission some four years ago?

The evidence suggests that a para-military police force, the RCMP, in cooperation with provincial and city forces, have taken it upon themselves to be the guardians of our political morality. Organized in a manner which develops an authoritarian mentality amongst its members, in its day-to-day activity, a police force tends to view the

---

[9] *Ibid.*, p. 73.
[10] Robert Gordon, "Warsaw Pact Not Invited to Party," *The Chronicle-Herald*, Nov. 9, 1984.
[11] Jean-Pierre Deslauriers, "The Totality of Totalitarianism," in Hewitt and Roussopoulos, *op. cit.*, p. 132.

rest of us as potential criminals. Their presumption must be that 'there are a lot of evil people out there' against whom society must be protected. And some of that 'evil out there' takes the form of political ideas and extra-parliamentary political activity. So, for example, to be active in the peace movement is regarded as just cause for tapping someone's phone — with or without a warrant, although these are easy to acquire from cooperative judges. [12]

The police in Canada have taken it upon themselves to 'target' political enemies of the State. Having done so, it has pursued the individuals involved by acting as *agents provocateurs*, destroying property, initiating break-ins into the offices of 'suspected' persons and institutions, stealing files and membership lists of political organizations (including those of the Parti Québécois), blackmailing people to force them to spy on their friends, falsifying tax returns, and even kidnapping people.

All of this has been discussed in detail elsewhere. It is not speculation, but reported fact. The question is — is this a deviation from the norm? Is police work fundamentally decent in our State and were the above facts exceptions to the rule? My contention is that this is not the case. The Security Service of the RCMP took 20% of the force's budget — as Svend Robinson revealed to the Commons in September 1983. Moreover, in 1982 they checked the political credentials of 76,521 federal civil servants — ensuring that they were not closet communists hawking secrets to the Russians. [13] Security is a serious and sweeping business.

Their zeal, however, was combined with incompetence. They got caught in the act of breaking laws which they were supposed to be keeping. This gave rise to a debate as to whether or not the police should be allowed to break the law in pursuit of their tasks — with former Solicitor-General Robert Kaplan taking the side of police powers beyond the restrictions of law. Protecting the State, rather than the people in it, the police should be free to do whatever they decide is for our own good. So goes the argument.

This interference into citizens' lives has, of course, supposedly been taken away from the para-military RCMP, and given over to a civilian

[12] Frank Harrison, "Orwell and Anarchy in 1984," *Ibid.*
[13] As reported by Gordon Fairweather, Human Rights Commissioner, to the Senate committee on national security, October 1983.

agency — the Canadian Security Intelligence Agency, that last product of a dying Liberal administration in June 1984. Let us not be persuaded that this will improve the situation. The new agency was created only because of political embarrassment, and its operatives are the very same people who were in the RCMP security service. Ted Finn, the first director of the agency, informs us that "slightly more than 90% of the members of the RCMP security service have decided to join the new agency...."[14]

So now we have our own secret police, the CSIS. There is also a secret court, with an anonymous membership drawn from the Federal Court of Canada, the purpose of which is "the official, legal targeting of groups and individuals considered serious threats to national security and thus deserving of the closest scrutiny — spies, terrorists and subversives."[15] There are no regulations controlling the choice of victims at the time of writing. Warrants can be issued to 'legalize' phone tapping, plant bugging devices, search, and obtain access to confidential records (such as medical files). The Tory Solicitor-General, Elmer MacKay, sees "nothing particularly sinister about it."[16] By the same measure, neither the CIA nor the KGB are particularly sinister — which is a good thing insofar as "intelligence agents of some foreign governments are free to carry out limited spying operations on residents of Canada..."[17] according to the head of the CSIS.

The new security agency, populated by ex-policemen, will continue to regard every citizen as a potential traitor. Its purpose is to collect information about anyone they have reason to suspect is a threat to 'national security'. The information is collected without our knowledge, is often imprecise or fallacious hearsay, and is compiled with suspicion and a desire to discover individual failings, to cast doubt on the individual's dependability as a good Canadian. In an era when the State's power extends to a control of ever-greater segments of the national product, and becomes the source of employment opportunity, these Thought Police threaten everyone, discouraging impure thoughts,

[14] See *The Globe and Mail*, July 13, 1984.
[15] Jeff Sallot, "Spy Court Wields Power Secretly, Without Regulation," *The Globe and Mail*, Jan. 24, 1985.
[16] See *The Globe and Mail*, Jan. 25, 1985.
[17] Patrick Martin, "Foreign Agents Free to Spy on Residents, Security Official Says," *The Globe and Mail*, Jan. 15, 1985.

and encouraging self-censorship as a means of safeguarding one's job. And as the micro-chip revolution continues, and information storage and retrieval becomes ever more efficient, the potential for supervising the private lives of citizens seems limitless.

The term 'national interest' is most useful to our self-styled guardians. First, it means that we can be kept in the dark, giving the political police a free hand. Second, it is frequently used to suggest that the victims of police surveillance are somehow un-Canadian, anti-democratic and pro-communist — potential traitors who hardly deserve a break. Third, it suggests a relationship to questions of such awe-inspiring importance that the so-called constitutional rights of a few individuals are worth the price. Fourth, it has a useful psychological effect on the operatives themselves; whose own sense of self-esteem is raised by the idea of watching over the nation's security.

In response to this, one should always ask exactly what is it that is being protected? What kind of knowledge? Or is it the established State structure itself? And from whom are we protecting it? — obviously not the Americans, who had access to 'our' secret police files even while our own intelligence agency was being denied them. [18] All in all, I have a strong suspicion that the 'national security' is a bit of a chimera, conjured up regularly as a means of justifying the arbitrary power of officers of the State. It is a legal fiction used to associate critics of the Canadian system with Communists, which means that they are helping the perceived enemy, the USSR.

What seems to have happened is that as the technology of control has developed, the State has used it. The police are an arm of the State in this operation of social integration and attack on nonconformity. As such, security activities are no more than an extension of already established methods of policing society. The very logic of the police is that of the State; which is to seize every opportunity for control. Presenting an unrealistic and jaundiced view of society, they suggest that all order would break down without their action as watchdogs — and even though they have not read Plato's *Republic*, they certainly see themselves filling the canine function. From this perspective, the radical actions of a peaceworker, organizing a demonstration against

---

[18] See Jeff Sallot, "FBI Already Given Data Link Denied to Ottawa Agency," *The Globe and Mail*, Oct. 17, 1984.

the Cruise missile, for example, are as disturbing as the actions of an axe murderer. Security work becomes an extension of ordinary police work.

To keep the public with a sense of insecurity, and a sense of need for a protector, is the goal of the State. At its most general level the suggestion is that the incidence of robbery, rape and violence in society would be unlimited if the police were not on the job. This reflects a judgement on human nature as pessimistic as that of any Thomas Hobbes, and is a source of the police tendency to regard all the public as potential criminals.

This argument is highly debatable. Crime is not a normal human response to a non-policed situation. To the extent that criminals exist, they are a product of the socio-political environment, reflecting the egoistic materialism of the capitalist culture. Who ends up in prison? — "…those who learn only too well the meaning and power of 'success' in this society, and who dare to use the same tactics of intimidation, violence and lack of concern for others to achieve it as do the political and economic élite, but are without access to their legalized means…."[19] And even then, most people do not resort to these means even when they get the opportunity — as during a police strike. We are, in fact, a remarkably sociable lot.

Rather than preventing crime, it might be argued that the police are involved in the reproduction of a criminal class — giving to society what society must then protect itself against through a police force. As I have said elsewhere.

> Harassment and intimidation is the police style. If you are young and driving an old car, and therefore probably working class, you will be stopped and searched. If you have open liquor or a marijuana joint, you are charged and acquire a criminal record. You become an immediate suspect for later petty crimes and, in the event of another minor offence, you can end up doing time. You are sent to the best school for criminality — the prison. Thereby, you become criminalized by the police system, one purpose of which is the reproduction of the group in society which justifies its existence.[20]

---

[19] Helen Durie in an unpublished article, quoted by Claire Culhane, "Prisons: 1984 and After," in Hewitt and Roussopoulos, *op. cit.*, p. 78.
[20] See Frank Harrison, "Orwell and Anarchy in 1984" *Ibid.*, p. 161.

In this manner, harassment by the police over trivial matters against arbitrarily chosen groups (particularly working-class males and racial minorities) can be seen as the daily norm — and harassment of political targets is merely its extension.

As for the prisons themselves, they can be seen as "an integral part of the growing drift towards authoritarianism that is taking place in our alieged liberal democracy."[21] We might well ask why our prisons hold 150 persons per 100,000 of the population — compared with 85 in England and Wales, 67 in France, and 28 in the Netherlands? We might also ask why those people are there, brutalized, being made into people who are incapable of being other than criminals, and certainly more capable of violence when they come out than when they went in. This is so very obvious that even the prison authorities themselves have suggested that as many as 90% of Canada's prison population ought not to be there.[22]

Perhaps it is because the logic of hierarchical organization is to maintain itself, and expand its influence. The State does this in alliance with that other hierarchy, the economic system. The economic élite and the political élite have much in common, and their membership interlocks at many points. Many laws are passed specifically for the benefit of the owners of property in our society. They are, however, capable of organizing themselves as distinct interests and competing with each other — as seems to be happening in Canada with this Tory government which, controlled by representatives of the economic hierarchy, are seeking to dismantle elements of State power. It is unlikely, however, that any government will reduce the policing function of the State. To the extent that the neo-conservatives in politics reduce the social programmes provided by the State, generating poverty and unemployment, they will need the police even more. And should massive internal dissent occur, they can always send us to concentration camps. Such camps are provided for by Order-in-Council 1981-1305, which gives the Solicitor-General powers (under the Emergency Powers Order):

> No. 6   To establish, administer and operate civilian internment camps;

---

[21] Culhane, *Ibid.*, p. 76.
[22] In 1983 the Correctional Service of Canada published "Incarceration: A Plea for Restraint" in which this conclusion in presented.

No. 7   To facilitate the selective reduction and transfer of prison population to provide for the establishment of civilian internment camps. [23]

When those camps are to be used, and against whom, is not indicated.

From the above we cannot but conclude that Canada has something of *1984* about it. It is not simply a capitalist State, for structures of power (hierarchy in any form) acquire their own *raison d'être*, interests, ideology and goals. As anarchists have always argued, this is particularly true of the State; and we have seen here how the Canadian State is sustained by both a narrow perception of reality and an identifiable system of police coercion. There are other hierarchies which compromise us fundamentally (such as capitalism and sexism), and which must also be demystified in the framework of our culture, as a precondition for their removal. What anarchism persuasively suggests is that neither one nor all of these structures can be replaced by resorting to hierarchical techniques of their own; and a revolution in one area can never in reality automatically remove dehumanization (meaning simply treating people as objects) everywhere. Anarchism becomes a multi-faceted critique of all forms of repression. The cultural realms of ideology and aesthetics, the economic realm of property and exploitation, the scientific realm which involves the technological distortion of a healthy ecological condition, the sexual realm of patriarchy and domination according to gender and age, and the political realm of the State: all are areas upon which anarchists may concentrate their attention. Fundamental to them all, however, is the view that neither a reformist nor a revolutionary State can be a vehicle for progressive change; for intrinsic to the State is its own hierarchical structure and assumptions.

To the extent that the State's position in and over modern society is considerably entrenched, the anarchist may be regarded as something of a radical pessimist; for the destruction of hierarchy is not just around the corner. However, this same position makes of him/her the only consistent critic of human oppression, unlikely to be confused by systems of authority implicit in the programmes of others, avoiding hierarchical directions in such organizations or movements in which he/she may choose to participate. The hope must be that anarchist

[23] Quoted by Culhane, *op. cit.*, p. 92.

perceptions rub off on others, and like a bacillus gradually disable the operation of those various systems of power within which we all find ourselves, and which are reinforced by their broad acceptance.

The anarchist is most often an advocate of discussion rather than dogma, emphasizing human variety against conformity, looking to a free individual as against one trapped in hierarchy. As a critic and a propagandist, he/she would probably have no difficulty in appreciating the view once stated by Leszek Kolakowski:

> ...in almost every epoch the philosophy of the priest and the philosophy of the jester are the two most general forms of intellectual culture. The priest is the guardian of the absolute; he sustains the cult of the final and the obvious as acknowledged by and contained in tradition. The jester is he who moves in good society without belonging to it, and treats it with impertinence; he who doubts all that appears self-evident.... He is motivated not by a desire to be perverse but by distrust of a stabilized system. [24]

Kolakowski was writing as a Marxist at the time, but that does not prevent him from appealing to all of us when he concludes, "We declare ourselves in favor of the jester's philosophy, and thus vigilant against any absolute...."

## APPENDIX I

You will note that in this paper my sources have frequently been Canadian newspapers, particularly the national edition of *The Globe and Mail*. It might well be argued that the very presence of the kind of controversial information found there militates against the argument that the media are principally involved in the politics of conformity. In response to this I would argue, first, that the 'impression' of a free press (unbiased and investigative) is of such value as integrative propaganda in the society, that it far outweighs any damage that minor revelations might have. Indeed, quite the opposite. It may lead people to believe that something is being done about such things as police harassment, invasion of privacy, and police brutality. Second, we are not to know how large is the submerged mass beneath the tip of the iceberg that is revealed by the media. Only a minority of crimes are solved by the police; how much smaller a percentage are solved when they themselves are the criminals? Third, and perhaps most important, the presentation of critical information

[24] Leszek Kolakowski, "The Priest and the Jester," in *Toward a Marxist Humanism*. New York: Grove Press, 1968, pp. 33-34.

concerning repression in the Canadian State is inconsistent, often lacking any analysis of its significance. Also, as news, it is essentially transitory, to be replaced by another story in the next pile of news releases. Further, it is hidden away amongst hundreds of other pieces of information about sports, the families of Prime Ministers, and the latest advertisements for vaginal sprays, etc. In this way the news is *trivialized*. It is well said that the attempt to follow socio-political events by reading a newspaper is like trying to tell time by looking at the second hand of a clock.

## APPENDIX II

As an anarchist, I would argue that the welfare State has indeed sapped the independence of individuals in society. As a result of the State's expanded role in education, medicine, social security, unemployment, etc., its hierarchy has become increasingly the main determinant in our lives. More than ever before are we its dependents; and it is our responsibility to think of ways in which the condition might be ameliorated.

This same welfare State which has increasingly drawn us into its institutional framework is also attacked by those who are called the new conservatives or new Right. In the USA they are typified by Reagan and his cohorts. In Canada the right wing of the Tory party has taken up the position.

Their emphasis is on the manner in which the enlarged modern State has influenced the economic sector, arguing that government regulations are stifling business initiative, hindering profit-making, and discouraging investment. We are told that welfare payments and unemployment insurance payments are discouraging people from working except for prohibitively high (for the employer) wages. Massive government spending also means massive borrowing, government debt, and a high price for money when the private sector seeks to borrow. Then, at a more general level, big government is seen to be a creeping socialism, involving a threat to private property and loss of personal freedoms. The political energy of the nation is sapped along with its economic resourcefulness — against which the only defence is to begin to dismantle the State.

These arguments of the neo-conservatives are, as I suggested in this article, an attack by the economic hierarchy upon the State hierarchy at a point where their interests conflict. It is very much a rebellion of capitalism against the State, seeking to remove State controls. In this way they wish to replace dependence on the State by dependence on the capitalist employer by *expanding the arbitrary power of employers*. It is a position shown clearly in the submission of the Canadian Manufacturing Association to the federal Cabinet and the Royal Commission on the Economy. Their demands, reported by Thomas Walkom in *The Globe and Mail*, involved the "loosening up of expensive laws dealing with child labor (sic), statutory holidays, minimum wages and health and safety standards..." Such things "get in the way of business" and lead to unemployment. Such was and is the argument (October 17, 1984).

This is the position of the right wing of the Tory party, which group would be taken to include the Finance Minister, Michael Wilson, Sinclair Stevens (Regional Industrial Expansion), Robert Coates (Defence), and Barbara McDougall (Finance). There are the makings here of a group who would follow the example of Margaret Thatcher in the U.K. They would privatize public companies and reduce involvement of the State in the economy generally. Wilson's mini-budget at the beginning of November 1984 indicated the first steps in that direction.

In all of this, what we should remember is that none of this right-wing enthusiasm has anything to do with anarchism. It is best seen as a narrow and reactionary position which will contribute nothing to human welfare. It is an attempt to increase the capacity for economic exploitation under the guise of encouraging investment. Its motivation is the distorted viewpoint of the economic élite masquerading under the guise of job creators.

To the extent that it is successful it must be regarded as regressive, generating greater hierarchical authority and coercion than is already present. Anarchists, like socialists and welfare State liberals, oppose it.

On the other hand, let us not be fooled into believing that these conservatives want smaller government. They want less government in some areas, but more in others. They are positively neanderthal when it comes to such questions as capital punishment and censorship. They support a strong police force to keep public order and defend property — especially in periods of high unemployment (which their economic prescriptions will do nothing to improve, given the labour-saving character of modern capital investment). They are rabid anti-communists, and want to participate in the international crusade against the USSR and its allies by increasing military expenditure. Therefore, the anti-State positions of the neo-conservatives will generate a stronger State in areas of traditional coercion. They are, therefore, the very antithesis of anarchists.

# PAUL GOODMAN:
# THE ANARCHIST AS CONSERVATOR
*George Woodcock*

Anarchism has sometimes been described, especially by the Marxists, as a regressive doctrine, and insofar as anarchists have never accepted the necessary desirability of progress, the criticism is justified, though to admit it does not mean admitting that anarchism is ahistorical. It means that the anarchist moves through history in a different way from the liberal or the socialist, who is always inclined to assume that the future necessarily promises the greater good. It means that, where the Marxist — for example — seems destined to carry to a further degree of efficiency the rationalization of human control over the material world which capitalism and the Nation-State achieved, the anarchist stands aside in criticism of the very concepts of efficiency and rationalization when they are derived only from a consideration of economic factors. Anarchism recognizes the perilous importance of the psychological element at work in the development of human institutions, the element whose dangers were best defined by that acute observer of political societies, Lord Acton, in his famous aphorism: "Power tends to corrupt, and absolute power corrupts absolutely." The anarchists have always seen the tragic flaw in social democracy as its assumption that by the use of power transferred from one élite to another, coercive institutions can be melted away — the State, as Engels once claimed, can paradoxically wither under the dictatorship of one class within it, the proletariat. The anarchists have recognized — and the history of socialist countries seems to have proved them right — that the use of power merely feeds the desire for power.

---

*George Woodcock is a journalist, poet and author of more than forty books, among them* Gandhi, Dawn and Darkest Hour: A Study of Aldous Huxley, Canada and Canadians, Anarchism, *and* The Crystal Spirit *(a biography of George Orwell).*

It is because the anarchists have never been able to accept the power-dominated politics of the world in which they live that they have so often — from Gerrard Winstanley down to Paul Goodman — seemed to assume a posture rather like the legendary position of Mahomet's coffin, suspended between its two lodestones in sacred Mecca. It is very easy to see the anarchist lodestones as an idealized future towards which they yearn without great hope and an ideal past to which they look back with frustrated longing.

In fact, the situation is somewhat less simple than that, since what the more perceptive anarchists actually believe is not that we have to yearn towards future or past, but that in any society there are really two kinds of presents between which we have to make our choice. One is the institutional present, that of the authoritarian structures under which we live and which atomize society and alienate individuals by weakening the sense of social responsibility that is innate in all people. For, as I have said elsewhere:

> All anarchists, I think, would accept the proposition that man naturally contains within him all the attributes that make him capable of living in freedom and social concord. They may not believe that man is naturally good, but they may believe very fervently that man is naturally social.... Not merely is man naturally social, the anarchists contend, but the tendency to live in society emerged with him as he evolved out of the animal world. Society existed before man, and a society living and growing freely would in fact be a natural society. *Anarchism*

Here we come to the second anarchist present. For, as thoughtful anarchists from Kropotkin onward have always argued, the institutions of power have never completely eliminated man's natural inclination to cooperate; if they did, George Orwell's nightmare of *1984* would indeed be fulfilled. In fact, it is because men carry on their benign way of free and natural cooperation parallel to the malign and coercive way of the State that society continues to exist as an endurable human environment. As Colin Ward put it in one of the more important theoretical works on the subject:

> An anarchist society, a society which organizes itself without authority, is always in existence, like a seed beneath the snow, buried under the weight of the state and its bureaucracy, capitalism and its waste, privilege and its injustices, nationalism and its suicidal loyalties, religious differences and their superstitious separatism. *Anarchy in Action*

What the anarchist seeks to do, according to this viewpoint, is not to destroy the present political order so that it may be replaced by a better system of organization; that is the Marxist fallacy which produced the tragic history of post-Tsarist Russia. Rather, anarchism proposes to clear the existing structure of coercive institutions so that the natural society which has survived in a largely subterranean way from earlier, freer and more originative periods can be liberated to flower again in a different future. The anarchists have never been nihilists, wishing to destroy present society entirely and replace it by something new, precisely because they have never been neophiliacs either, who see virtue only in what is novel. The anarchists have always valued the endurance of natural social impulses and of the voluntary institutions they create, and it is to liberating the great network of human cooperation that even now spreads through all levels of our lives rather than to creating or even imagining brave new world that they have bent their efforts. That is why there are so few utopian writings among the anarchists; they have always believed that human social instincts, once set free, could be trusted to adapt society in desirable and practical ways without plans — which are always constructive — being made beforehand.

To declare that the capacity to live a free life — and the rudimentary institutions for it — exists among us and needs to be liberated and encouraged, is at once revolutionary and conservative: revolutionary in the sense that the destruction or at least the erosion of a whole structure of power is contemplated; and conservative in the sense that the successful outcome of the revolution is seen in terms of the preservation and renewal of something that already exists. For the fact that authoritarian institutions are dismissed by anarchists as transient aberrations which, as Godwin put it, "reverses the genuine propensities of mind," does not lessen the conservative element within the divided heart of anarchism, since all conservatives regard what they condemn as transient and aberrant. And in this sense anarchism is not merely conservative.

In terms of popular ideas of progress, anarchism is indeed regressive. Its proponents have always seen liberation in terms of simplification rather than complication. Where the price of affluence is the progressive loss of freedom to develop — to use Paul Goodman's terminology — as 'people' rather than 'personnel,' they have always, from Proudhon onwards, praised the virtues of poverty (as distinct from pauperism) and where possible (as in peasant collectives in the Spanish civil war) sought to achieve them in austere practice. They have always favoured decentralization (being the true originators of the idea that 'small is beautiful'), and in the organizational sense decentralism means devolution, however much its defenders may see it as favourable to the creative and spiritual evolution of humanity.

It is not, therefore, entirely accidental that a conservative like Lord Acton, a Catholic who saw the declaration of Papal Infallibility in 1869 as an insufferable imposition on his own spiritual freedom, should in his remarks on power have given the most eloquent expression to one of the central anarchist beliefs. Nor is it a matter of caprice that a latter-day anarchist like Paul Goodman, one of the most painstakingly honest intellectuals of his time, should say, and be right in saying: "I am anarchistic and agitational, and I am conservative and traditional" (*Creator Spirit, Come*), and, not long before his death and in a book he sub-titled *Notes of a Neolithic Conservative*:

> I am not a 'romantic': what puts my liberal and radical critics off is that I am a conservative, a conservationist. I do use the past: the question is how. *New Reformation*

What I propose in the rest of this essay is to examine, in an appropriately desultory manner, how Goodman does in fact use the past, and how in doing so he continues and extends one of the vital currents in anarchist thought — the current which, to use terms that seem at variance with most commonly held views of anarchism, is both traditional and aristocratic. For a viewpoint that treasures the past (as Kropotkin and Herbert Read as well as Goodman did) for the social virtues that have been destroyed or are threatened by authority obviously does not seek to level people down to the common denominator of the proletarian (the alienated of the industrial revolution). Rather, it is a matter of being raised to a cultural level once enjoyed only by the rich and powerful, for, as I once suggested:

> In reality the ideal of anarchism, far from being democracy carried to a logical end, is much nearer to aristocracy universalized and purified. The spiral of history here has turned full circle, and where aristocracy — at its highest point in the Rabelaisian vision of the Abbey of Thelème — called for the freedom of noble men, anarchism has always declared the nobility of free men. *Anarchism*

It is an aristocracy purged of privilege, whose demand on the material world is no more than "the sufficiency that will allow men to be free"

*(Anarchism)*, or what Goodman repeatedly called "decent poverty"; it is, as Goodman further defined it, "aristocratic equality."

Within this pattern Goodman saw himself — in the words of the editor of his essays, Taylor Stoehr — as "the poor scholar, ragged but learned, able to philosophize with newsboys as well as clerics," the equivalent of the Greek philosopher who — as Goodman remarked more than once in his books on education — turned unpromising boys into men of true culture by wandering through the streets with them and mingling his discourses with the observation of actual daily life in all its forms.

As for the tradition to which Goodman saw himself belonging — and the past he used — Goodman defined it in a passage that is worth quoting at length because it defines and differentiates so well both the sources of his knowledge and the framework within which his insights emerge.

> The culture I want to teach — I am myself trapped in it and cannot think or strive apart from it — is our Western tradition: the values of Greece, the Bible, Christianity, Chivalry, the Free Cities of the Twelfth century, the Renaissance, the heroic age of Science, the Enlightenment, the French Revolution, early nineteenth-century Utilitarianism, late nineteenth-century Naturalism.
>
> To indicate what I mean, let me mention a typical proposition about each of them. The Greeks sometimes aspire to a civil excellence in which mere individual success would be shameful. The Bible teaches that there is a created world and history in which we move as creatures. Christians have a spirit of crazy commitment because we are always in the last times. Chivalry is personal honour and loyalty, in love or war. Free cities have invented social corporations with juridical rights. The Renaissance affirms the imperious right of gifted individuals to immortality. Scientists carry on a disinterested dialogue with nature, regardless of dogma or consequence. The Enlightenment had decided that there is a common sensibility of mankind. The Revolution has made equality and fraternity necessary to liberty. Utilitarian economy is for tangible satisfactions, not busy work, money or power. Naturalism urges us to an honest ethics, intrinsic in animal and social conditions.
>
> Needless to say, these familiar propositions are often in practical and theoretical contradiction with one another; but that conflict too is part of the Western tradition. And certainly they are only ideals — they never did exist on land or sea — but they are the inventions of

the holy spirit and the human spirit that constitute the university, which also *is* an ideal.

Naturally, as a teacher, I rarely mention such things; I take them for granted as assumed by everybody. But I am rudely disillusioned when I find that both my students and my younger colleagues take quite different things for granted. *Compulsory Miseducation*

This passage, from a book first published in 1962 and revised in 1964, not only helps us define Goodman's position as a humanist scholar in relation to the academic situation in the early 1960s. It also provides a starting point for assessing his position within the tradition of anarchism.

Goodman saw himself as a humanist rather than as an academic, and as a writer rather than as a professor, in which role — despite the excellence of his teaching — he turned out somewhat too eccentric in behaviour for the academic community to assimilate easily. Nevertheless, the universities were for him one aspect of the culture he valued, even if he felt that he stood outside them.

When I consider the long lineage: Paris manned Oxford, and Oxford manned Cambridge, and Cambridge Harvard, and Harvard Yale, and Yale Chicago, etc., I realize that I am not a scholastic nor a university man though I ceremonially defend them. I am a humanist, that kind of Renaissance free-lance. At present I seem to be seeking a different lineage: Charcot to Freud, Freud to Reich, and so forth; but I am significantly unable to belong to it. In fact, I was born fatherless. *Nature Heals*

It is here, in this context of the universities and of education in general, that we see Goodman taking some of his great steps into the past. Constantly, he urges on the universities that their duty was to conserve the Western tradition which he believed had shaped him. He takes up what he defines as "a very old-fashioned topic of educational theory, how to transmit Culture with a big C, the greatness of man..." (*New Reformation*). He upbraids the universities for their acceptance of army subsidies, which he denounces as "the end of free research and liberal education, for he who pays the piper calls the tune." And he calls for a revivification of the humanities within the academies, since it is only if we understand and use language clearly and expansively, and not merely as a "code to render information narrowly," that we shall be able to understand and

> manage the exploding scientific technology and the collectivism which
> are the conditions of the foreseeable future.... Just now the method of
> literature is indispensable: to find and say the humanities in new
> science, the morality in technology, and the community and individualism
> in collectivism. *New Reformation*

Such views resemble in many ways those of educational conservatives
with the difference that Goodman embodies them in a generally libertarian theory of education. Education in the humanities is essential
to the health of society, but this does not mean that all people are
adapted mentally to absorb in academic form what their culture has
to offer.

And of course, while most educational conservatives seek the rigidities
of past systems of teaching and educational organization which were
little better than what we have, Goodman sought a decentralization
and diversification and deinstitutionalization of education that is entirely
in keeping with his anarchism. *Growing Up Absurd* (1960) showed
how 'problem children' were held in that role because their 'problems'
were institutionalized in the kind of schools that purported to 'treat'
them. *The Community of Scholars* revealed Goodman as an advocate of
free and highly experimental forms of education, though he was by
no means a single-minded advocate of the progressive school movement,
which he recognized developed its own rigidities. Yet when he wrote
of the universities in this book and elsewhere, it was clear that he in
no way aspired to destroy the tradition of education as transmitted by
the academies, or the high tradition of Western culture which at its
best he felt it expressed and transmitted. What he attacked was the
physical gigantism and the bureaucratic inhumanity of the multiversities.
In its place he suggested a return to the medieval kind of college in
which bands of teachers and students came together to teach and learn,
with a recognition that those who know most must in the field of
learning — but there alone — be regarded as the masters.

Goodman was always hoping to find this kind of community of
scholars. He hoped he might encounter it at Black Mountain College,
whose informal structure attracted him, but, quite apart from the
vestigial moralism of the place, which led to his being eased out for
his frank expression of homosexual desires, Goodman found a 'feebleness'
in the presentation of traditional humanities there and insisted on
teaching more scholastically than his fellows. Going to Berkeley at

the height of the Free Speech movement in February 1965 to report on it for *Dissent*, he found:

> ...an uncanny re-emergence of the primitive medieval University, with its fat-cat professors lecturing in the central halls, a ragged student community living in its own neighbourhood, and, astoundingly, a new student leadership by the graduates and teaching-assistants, the very Masters of Arts who used to cause all the trouble in 1200! One would have expected, in the era of the Organization Man, that precisely the bright graduate-students, the junior-executives, would be the most conformist, to protect their status and advancement; yet we see at Berkeley that the teaching-assistants provided leaders and almost unanimously went on strike.

Yet he had to admit wryly that when he said all this to the students, they were not entirely responsive:

> To my surprise, the students did not dig what I was saying; they do not have much memory of the tradition of the West. They know what freedom is, yes, they do — but they don't really know what a University is.

And, indeed, it was not long after 1965 that Goodman began to realize that, for all the anarchistic elements in the student revolt of the early 1960s, many of the activists did not know enough about politics or history to prevent their sliding into authoritarian, neo-Leninist political stances, while the rest of the students revealed themselves as — in his view — virtual philistines because of their unawareness of the tradition he treasured and in which he had grown up. By 1969 he was talking like this:

> When I speak at a college, I pepper the discussion with references to Spinoza, Beethoven and Milton, hoping that the students will learn that former great men were real human beings, but the poignant effect is that they regard me wistfully because I seem to have a past, and they are more forlorn than ever. If I try to analyze a text in its own terms, to find a human spirit coping with its particulars and *therefore* relevant to us, it is taken as an irrelevant exercise in order to avoid present gut issues. Naturally, inability to read a book is cumulative. Since there is no belief in the tradition or habituation in its ways, it becomes a chore to read the sentences, and why bother? *New Reformation*

But, as we realize from reading Goodman's essays on education, and particularly those collected in *Compulsory Miseducation*, he is not blaming the students who react in this way so much as the system that has taken them out of a natural social situation and put wrong demands on them. For instead of being oriented towards creating a human being capable at the earliest possible stage of playing a productive and therefore satisfying role in his world, contemporary education — in Goodman's view — has become a holding operation by which millions of young people are kept out of mischief and out of the labour market until they have reached their early twenties and by any normal standards are well into adulthood. In this system, whether education benefits the students emotionally or intellectually has become irrelevant.

Thus we see Goodman advocating, time and again, that it might be a good idea if we were to step backward mentally in time, reconsider our thoughts on education and perhaps start off again from scratch. So, at the same time as he suggests that the universities should devolve from vast expansive multiversities (where overheads cost three times as much as the actual teaching) into something small and intimate like the medieval universities, Goodman is also pointing out that even in our present century enormous numbers of people did very well for themselves and enriched society with only a fraction of the time in school (as distinct from real education) that their descendants endure.

> When there was academic instruction for many for a short time, or for a few for a longer time, it is possible that some academic education occurred. To be sure, most education for most people happened by means other than schools. Society functioned very well and many people became very expert and learned without going to school — in 1900, 6 per cent graduated from high school and less than half of 1 per cent went to college. Now, however, 100 per cent are forced to go to high school and last year 75 per cent graduated. On this scale, it is my observation as reporter, very little education is occurring. For academic purposes, we might do just as well if we closed all the schools, though of course they serve for baby sitting, policing and so forth. We could surely provide all the academic instruction that is achieved by far simpler and cheaper methods. *Compulsory Miseducation*

George Orwell made a very similar point when he remarked in *The Road to Wigan Pier* on the irrelevance of academic education to the life of the workers, pointing out that the normal English working-class boy of the 1930s longed for the day he would leave school and be "doing real work," as a result of which at eighteen he was a man with adult responsibilities, while a middle-class boy of the same age attending a public school was little more than a baby. Goodman's ultimate position is not far from Orwell's, since he concludes that real education is not what goes on in the school.

> It is a natural community function and occurs inevitably, since the young grow up on the old, towards their activities, and into (or against) their institutional; and the old foster, teach, train, exploit and abuse the young. Even neglect of the young, except physical neglect, has an educational effect — not the worst possible. *Compulsory Miseducation*

What Goodman really proposes is that education should once again be an extension of activities that normally take place in a healthy society outside the schoolroom, and therefore, for the majority of children (those with no aptitude for scholarship or the arts) of learning by experiencing and doing, which means being an apprentice more than a student in the academic sense, and in the case of town children, learning the processes of cultivation and growth by living and working for long periods on renovated marginal farms. The desystematization of education, the breaking up of the learning process into a multitude of improvized responses to particular situations, would allow such a flexible approach.

An implication of such a concept of education is that the function of the scholar and the artist are detached from the role of teaching the young, as they were in the medieval universities, and consequently one never encounters in Goodman's writings that bogus cultural democracy which denounces as elitism any regard for high culture or for the literary tradition. The culture and the tradition are there for those who wish to pursue them, but the elimination of compulsory education would make it a matter of free choice. It is true that as an artist Goodman was not notably experimental, and he was inclined to identify with Wordsworth's "simplification of vocabulary, and the connection of this with the speech of unsophisticated people and the expression of feeling." But he also remarked that the great thing about Wordsworth was something much more recondite, his "exquisite syntax," and he added a remark about the great Romantic poet that is germane to what I have been saying about his own views on the nature of a libertarian education:

> In my opinion, his idea of pedagogy is true and primary; it *is* the beauty of the world and simple human affections, that develop great-souled and disinterested adults. *Creator Spirit, Come*

Anarchists, always seeking a way to liberate natural social urges other than the suicidal course of political revolution, have been greatly concerned with education, not merely as a means of drawing out the natural capabilities of young people in society as it exists, but also as one of the ways to transform society. It is significant that this preoccupation has been strongest among non-violent anarchists, like William Godwin and Leo Tolstoy, or among anarchists in general at times when the movement was not collectively dominated by myths of violence, as in France after terrorism died down during the later 1890s, when a notable libertarian educational movement arose under the leadership of Sebastian Faure and Elisée Reclus, and as in England during and after World War II, when Herbert Read published *Education through Art* and *The Education of Free Men*, and other anarchists like Tony Weaver, Tony Gibson and Tom Earley — all of them involved in practical teaching — wrote extensively on free forms of education based on a re-immersion of the child in natural social processes.

In many ways Goodman's approach resembles that of the English anarchists. He would certainly synpathize with Herbert Read's basic statement:

> To neglect the senses, either through ignorance of their significance or from mere puritanical prejudice, is to neglect one half of our being. Neither in teaching nor in learning, neither in making things nor in our dealings with one another, can we afford to ignore the sensuous reactions that record the quality of experience. It follows that in any ideal system of education we should educate the senses, and to this end each of the arts should have its appropriate place in the curriculum.

Yet there are points at which Read's and Goodman's views do not entirely accord. Goodman's idea of educating the senses goes a good deal beyond the arts, which he would perhaps not give the over-riding importance they have in Read's rather more systematic proposals for the reform of education, largely, I think, because though he would agree that the education of the senses should precede the education of the intellect, Goodman recognizes that there are many people who can get along and live a full and happy life without being even minimally involved in the arts. They can, for example, be immersed from the beginning in all-absorbing occupations like farming or certain forms of craftsmanship or even the kind of mechanical work that demands intelligent attention. Here Goodman perhaps also differs from Read

in the stress that — like Kropotkin and Fourier and Proudhon — he
lays on the importance of productive work, as distinct from toil, in
giving meaning to human life. Though I have found no mention of
it in Goodman's writings, he must have found little to disagree with
in William Morris's *Useful Work versus Useless Toil.*

Goodman's views on education show, admirably, the nature of both
his conservatism and his traditionalism. He recognizes and lives by
the great philosophies and the great poetry of the past, and what he
perceives with apprehension is the way modern methods and systems
of education have broken the lines of connection by which mankind's
total achievement over the centuries can remain a living part of the
present. One alarming result of this kind of alienation is that science
has escaped from the modifying and moralizing influence of the humanities. And so he commends not the invention of new systems, but
experiments in simplification, for, as he has said:

> A free society cannot be the substitution of a 'new order' for the old
> order; it is the extension of spheres of free action until they make up
> most of the social life. *Drawing the Line*

And often freedom can involve a stepping back rather than a stepping
forward so that it becomes appropriate to consider how the medieval
universities operated without the crushing superstructures of modern
academic institutions, and how the guild systems of apprenticeship
produced not merely good workmen but also well-rounded intelligences,
so that we owe to the free cities of the middle ages so many of the
innovations that led to the enlargement of life during the modern era.

This seems an appropriate place to turn from conservative aspects
of Goodman's views on education to this relationship with anarchist
traditionalism in the larger sense. Anarchists often deny tradition,
since the appeal to the past seems to them a way of admitting the
validity of authority. Yet no observer of the movement can fail to note
how interested they are in the ancestry of their teachings, and how
much attention those among them with a historical bent — like
Kropotkin, Max Netlau and Rudolf Rocker — have given to the
constructions of family trees reaching back not merely to the French
Revolution or to the Diggers in the English Revolution but to distant
forebears like Zeno the Stoic and Lao-Tse and Jesus Christ, whose
apostles, according to one French historian of the movement, formed
"the first anarchist society."

In attempting to give a scientific and historical basis to anarchism that might help it compete with the 'scientific socialism' of Marx, the two great anarchist geographers, Peter Kropotkin and Elisée Reclus, formulated the doctrine of mutual aid, which held that one of the great factors of evolution was a social instinct which made cooperation within the species as important in the scheme of nature as the struggles with adverse conditions and between species that neo-Darwinists like Thomas Henry Huxley had stressed. In a way, the theory of mutual aid was an extension into the whole animal world of Proudhon's earlier teaching of mutualism, which had already posed the existence of a natural social order that was weakened by the imposition of artificial institutions like the State and other forms of government.

In the historical, as distinct from the biological sense, what the theory of mutual aid gave to anarchism was a ready-made substitute for a tradition; a positive outlook on the past; and a reason for conservatism in the sense that Goodman meant when he said:

> Edmund Burke had a good idea of conservatism, that existing community bonds are destroyed at peril; they are not readily replaced, and society becomes superficial and government illegitimate.

Kropotkin and his followers taught that the urge to cooperation existed among the animals, so that people did not become social beings at the point where they emerged into social consciousness as we know it; sociability was one of the gifts he inherited from our animal ancestors, as were those complementary urges towards free cooperation and towards authority, which we see Kropotkin evoking with a curious Manichean vision when he claimed for anarchism a record as long as that of mankind and of the opposing current of government and coercion.

> It is evident that Anarchy represents the first of these two currents, that is to say, the creative constructive force of the masses, who elaborated common-law institutions in order to defend themselves against a domineering minority. It is also by the creative and constructive force of the people, aided by the whole strength of modern science and technique, that today Anarchy strives to set up institutions that are indispensable to the free development of society, in opposition to those who put their hope in laws made by governing minorities. We can therefore say that from all times there have been Anarchists and Statists.

Kropotkin observes that in human societies there have been certain periods when the nature of society has extraordinarily liberated the

cooperative spirit in constructive ways, such as the time when the
barbarians established their village communes all over Europe, and
the later era when the free cities of Europe flourished as centres of
medieval civilisation. The village communes of the barbarians became
subordinate to the patterns of graduated authority introduced by feu-
dalism, and the free cities were largely robbed of their liberties and
their originative vision by the rise of the Nation-State in the seventeenth
century.

In much of this kind of interpretation of history, Goodman follows
Kropotkin, and especially in his evaluation of what he called the 'high
Middle Ages,' which he regarded as a period of searching and seminal
thought and practice rather than — as it has so often been represented
— of mental stasis. The picture he gives in *New Reformation* is, if
anything, even more favourable than Kropotkin's, since Goodman was
versed in areas of medieval philosophy which had comparatively little
meaning for his more scientifically minded predecessor:

> ...the organization of society was pluralistic and pragmatic; the moral
> sciences came alive, and in the physical sciences, there began to be
> widespread experimentation.
>
> In the heterogenous political structure of feudalism, national states,
> city states, municipal councils, craft guilds, trade associations, the
> international church, and the ghost of the international empire, there
> was a thriving moral philosophy and law, inventive and probing.
> Today, in every kind of moral inquiry, religious or secular, the medieval
> analyses reappear, in commercial transactions, craft regulation, sexual
> morality, rules of war, university polity and privilege, discussions of
> sovereignty and legitimacy.
>
> In form, medieval moral philosophy was apparently systematic rather
> than experimental, aiming at the *summum bonum* of salvation. But in
> the great variety of occasions and jurisdictions, casuistry made moral
> inquiry concrete and pragmatic. Scholasticism and legalism provided
> a consensual language that made thought precise, rather than stifling.
> Arts and crafts, technology, were, like all other activities, personal,
> moral and responsible, e.g. in determining quality and just price and
> in guild and building-gang organization. Indeed, the free-city guilds
> were the closest we have yet come to workers' management.
>
> On to this pluralistic and pragmatic scene appeared the dramatic
> new force of experimental science; but the opposite of our situation,
> it was in the context of prudence and morals. *Prima facie*, experimentation

was making and doing, a branch of moral philosophy, liable to moral judgement and not merely a means of knowing; nor were its findings acceptable in style to orthodox academic natural philosophy. One important source of experimentation was the arts and crafts revived or newly invented by self-directed artisans who were both highly cooperative and highly competitive, producing for their own purposes and judging what they were doing, an excellent set-up for learning new science without bookish scientific preconceptions, and strictly prudential.

If the Middle Ages, where so much was 'personal, moral and responsible,' as well as genuinely experimental, fitted into Goodman's sense of a libertarian tradition as much as it did into Kropotkin's, he diverged into the history of his own environment to find the same virtues at the roots of the American experiment in liberation. He had very little to say, indeed, about the native American anarchists who in many ways were his intellectual forebears, like Josiah Warren and Lysander Spooner and Benjamin Tucker, but this was mainly because he saw in the whole American tradition a libertarian impulse that was far broader than the movement which the theoreticians I have mentioned represented. Here, for example, is one of his mental pictures of the early years of the United States.

> During the first thirty years of the Republic only 5 to 10 per cent were enfranchised and as few as 2 per cent bothered to vote. But the conclusion to be drawn from this is not necessarily that society was undemocratic. On the contrary, apart from the big merchants, planters, clerics and lawyers, people were likely quite content, freed from the British, to carry on their social affairs in a quasi-anarchy, with unofficial, decentralized and improvised political forms. It was in this atmosphere that important elements of our American character were developed.
> *Creator Spirit, Come*

And elsewhere he sketched out a pluralistic network of social forms which arose in revolutionary America and enjoyed an existence parallel to but independent of the formal structures that were created to replace the British apparatus of rule.

> When the revolution of 1776-83 removed the top structure of British authority from the American colonies, this country was fundamentally organized as a network of highly structured face-to-face communities, each fairly autonomous; town-meetings, congregational parishes, gentry families and yeoman families. These had hierarchical structures: master and apprentice, indentured servants, family slaves, professionals and

their clients, pastors and parishes; but each person was in frequent contact with those who initiated and decided.

For the first twenty-five years of the republic, in important respects there was virtually a community anarchy with regard to the central and state governments.

For immigrants and for the poor who felt too disadvantaged in the existing structured communities, the frontier was an open area for independence. *Drawing the Line*

In Goodman's view, this healthy, pluralist, early American society was destroyed by the trend towards centralization, in government and industry alike, set into motion by the Civil War, and it is notable that he sees its last forlorn fling, not in the native or immigrant anarchists, but in the Populist movement.

More than the beginnings of the modern labour movement during the same period, and certainly more than Reform politics, Populism clearly saw the closing trap of interlocking centralization... Now the free market was restrained by trusts and ever higher tariffs... The political parties became increasingly massified and distantly controlled, and there were alliances between government and the monopolies. To all this the Populists responded with heroic self-reliance, and tragic paranoia and political confusion.

In my opinion, this was the last American political movement to face squarely the crucial dilemma of modern society: how to preserve practical democracy in high industrial conditions. For a couple of decades, Populism saw the answer: the Jacksonian Party democracy could not work; one had to start anew from below. *People or Personnel*

The facets of any seminal work change in relative importance according to the times. When *Mutual Aid* was published, its immediate significance lay in its correction of the Huxleyan distortions of evolutionary doctrine, but it also had importance in giving scientific support to anarchist arguments about the possibility of human societies existing and succeeding without coercive institutions. In our day, when most anarchists no longer foresee the destruction of government ushering in a completely free society, *Mutual Aid* is most inspiring for its revelation that, even in times when authoritarian structures dominate society, the institutions created by voluntary cooperation still survive and prevent the collapse of society. Kropotkin's words, when he chronicled the decline of the once splendid free cities of Europe, carry the seed of the hope that has inspired contemporary writers like Paul Goodman and Colin Ward who seek within our society the elements that can be preserved and nurtured with a view to evolving a free and more natural way of living.

> And yet, the current of mutual aid and support did not die out in the masses; it continued to flow even after that defeat. It rose up again with a formidable force, in answer to the communist appeals of the first propagandists of the reform, and it continued to exist even after the masses, having failed to realize the life which they hoped to inaugurate under the inspiration of a reformed religion, fell under the dominions of an autocratic power. It flows still even now, and it seeks its way to find out a new expression which would not be the State, nor the medieval city, nor the village community of the barbarians, nor the savage clan, but would proceed from all of them, and yet be superior to them in its wider and more deeply human conceptions. *Mutual Aid*

The recognition that Kropotkin was right in his assessment of the tenacity of mutual aid as a manifestation of human sociality led Colin Ward to declare in *Anarchy in Action* that anarchism exists already in our society and Paul Goodman to explore ways in which — even without any recognizable revolution, constructive social tendencies can be liberated by piecemeal change, by what he often wryly called 'tinkering.' Here, in this desire to foster and to revive social manifestations so constant in history that they can be called traditional, lies the essence of Paul Goodman's conservatism, the necessary conservatism of an anarchist in our own day.

This conservationist conservatism is manifest in aspects of Goodman's thought and action too varied and too broad to be more than mentionable in the present essay; in his advocacy of decentralization, meaning the breaking down of structures too large for the human scale; his demands for a readjustment of the balance between rural and urban ways of living through repopulating the country, reviving village life, bringing the marginal land back into cultivation through new forms of mixed farming; in his many proposals for the humanizing of city life; in his preference for guild over trade union ethics; in his preference for the college over the multiversity, for the storefront school over the massive modern educational plant, and for apprenticeship over the barren perversion of academic education that turns the schools into detention places for young people who would be better off and of more use to the community if they were put to work. All these proposals involve piecemeal changes, major or minor, and in most cases the idea is to return to a simpler state of affairs in which a freer form of action can be initiated.

Perhaps Goodman is most differentiated from the old-style fundamentalist anarchist in his recognition that the changeover to a totally free society is not a possible revolution, and that the gradualism which earlier anarchists contemptuously rejected has to be accepted for anything to be achieved in the real world. He constantly uses phrases like "adjustments and transformations of historical conditions," and he recognizes that no process which is not gradual can hope to carry the people with it, which is necessary if one is not to resort to Bolshevik methods.

> The best period is one in which every new work destroys the convention of predecessors, yet advancing to just the next step — the result of an achieved habit and assimilated tradition — it carries its audience along. *Creator Spirit, Come*

It is, Goodman believes, of the essence of anarchism that its principle is always manifested in relation to the actual situation, and so remarks that "there *cannot* be a history of anarchism in the sense of establishing a permanent state of things called 'anarchist'." (*Drawing the Line*) In the foreseeable future, a mixed society seems inevitable, and what the anarchist must do is to decide where to 'draw the line,' where to go beyond 'tinkering,' where to disturb the peace, for:

> Useful services must not be neglected because they are inappropriate to the dominant style, and basic necessities must not depend on the smooth working of the economy. *People or Personnel*

The nature of anarchism is to resist change that reduces the naturalness of a society (which is a conservative act) and to promote change that makes society more free (which is a radical act). The process of anarchism

> is always a continual coping with the next situation, and a vigilance to make sure that past freedoms are not lost and do not turn into the opposite, as free enterprise turned into wage-slavery and monopoly capitalism, or the independent judiciary turned into a monopoly of courts, cops and lawyers, or free education turned into School Systems.

In the end, it was the conservative in Goodman, his impulse to found everything in tradition, his recognition that people live largely by anarchist principles even in the most authoritarian society, his knowledge that small steps in the direction of simplification often immensely enlarge the scope of freedom, and his realistic awareness that in the foreseeable future the best we can expect is a vigorously pluralist society. This perspective preserved Goodman from the despairing inertia of the purist anarchist or the idealist futility of those who, as Herbert Read did in his last years, see the fulfilment of anarchist expectations as a distant point on a far horizon. Goodman saw it as part of the personal struggle of day-to-day living, permeating everything he did and said and wrote, and nourished by all that remains natural and free in human living. It was this that made him, by any standards, so interesting and stimulating a social critic. He was never afraid of the apparent contradictions of his position; he knew that in our era the anarchist and the true conservative must live within the same mind and work upon each other.

# THE FATE OF MARXISM
*Cornelius Castoriadis*

For anyone seriously concerned with the social question, an encounter with Marxism is both immediate and inevitable. It is probably even wrong to use the word 'encounter,' in that such a term conveys both something external to the observer and something that may or may not happen. Marxism today has ceased to be some particular theory or some particular political programme advocated by this or that group. It has deeply permeated our language, our ideas, and the very reality around us. It has become part of the air we breathe in coming into the social world. It is part of the historical landscape in the backgrounds of our comings and goings.

For this very reason to speak of Marxism has become one of the most difficult tasks imaginable. We are involved in the subject matter in a hundred different ways. Moreover, this Marxism, in realizing itself, has become impossible to pin down. For with which Marxism should we deal? With the Marxism of Khrushchev or with the Marxism of Mao Tse Tung? With the Marxism of Togliatti or with that of Thorez? With the Marxism of Castro, of the Yugoslavs, or of the Polish revisionists? Or should one perhaps deal with the Marxism of the Trotskyists (although here too the claims of geography reassert themselves: British and French Trotskyists, Trotskyists in the United States and Trotskyists in Latin America tear one another to pieces, mutually denouncing one another as non-Marxist). Or should one deal

*Cornelius Castoriadis is widely published in France. His works include* Mai 1968 *(with Edgar Morin and Claude Lefort), a multi-volume series* Socialisme ou Barbarie, L'Institution imaginaire de la société, Les Carrefours du Labyrinthe, *and* Devant la Guerre. *The first book in English of Castoriadis' political writings,* Redefining Revolution, *is in preparation by Black Rose Books.*

with the Marxism of the Bordighists or of the SPGB, of Raya Dunayevskaya or of C.L.R. James, or of this or that other still smaller group of the extreme 'left'? As is well known, each of these groups denounces all others as betraying the spirit of 'true Marxism,' which it alone apparently embodies. A survey of the whole field will immediately show that there is not only the abyss separating 'official' from 'oppositional' Marxisms. There is also the vast multiplicity of both 'official' and 'oppositional' variants, each seeing itself as excluding all others.

There is no simple yardstick by which this complex situation could be simplified. There is no 'test of events which speaks for itself.' Both the Marxist politician enjoying the fruits of office and the Marxist political prisoner find themselves in specific social circumstances, and in themselves these circumstances confer no particular validity to the particular views of those who expound them. On the contrary, particular circumstances make it essential to interpret carefully what various spokesmen for Marxism say. Consecration in power gives no more validity to what a man says than does the halo of the martyr or irreconcilable opponent. For does not Marxism itself teach us to view with suspicion both what emanates from institutionalized authority and what emanates from oppositions that perpetually fail to get even a toe-hold in historical reality?

## A Return to the Sources

The solution to this dilemma cannot be purely and simply a 'return to Marx.' What would such a return imply? Firstly it would see no more, in the development of ideas and actions in the last eighty years, and in particular in the development of social democracy, Leninism, Stalinism, Trotskyism, etc., than layer upon layer of disfiguring scabs covering a healthy body of intact doctrine. This would be most unhistorical.

It is not only that Marx's doctrine is far from having the systematic simplicity and logical consistency that certain people would like to attribute to it. Nor is it that such a 'return to the sources' would necessarily have something academic about it (at best it could only correctly re-establish the theoretical content of a doctrine belonging to the past — as one might attempt to do, say, for the writings of Descartes or St. Thomas Aquinas). Such an endeavour could leave the main problem unsolved, namely that of discovering the significance of Marxism for contemporary history and for those of us who live in the world of today.

The main reason why a 'return to Marx' is impossible is that under the pretext of faithfulness to Marx — and in order to achieve this faithfulness — such a 'return' would have to start by violating one of the essential principles enunciated by Marx himself. Marx was, in fact, the first to stress that the significance of a theory cannot be grasped independently of the historical and social practice which it inspires and initiates, to which it gives rise, in which it prolongs itself and under cover of which a given practice seeks to justify itself.

Who, today, would dare proclaim that the only significance of Christianity for history is to be found in reading unaltered versions of the Gospels or that the historical practice of various Churches over a period of some 2,000 years can teach us nothing fundamental about the significance of this religious movement? A 'faithfulness to Marx' which would see the historical fate of Marxism as something unimportant would be just as laughable. It would in fact be quite ridiculous. Whereas for the Christian the revelations of the Gospels have a transcendental kernel and an intemporal validity, no theory could ever have such qualities in the eyes of a Marxist. To seek to discover the meaning of Marxism only in what Marx wrote (while keeping quiet about what the doctrine has become in history) is to pretend — in flagrant contradiction with the central ideas of that doctrine — that real history doesn't count and that the truth of a theory is always and exclusively to be found 'further on.' It finally comes to replacing revolution by revelation and the understanding of events by the exegesis of texts.

All this would be bad enough. But there is worse. The insistence that a revolutionary theory be confronted, at all stages, by historical reality[1] is explicitly proclaimed in Marx's writings. It is in fact part of the deepest meaning of Marxism. Marx's Marxism did not seek to be — and could not be — just one theory among others. It did not seek to hide its historical roots or to dissociate itself from its historical

---

[1] By 'historical reality' we obviously do not mean particular events, separated from all others. We mean the dominant tendencies of social evolution, after all the necessary interpretations have been made.

repercussions. Marxism was to provide the weapons not only for interpreting the world but for changing it.[2] The fullest meaning of the theory was, according to the theory itself, that it gave rise to and inspired a revolutionary practice. Those who, seeking to exculpate Marxism theory, proclaim that none of the historical practices which for 100 years have claimed to base themselves on Marxism are 'really' based on Marxism, are in fact reducing Marxism to the status of a mere theory, to the status of a theory just like any other. They are submitting Marxism to an irrevocable judgement. They are in fact submitting it, quite literally, to a 'Last Judgement.' For did not Marx thoroughly accept Hegel's great idea: *'Weltgeschichte ist Weltgericht.'*[3]

## Marxism as Ideology

Let us look at what happened in real life. In certain stages of modern history a practice inspired by Marxism has been genuinely revolutionary. But in more recent phases of history it has been quite the opposite. And while these two phenomena need interpreting (and we will return to them) they undoubtedly point to the fundamental ambivalence of Marxism. It is important to realize that in history, as in politics, the present weighs far more than the past. And for us, the present can be summed up in the statement that for the last forty years Marxism has become an *ideology* in the full meaning that Marx himself attributed to this word. It has become a system of ideas which relate to reality not in order to clarify it and to transform it, but on the contrary in order to mask it and to justify it in the abstract. It has become a means of allowing people to say one thing and to do another, to appear other than they are.

In this sense Marxism first became ideology when it became Establishment dogma in countries paradoxically called 'socialist.' In these countries 'Marxism' is invoked by governments which quite obviously do not incarnate working class power and which are no more controlled by the working class than is any bourgeois government. In these

---

[2]  K. Marx. Eleventh Thesis on Feuerbach.

[3]  'Universal History is the Last Judgement.' Despite its theological form, this statement expresses one of Hegel's most radically atheistic ideas. It means that there is nothing transcendental; that there is no appeal against what happens here and now. We are, definitively, what we are in the process of becoming, what we shall have become.

countries 'Marxism' is represented by 'leaders of genius' — whom their successors call 'criminal lunatics' without more ado. 'Marxism' is proclaimed the ideological basis of Tito's policies *and* of those of the Albanians, of Russian policies *and* of those of the Chinese. In these countries Marxism has become what Marx called the 'solemn complement of justification.' It permits the compulsory teaching of 'State and Revolution' to students, while maintaining the most oppressive and rigid State structure known to history. It enables a self-perpetuating and privileged bureaucracy to take refuge behind talk of the 'collective ownership of the means of production' and 'abolition of the profit motive.'

But Marxism has also become ideology insofar as it represents the doctrine of the numerous sects, proliferating on the decomposing body of the 'official' Marxist movement. For us the word 'sect' is not a term of abuse. It has a precise sociological and historical meaning. A small group is not necessarily a sect. Marx and Engels did not constitute a sect, even when they were most isolated. A sect is a group which blows up into an absolute single side, aspect or phase of the movement from which it developed, makes of this the touchstone of the truth of its doctrine (or of the truth, full stop), subordinates everything else to this 'truth' and in order to remain 'faithful' to it is quite prepared totally to separate itself from the real world and henceforth to live in a world of its own. The invocation of Marxism by the sects allows them to think of themselves and to present themselves as something other than what they are, namely as the future revolutionary party of that very proletariat in which they never succeed in implanting themselves.

Finally, Marxism has become ideology in yet another sense. For several decades now it has ceased to be a *living* theory. One could search the political literature of the last thirty years in vain even to discover fruitful applications of the theory, let alone attempts to extend it or to deepen it.

We don't doubt that what we are now saying will provoke indignant protests among those who, while professing to 'defend Marx,' daily bury his corpse a little deeper under the thick layers of their distortions and stupidities. We don't care. This is no personal quarrel. In analyzing the historical fate of Marxism we are not implying that Marx had any kind of *moral* responsibility for what happened. It is Marxism itself, in what was best and most revolutionary in it, namely its pityless denunciation of hollow phrases and ideologies and its insistence on permanent self-criticism, which compels us to take stock of what Marxism has become in real life.

It is no longer possible to maintain or to rediscover some kind of 'Marxist orthodoxy.' It cannot be done in the ludicrous (and ludicrously linked) way in which the task is attempted by the high priests of Stalinism and by the sectarian hermits, who see a Marxist doctrine which they presume intact, but 'amend,' 'improve' or 'bring up to date' on this or that specific point, at their convenience. Nor can it be done in the dramatic and ultimatistic way suggested by Trotsky in 1940,[4] who said, more or less: 'We know that Marxism is an imperfect theory linked to a given period of history. We know that theoretical elaboration should continue. But today, the revolution being on the agenda, this task will have to wait.' This argument is conceivable — although superfluous — on the eve of an armed insurrection. Uttered a quarter of a century later it can only serve to mask the inertia and sterility of the Trotskyist movement, since the death of its founder.

## A Marxist 'Method'?

Some will agree with us so far, but will seek final refuge in the defence of a 'Marxist method,' allegedly unaffected by what we have just discussed. It is not possible, however, to maintain 'orthodoxy' as Lukacs attempted long before them (in 1919, to be precise), by limiting it to a Marxist *method*, which could somehow be separated from its content and which could somehow be neutral in relation to this content.[5]

Although a step forward in relation to various kinds of 'orthodox' cretinism, Lukacs' position is basically untenable. It is untenable for a reason which Lukacs forgets, despite his familiarity with dialectical thinking, namely that it is impossible, except if one takes the term 'method' at its most superficial level, to separate a method from its content, particularly when one is dealing with historical and social theory.

---

[4] In his *In Defence of Marxism*.
[5] See the essay "What Is Orthodox Marxism?" in Lukacs' book *History and Class Consciousness*. An English translation of this essay was recently published by *International Socialism*, Nos. 24 and 25. C. Wright Mills adopts a rather similar viewpoint in his book *The Marxists*.

A method, in the philosophical sense, is defined by the sum total of the categories it uses. A rigid distinction between method and content only belongs to the more naïve forms of transcendental idealism (or 'criticism'). In its early stages this method of thought sought to separate and to oppose matter or content (which were infinite and undefined) to certain finite operative categories. According to this view the permanent flux of the subject matter could not alter the basic categories which were seen as the form without which the subject matter could not be grasped or comprehended.

But this rigid distinction between material and category is already transcended in the more advanced stages of 'criticist' thought, when it comes under the influence of dialectical thought. For immediately the problem arises: how do we determine which is the appropriate analytical category for this or that type of raw material? If the raw material carries within itself the appropriate 'hallmark' allowing it to be placed in this or that category, it is not just 'amorphous'; and if it is genuinely amorphous then it could indifferently be placed in one category or in another and the distinction between true and false breaks down. It is precisely this contradiction which, at several times in the history of philosophy, has developed from a criticist type of thinking of a dialectical type.[6]

This is how the question is posed at the level of logic. When one considers the growth of knowledge as *history*, one sees that it was often the 'development of the subject matter' that led to a revision of the previously accepted categories or even to their being exploded and superseded. The 'philosophical' revolutions produced in modern physics by relativity theory or by quantum theory are just two examples among many.[7]

---

[6] The classical example of such a transition is the passage from Kant to Hegel, via Fichte and Schelling. But the basic pattern can be discerned in the later works of Plato, or among the neo-Kantians, from Rickert to Last.

[7] It is obviously not just a question of turning things upside down. Neither logically nor historically have the categories of physics been 'simply a result' (and even less 'simply a reflection') of the subject matter. A revolution in the realm of categories may allow one to grasp raw material which hitherto defied definition (as happened with Galileo). Moreover, advances in experimental technique may at times 'compel' new material to appear. There is therefore a two-way relationship — but certainly no independence — between categories and subject matter.

The impossibility of establishing a rigid separation of method and content, between categories and raw material, becomes even more obvious when one passes from knowledge of the physical world to the understanding of history. A deeper enquiry into already available material — or the discovery of new material — may lead to a modification of the categories and therefore of the method. But there is, in addition, something much more fundamental, something highlighted precisely by Marx and by Lukacs themselves. [8] This is the fact that *the categories through which we approach and apprehend history are themselves real products of historical development*. These categories can become clear and effective methods of historical knowledge only when they have to some extent become incarnated or fulfilled in *real* forms of social life.

Let us give a simple example. In the thinking of the ancient Greeks the dominant categories defining social relations and history were essentially *political* (the power of the city, relations between cities, relations between 'might' and 'right', etc.). The economy received only marginal attention. This was not because the intelligence or insight of the Greeks were less 'developed' than those of modern man. Nor was it because there were no economic facts, or because economic facts were totally ignored. It was because in the social reality of that particular epoch the economy had not yet become a separate, autonomous factor (a factor 'for itself,' as Marx would say) in human development. A significant analysis of the economy and of its importance for society could take place only in the 17th century and more particularly in the 18th century. It could take place only in parallel with the real development of capitalism which made of the economy the dominant element in social life. The central importance attributed by Marx and the Marxists to economic factors is but an aspect of the unfolding of this historical reality.

It is therefore clear that there cannot exist a 'method' of approaching history, which could remain immune from the actual development of history. This is due to reasons far more profound than the 'progress of knowledge' or than 'new discoveries,' etc. It is due to reasons pertaining directly to the very structure of historical knowledge, and first of all to the structure of its object: the mode of being of history. What is the object we are trying to know when we study history?

---

[8] See Lukacs, *The Changing Function of Historical Materialism (loc. cit.).*

What is history? History is inseparable from meaning. Historical facts are historical (and not natural, or biological) inasmuch as they are interwoven with meaning (or sense). The development of the historical world is, *ipso facto*, the development of a universe of meaning. Therefore, it is impossible radically to separate fact from meaning (or sense), or to draw a sharp logical distinction between the categories we use to understand the historical material, and the material itself. And, as this universe of meaning provides the environment in which the 'subject' of the historical knowledge (i.e. the student of history) lives, it is also necessarily the means by which he grasps, in the first instance, the whole historical material. No epoch can grasp history except through its own ideas about history; but these ideas are themselves a product of history and part and parcel of the historical material (which will be studied as such by the next epoch). Plainly speaking, the method of the biologist is not a biological phenomenon; but the method of the historian is a historical phenomenon.[9]

Even these comments, however, have to be seen in proper perspective. They don't imply that at every moment, every category and every method are thrown into question. Every method is not transcended or ruined by the development of real history at the very instant it is being utilized. At any given moment, it is always a practical question of knowing if historical change has reached a point where the old categories and the old method have to be reassessed. But this judgement cannot be made independently of a discussion of the content. In fact, such an assessment is nothing other than a discussion on content which, starting with the old categories, comes to show, through its dealings with the raw material of history, that one needs to go beyond a particular set of categories.

Many will say: 'To be Marxist is to remain faithful to Marx's *method*, which remains valid.' This is tantamount to saying that nothing has happened in the history of the last 100 years which either permits one or challenges one to question Marx's categories. It is tantamount to implying that everything will forever be understood by these categories. It is to take up a position in relation to content and categories, to have a static, non-dialectical theory concerning this relationship, while at the same time refusing openly to admit it.

---

[9] These considerations are developed more fully on p. 20 *et seq.* of the French text.

## Conclusion

In fact, it is precisely the detailed study of the content of recent history which compelled us to reconsider the categories — and therefore the method of Marxism. We have questioned these categories not only (or not so much) because this or that particular theory of Marx — or of traditional Marxism — had been proved 'wrong' in real life, but because we felt that history as we were living it could no longer be grasped through these traditional categories, either in their original form[10] or as 'amended' or 'enlarged' by post-Marxian Marxists. The course of history, we felt, could neither be grasped, *nor changed*, by these methods.

Our re-examination of Marxism does not take place in a vacuum. We don't speak from just anywhere or from nowhere at all. We started from revolutionary Marxism. But we have now reached the stage where a choice confronts us: to remain Marxists or to remain revolutionaries. We have to choose between faithfulness to a doctrine which, for a considerable period now, has no longer been animated by any new thought or any meaningful action, and faithfulness to our basic purpose as revolutionaries, which is a radical and total transformation of society.

Such a radical objective requires first of all that one should understand that which one seeks to transform. It requires that one identifies what elements, in contemporary society, genuinely challenge its fundamental assumptions and are in basic (and not merely superficial) conflict with its present structure. But one must go further. Method is not separable from content. Their unity, namely theory, is in its turn not separable from the requirements of revolutionary action. And anyone looking at the real world must conclude that meaningful revolutionary action can no longer be guided by traditional theory. This has been amply demonstrated for several decades now both by the experience of the mass parties of the 'left' and by the experience of the sects.

---

[10] In the present article we cannot enter into a detailed discussion as to which of the concepts of classical Marxism have today to be discarded for a real grasp of the nature of the modern world and of the means of changing it. The subject is discussed in detail in an article "Recommencer la Révolution" (published in January 1964 in issue No. 35 of *Socialisme ou Barbarie* of which we hope to publish extracts in forthcoming issues).

# THE MANUFACTURE OF CONSENT
## Noam Chomsky

Recently, I took a walk with some friends and family in a National Park. We came across a gravestone, which had on it the following inscription: "Here lies an Indian woman, a Wampanoag, whose family and tribe gave of themselves and their land that this great nation might be born and grow."

Of course, it is not quite accurate to say that the indigenous population gave of themselves and their land for that noble purpose. Rather, they were slaughtered, decimated and dispersed in the course of one of the greatest exercises in genocide in human history. Current estimates suggest that there may have been about 20 million Native Americans in Latin America when Columbus discovered the continent — as we say — and about twelve to fifteen million more north of the Rio Grande. By 1650, about 95% of the population of Latin America had been wiped out and by the time the continental borders of the United States had been established, some 200,000 were left of the indigenous population. In short, mass genocide, on a colossal scale, which Americans celebrate each October when we honour Columbus — a notable mass murderer himself — on Columbus Day.

*Noam Chomsky is Professor of Linguistics and Philosophy, and Institute Professor at M.I.T.; recipient of honorary degrees from the University of London, University of Chicago, Delhi University and four other colleges and universities; fellow of the American Academy of Arts and Sciences and member of the National Academy of Arts and Sciences and member of the National Academy of Science; author of numerous books (and articles) on linguistics, philosophy, intellectual history and contemporary issues, including* At War with Asia, Peace in the Middle East?, Human Rights and American Foreign Policy, The Political Economy of Human Rights *(2 volumes with E. S. Herman)*, Toward a New Cold War, Radical Priorities, Binding, *and* The Fateful Triangle: The U.S., Israel and the Palestinians.

Hundreds of American citizens, well-meaning and decent people, troop by that gravestone, regularly, and read it, apparently without reaction; except, perhaps, a feeling of satisfaction that at last we are giving some due recognition to the sacrifices of the Native peoples, presumably the reason why it was placed there. They might react differently if they were to visit Auschwitz or Dachau and find a gravestone reading: "Here lies a woman, a Jew, whose family and people gave of themselves and their possessions that this great nation might grow and prosper."

The truth is not entirely suppressed. The distinguished Harvard historian and Columbus biographer Samuel Eliot Morrison does comment that "The cruel policy initiated by Columbus and pursued by his successors resulted in complete genocide." This statement is "buried halfway into the telling of a grand romance," Howard Zinn observes in his *People's History of the U.S.*, noting that in the book's last paragraph, Morrison sums up his view of Columbus as follows:

> He had his faults and his defects, but they were largely the defects of the qualities that made him great — his indomitable will, his superb faith in God and in his own mission as the Christ-bearer to lands beyond the seas, his stubborn persistence despite neglect, poverty and discouragement. But there was no flaw, no dark side to the most outstanding and essential of all his qualities — his seamanship.

I omit the corresponding paragraph that some acolyte might compose about other practitioners of "complete genocide" or even lesser crimes or the reaction that this would arouse among us if such examples existed.

The sentiment on the gravestone of the Wampanoag woman is not original. One hundred and sixty years ago, John Quincy Adams explained in a Fourth of July address that the U.S. government is superior to all others because it was based upon consent, not conquest:

> The first settlers... immediately after landing, purchased from the Indian natives the right of settlement upon the soil. Thus was a social compact formed upon the elementary principles of civil society, in which conquest and servitude had no part. The slough of brutal force was entirely cast off: all was voluntary: all was unbiased consent: all was the agreement of soul with soul.

Citing these remarks by a President known as a legalist who respected Indian treaties, T. D. Allman observes that "the American national

experience of genocidal slaughter of the Indian" is "nearly nonexistent...
They were not human beings; they were only obstacles to the inexorable
triumph of American virtue, who must be swept away to make room
for a new reality of American freedom." The consensus has been that
"our own solemnly proclaimed rights to life, liberty and the pursuit
of happiness totally superseded the rights of the peoples whose lives,
liberties and happiness we were expunging from the face of the earth."
The Indians were the first 'aggressors' who had to be faced in our
celebration of freedom, the definition of 'aggressor' being that we have
attacked them, to be followed by Mexicans, Filipinos, Vietnamese,
Nicaraguans, and many others. It may be added that U.S. history is
hardly unique in this respect, down to the present day.

The sense in which the Native population had given 'unbiased
consent' in this "agreement of soul with soul" was explained further
by one of the early American sociologists, Franklin Henry Giddings,
at the time when we were obtaining the consent of the Filipinos at
the turn of the century. He coined the phrase "consent without consent"
to deal with the achievement of the British in extending the "English
sacredness of life" and the "requirement of social order" to "racially
inferior types." "If in later years," he wrote, the colonized "see and
admit that the disputed relation was for the highest interest, it may
be reasonably held that authority has been imposed with the consent
of the governed" — just as we may say that a young child gives
"consent without consent" when its parents prevent it from running
into the street.

During a visit to a fine and much-respected American college some
time ago, I was taken on a tour of the college cathedral and shown
the series of stained glass windows recording the history of the college
from the days when it was attacked by union soldiers to the present.
One panel was devoted to the founding of the Air Force ROTC chapter
shortly after the Second World War. It showed a man sitting at a
desk signing some document, with an Air Force officer standing nearby.
An American bomber was shown in the background and on a blackboard
we read: E equals $mc^2$. Though it is difficult to believe at first, the
stained glass window in this cathedral is celebrating the atomic bombing
of Hiroshima and Nagasaki, what Truman described at the time as
"the greatest thing in history."

Not everyone, incidentally, felt quite that way. The distinguished
Indian Jurist Radhabinod Pal, in his dissenting opinion at the Tokyo

Tribunal that assessed Japanese war guilt, wrote that "if any indiscriminate destruction of civilian life and property is still illegitimate in warfare, then in the Pacific war, this decision to use the atom bomb is the only near approach to the directives... of the Nazi leaders during the Second World War. Nothing like this could be traced to the credit of the present accused." He did not expand on what it implies with regard to war crimes trials. But such perceptions are remote from the consciousness of the victors, and perhaps we should not be surprised that "the greatest thing in history" merits a stained glass window in the cathedral of a college dedicated to humane values and religious devotion.

The process of creating and entrenching highly selective, reshaped or completely fabricated memories of the past is what we call 'indoctrination' or 'propaganda' when it is conducted by official enemies, and education, moral instruction or 'character building', when we do it ourselves. It is a valuable mechanism of control, since it effectively blocks any understanding of what is happening in the world. One crucial goal of successful education is to deflect attention elsewhere — say, to Vietnam, or Central America, or the Middle East, where our problems allegedly lie — and away from our own institutions and their systematic functioning and behaviour, the real source for a great deal of the violence and suffering in the world. It is crucially important to prevent understanding and to divert attention from the sources of our own conduct, so that élite groups can act without popular constraints to achieve their goals — which are called 'the national interest' in academic theology.

The importance of blocking understanding, and the great successes that have been achieved, are very well illustrated in current affairs. Last fall, the World Court rejected the American contention that it had no jurisdiction with regard to the Nicaraguan complaint concerning U.S. aggression against Nicaragua. The issue arose in April 1984, when Nicaragua brought to the Court its charge that the U.S. was mining its harbours and attacking its territory. With exquisite timing, President Reagan chose that very day to issue a Presidential Proclamation designating May 1 as 'Law Day 1984.' He hailed our "200-year-old partnership between law and liberty," adding that without law, there can be only "chaos and disorder." The day before, as part of his tribute to the Rule of Law, he had announced that the U.S. would not recognize any decision of the World Court.

These events aroused much anger. In the *New York Times*, Anthony Lewis decried Reagan's "failure to understand what the rule of law has meant to this country." He observed that Senator Moynihan had "made the point with great power" in a Law School address in which he criticized the Reagan Administration for "forsaking our centuries-old commitment to the idea of law in the conduct of nations" and for its "mysterious collective amnesia," its "losing the memory that there once was such a commitment." Our U.N. Delegation, Moynihan said, "does not know the history of our country."

Unfortunately, it is Ronald Reagan and Jeane Kirkpatrick who understand what the rule of law has meant to this country, and it is Anthony Lewis and Senator Moynihan who are suffering from a mysterious collective amnesia. The case they are discussing is a good example. It happened before, in almost exactly the same way. The story is told by Walter LaFeber, in his valuable book *Inevitable Revolutions*. In 1907, a Central American Court of Justice was established at the initiative of Washington to adjudicate conflicts among the states of the region. "Within nine years," LaFeber observes, "the institution was hollow because twice — in 1912 and 1916 — the United States refused to recognize Court decisions that went against its interests in Nicaragua." In 1912, the Court condemned U.S. military intervention in Nicaragua; Washington simply ignored the ruling. In 1916, the Court upheld a Costa Rican claim that U.S. actions in Nicaragua infringed its rights, and again the U.S. simply disregarded the decision, effectively destroying the Court. "In establishing its control over Central America," LaFeber comments, "the United States killed the institution it had helped create to bring Central America together." A final blow was administered in 1922 when Secretary of State Charles Evans Hughes convened a conference of Central American states in Washington. LaFeber comments:

> The occasion was not to be a replay of the 1907 conference, when the Central Americans had come to their own conclusions. Now the United States, with the help of faithful (and marine occupied) Nicaragua, set the agenda, which included the admonition that no one mention the late, unlamented Central American Court.

There are, to be sure, differences between the earlier case and today's, though not those that our current historical amnesia would suggest. Now, Nicaragua is not under marine occupation — merely under military attack by a U.S. mercenary army called 'freedom fighters';

and the U.S. is not powerful enough simply to disband the World
Court.

It is, incidentally, a little difficult to believe that Senator Moynihan
was serious in his reference to our commitment to the rule of law;
more likely these remarks were produced with tongue in cheek, or
intended as an example of his Irish wit. In his memoir of his tenure
as U.N. Ambassador, Moynihan gives graphic examples of this commitment to the rule of law, particularly to the United Nations charter
which forbids the use of force in international affairs. Thus, when
Indonesia invaded East Timor in 1975, illegally using U.S. arms and
obviously with the blessing of the United States, Moynihan dedicated
his efforts to blocking any moves by the United Nations to deter the
crime of aggression — for which people were hanged at Nuremberg
— and takes great pride in his success in this endeavour, which, as
he observes, led to a huge massacre. It is of some interest that his
pride in his complicity in war crimes does not affect his reputation as
a leading advocate of the sanctity of the rule of law among American
liberals.

The World Court incident provides some lessons concerning the
system of indoctrination. It is easy enough to make fun of Ronald
Reagan, but that is itself a diversion from the main point. Violence,
deceit and lawlessness are natural functions of the State, any State.
What is important in the present context is the contribution of the
harshest critics (within the mainstream) to reinforcing the system of
indoctrination, of which they themselves are victims — as is the norm
for the educated classes, who are typically the most profoundly indoctrinated and, in a deep sense, the most ignorant group, the victims
as well as the purveyors of the doctrines of the faith. The great achievement
of the critics is to prevent the realization that what is happening today
is not some departure from our historical ideals and practice, to be
attributed to the personal failings of this or that individual. Rather,
it is the systematic expression of the way our institutions function and
will continue to function unless impeded by an aroused public that
comes to understand their nature and their true history — exactly
what our educational institutions must prevent if they are to fulfill
*their* function, namely, to serve power and privilege.

A useful rule of thumb is this: If you want to learn something
about the propaganda system, have a close look at the critics and their

tacit assumptions. These typically constitute the doctrines of the State religion.

Let's take another current case. The justification of our attack against Nicaragua is that Nicaragua is a Soviet proxy, threatening Mexico, ultimately the United States itself. It is worth emphasizing that the basic assumptions of this doctrinal system extend across the political spectrum. Consider the tale of the Russian MIGs allegedly sent to Nicaragua, a fable nicely timed to divert attention from the Nicaraguan elections that we had sought to undermine and from the fact that we are sending advanced aircraft to El Salvador to facilitate the massacre of peasants; this is now conducted with improved efficiency thanks to the direct participation of U.S. military forces based in our Honduran and Panamanian sanctuaries, who coordinate bombing strikes on villages and fleeing peasants while we debate the profound question whether Nicaragua is obtaining aircraft that might enable it to defend itself against an attack by our mercenary army, not 'guerrillas,' but rather a well-equipped military force that in some respects outmatches the arms of Nicaragua in the level and quality of its armaments.

When the neatly timed MIG story was leaked by the Administration, thus setting the framework for further discussion of the issues within the ideological system, Senatorial doves made it clear that if MIGs were indeed sent, then we have a right to bomb Nicaragua because of the threat they pose to us. Senator Dodd stated that the U.S. would "have to go in and take [them] out — you'd have to bomb the crates." Senator Tsongas added:

> You just could not allow them to put those MIGs together, because the MIGs are not o..!y capable *vis-à-vis* El Salvador and Honduras, they're also capable against the United States and Nicaraguans knew for a long time that they could not do this without violating a clear sense of the sort of U.S. sphere of influence. (Boston *Globe*, Nov. 9).

Let us put aside the quaint idea that the Nicaraguans would be 'escalating' illegitimately by obtaining aircraft to defend themselves against our military attacks or that they might attack Honduras and El Salvador — while the U.S. stands by, a pitiful helpless giant, as Nixon once whined. Consider the threat that Nicaragua poses to us. By these standards, the USSR has a right to bomb Denmark, which is no less a threat to them than Nicaragua is to us — a far greater threat, in fact, because it is part of a hostile military alliance of great power — and it surely has the right to bomb Turkey, on its border, with its major NATO bases threatening the security of the Soviet Union. Fifty years ago, Hitler warned that Czechoslovakia was a dagger pointed at the heart of Germany, an intolerable threat to its security. By our standards, Hitler appears to have been rather sane. Again, it is the contribution of the critics that is noteworthy.

But let us return to the claim that Nicaragua is a Soviet proxy, threatening Mexico. In 1926, the Marines were sent back to Nicaragua, which they had occupied through much of the century, to combat a Bolshevik threat. Then Mexico was a Soviet proxy, threatening Nicaragua, ultimately the U.S. itself. "Mexico is on trial before the world," President Coolidge proclaimed as he sent the Marines to Nicaragua, once again, an intervention that led to the establishment of the Somoza dictatorship with its terrorist U.S.-trained National Guard and the killing of the authentic Nicaraguan nationalist Sandino. Note that though the cast of characters has changed, the bottom line remains the same: kill Nicaraguans.

What did we do before we could appeal to the Bolshevik threat? Woodrow Wilson, the great apostle of self-determination, celebrated this doctrine by sending his warriors to invade Haiti and the Dominican Republic, where they re-established slavery, burned and destroyed villages, tortured and murdered, leaving in Haiti a legacy that remains today in one of the most miserable corners of one of the most miserable parts of the world, and in the Dominican Republic, setting the stage for the Trujillo dictatorship established after a brutal war of counter-insurgency that has virtually disappeared from American history; the first book dealing with it has just appeared, after sixty years. There were no Bolsheviks then to justify these actions, so we were defending ourselves from Huns. Marine Commander Thorpe described how he told new Marine arrivals "that they were serving their country just as valuably as were their fortunate comrades across the seas, and the war would last long enough to give every man a chance against the Hun in Europe as against the Hun in Santo Domingo." The hand of the Huns was particularly evident in Haiti. Thrope explained: "Whoever is running this revolution is a wise man; he certainly is getting a lot out of the niggers... It shows the handwork of the German." "If I do a good job of clearing these... provinces of insurgents and kill a lot," he added, "it ought to demonstrate I'd be a good German-killer."

In earlier years, we were defending ourselves against other aggressors. When Polk stole a third of Mexico, we were defending ourselves against Mexican 'aggression' (initiated well inside Mexican territory); we had to take California to protect ourselves from a possible British threat to do so. The Indian wars were also defensive; the Indians were attacking us from their British and Spanish sanctuaries, so we were compelled to take Florida and the West, with consequences for the Native population that are, or should be, well-known. Before that, the doctrine of moralist Cotton Mather sufficed: he expressed his pleasure that "the woods were almost cleared of those pernicious creatures, to make room for a better growth." These, incidentally, were the pernicious creatures who "gave of themselves and their land that this great nation might be born and grow." The job was done so well that we no longer slaughter Indians here, though in areas where the task has not yet been successfully consummated, as in Guatemala, we continue to support massacres that the conservative Church hierarchy calls 'genocide,' within the 'sphere of influence' that we must 'defend,' according to Senatorial doves, just as we have 'defended' it — from its own population— so effectively in past years.

Looking at the real history, we see the current attack on Nicaragua in a perspective different from the conventional one and we can come to understand its causes in the normal and essentialy invarient functioning of our own institutions. And we can also come to understand the brain-washing techniques employed to conceal what is happening before our eyes. It is a relatively simple exercise to refute the Administration case, though one that must be constantly undertaken in a highly indoctrinated society where elementary truths are easily buried. What is more to the point is to recognize that this case is just another contribution to familiar historical fraud,while the events themselves are just another chapter in a shameful and sordid history, concealed from us by a contrived history framed in terms of such ideals as the rule of law, Wilsonian principles of self-determination, democracy and human rights, and others like them, which bear to American history the relation of irrelevance, under an interpretation that is rather too charitable.

How is this remarkable collective historical amnesia achieved? To better understand the system, let us first take a look at the way the process works in a totalitarian society, poles apart from our own in its internal order.

In May 1983, a remarkable event took place in Moscow. A courageous newscaster, Vladimir Danchev, denounced the Russian invasion of Afghanistan in five successive radio broadcasts extending over five days, calling upon the rebels to resist. This aroused great admiration in the West. The *New York Times* commented accurately that this was a departure from the "official Soviet propaganda line," that Danchev had "revolted against the standards of double-think and newspeak." In Paris a prize was established for a "journalist who fights for the right to be informed." Danchev was taken off the air and sent to a psychiatric hospital. He was returned to his position in December. A Russian official was quoted as saying that "he was not punished, because a sick man cannot be punished."

In the West, all of this was understood as a glimpse into the world of 1984. Danchev was admired for his courage, for a triumph of the human will, for his refusal to be cowed by totalitarian violence. All of this is fair enough.

What was particularly remarkable about Danchev's radio broadcasts was not simply that he expressed opposition to the Soviet invasion and called for resistance to it, but that he called it an 'invasion.' In Soviet theology, there is no such event as the Russian invasion of Afghanistan; rather, there is a Russian *defence* of Afghanistan against bandits operating from Pakistani sanctuaries and supported by the CIA and other warmongers. The Russians claim that they were invited in, and in a certain technical sense this is correct. But as the London *Economist* grandly proclaimed, "An invader is an invader unless invited in by a government with a claim to legitimacy," and the government installed by the USSR to invite them in can hardly make such a claim, outside of the world of Orwellian Newspeak.

Implicit in the coverage of the Danchev affair in the West was a note of self-congratulation: it couldn't happen here; no American newscaster has been sent to a psychiatric hospital for calling an American invasion 'an invasion' or for calling on the victims to resist. We might, however, inquire further into just why this has never happened. One possibility, at least an abstract possibility, is that the question has never arisen because no American journalist would ever mimic Danchev's courage, or could even perceive that an American invasion of the Afghan type is in fact an invasion or that a sane person might call on the victims to resist. If so, this would be a stage of indoctrination well beyond what has been achieved under Soviet terror, well beyond anything that Orwell imagined. Is this merely an abstract possibility, or is it an uncomfortably true portrayal of the actual circumstances in which we live?

Consider the following facts. In 1962, the United States attacked South Vietnam. In that year, President Kennedy sent the U.S. Air Force to attack rural South Vietnam, where more than 80% of the population lived, as part of a programme intended to drive several million people to concentration camps (called 'strategic hamlets') where they would be surrounded by barbed wire and armed guards and 'protected' from the guerrillas who, we conceded, they were willingly supporting. This was similar to what we are doing today in El Salvador, though in the Vietnamese case U.S. pilots were directly engaged in bombing of civilian targets and defoliation instead of merely guiding and coordinating air strikes against civilians and other military actions undertaken by the forces we train and arm. The direct U.S. invasion of South Vietnam followed our support for the French attempt to reconquer their former colony, our disruption of the 1954 'peace process,' and a terrorist war against the South Vietnamese population that had already left some 75,000 dead while evoking domestic resistance, supported from the northern half of the country after 1959, which threatened to bring down the terrorist régime that the U.S. had established. In the following years, the U.S. continued to resist every attempt at peaceful settlement and in 1964 began to plan the ground invasion of South Vietnam which took place in early 1965, accompanied by bombing of North Vietnam and an intensification of the bombing of the south, at triple the level of the more-publicized bombing of the north. The U.S. also extended the war to Laos, then Cambodia.

The U.S. protested that it was invited in, but as the London *Economist* recognized in the case of Afghanistan (never, in the case of Vietnam), "an invader is an invader unless invited in by a government with a claim to legitimacy," and outside the world of Newspeak, the client régime established by the U.S. had no more legitimacy than the Afghan régime established by the USSR. Nor did the U.S. regard this government as having any legitimacy; in fact, it was regularly overthrown and replaced when its leaders appeared to be insufficiently enthusiastic about U.S. plans to escalate the terror, or when they were feared to be considering a peaceful settlement. The U.S. openly recognized throughout that a political settlement was impossible, for the simple reason that the 'enemy' would win handily in a political competition, which was therefore unacceptable. The conflict had to be restricted to the military dimension, where the U.S. could hope to reign supreme. In the words of U.S. government scholar Douglas Pike, now head of the Indochina archives at Berkeley and much revered in mainstream journalism as one of a new breed of 'nonideological' scholars, the South Vietnamese enemy "maintained that its contest with the [U.S.-installed government and the] United States should be fought out at the political level and that the use of massed military might was in itself illegitimate" until forced by the U.S. "to use counter-force to survive."

For the past twenty-two years I have been searching to find some reference in mainstream journalism or scholarship to an American invasion of South Vietnam in 1962 (or ever), or an American attack against South Vietnam, or American aggression in Indochina — without success. There is no such event in history. Rather, there is an American *defence* of South Vietnam against terrorists supported from outside (namely, from Vietnam), a defence that was unwise, the doves maintain.

In short, there are no Danchevs here. Within the mainstream, there is no one who can call an invasion 'an invasion,' or even perceive the fact; it is unimaginable that any American journalist would have publicly called upon the South Vietnamese to resist the American invasion. Such a person would not have been sent to a psychiatric hospital, but he would surely not have retained his professional position and standing. Even today, those who refer to the U.S. invasion of South Vietnam in 1962, intensified in 1965, are regarded with disbelief; perhaps they are confused, or perhaps quite mad. Note that here it takes no courage to tell the truth, merely honesty. We cannot plead fear of State violence, as followers of the Party Line can in a totalitarian State.

Just to add a personal note, in a book I wrote shortly after the Russian invasion of Afghanistan, I compared it to the U.S. invasion of South Vietnam, and discussed more generally the responsibility of both superpowers for the Cold War system of conflict and intervention. American reviewers were unable to see the words, and complained that while there might be something to what I wrote, it would be more convincing if the story had been told "a little more evenhandedly" (Christopher Lehmann-Haupt in the *New York Times*) or that I was guilty of a "double moral standard" (James Fallows in the *Atlantic Monthly*). The same book was reviewed in the Communist press, which dismissed my "far-fetched and groundless concept that both powers have a vested interest in the Cold War" (James West of the American Communist Party Political Bureau, in the *World Marxist Review*), offering arguments that this was solely an American affair. What is of interest is that the Communist commentary, while incorrect, is at least rational, while the mainstream U.S. commentary reflects the kind of incapacity to perceive or think about simple issues that is sometimes found in the more fanatical religious cults.

It is common now to deride any analogy between the Soviet invasion of Afghanistan and the U.S. invasion of Grenada, and indeed they differ radically in scale and character. A comparison to the U.S. invasion of South Vietnam would be more appropriate, but is inconceivable within the mainstream. We incidentally see here another typical device of the well-indoctrinated intellectual (a somewhat redundant locution): select or concoct some weak criticism of the Holy State and dismiss it with contempt, thus displacing rational critical analysis and dispelling the threat of understanding.

In their important study *Demonstration Elections*, Edward Herman and Frank Brodhead include a photograph of Notre Dame President Theodore Hesburgh contemplating a ballot box while he was serving as an observer during the 1982 election in El Salvador, much heralded as a step toward something that we call 'democracy.' The caption reads: "The Rev. Theodore Hesburgh, 'observing' the Salvadoran election, but not 'seeing' the transparent voting box," plainly shown in the photograph. One of the central tasks of a successful educational system is to endow its victims with the capacity to observe, but not to see, a capacity that is the hallmark of the 'responsible intellectual.'

There did, of course, develop a kind of opposition to the Vietnam war in the mainstream, but it was overwhelmingly 'pragmatic,' as the critics characterized it with considerable self-adulation, distinguishing themselves from the 'emotional' or 'irresponsible' opponents who objected to the war on principled grounds. The 'pragmatic' opponents argued that the war could not be won at an acceptable cost, or that there was unclarity about goals, or duplicity, or errors in execution. On similar grounds, the German general staff was no doubt critical of Hitler after Stalingrad. Public attitudes, incidentally, were rather different. As recently as 1982, over 70% of the population held that the war was "fundamentally wrong and immoral," not merely a 'mistake,' a position held by far fewer 'opinion leaders' and by virtually none of the articulate intelligentsia, even at the height of opposition to the war in 1970.

How has this remarkable subservience to the doctrinal system been achieved? It is not that the facts were unavailable, as is sometimes the case. The devastating bombing of northern Laos and the 1969 bombing and other attacks was suppressed by the media, a fact that is suppressed within the mainstream until today (these are called 'secret wars,' meaning that the government kept the secret — as it did, with the complicity of the media). But in the case of the American attack against South Vietnam, sufficient facts were always available. They were observed, but not seen.

American scholarship is particularly remarkable. The official historian of the Kennedy Administration, Arthur Schlesinger, regarded as a leading dove, does indeed refer to aggression in 1962. "1962 had not been a bad year," he writes in his history *A Thousand Days*: "aggression [was] checked in Vietnam." That is, the year in which the U.S. undertook direct aggression against South Vietnam was the year in which aggression was *checked* in Vietnam. Orwell would have been impressed. Another respected figure in the liberal Pantheon, Adlai Stevenson, intoned at the United Nations that in Vietnam we were combatting "internal aggression," another phrase that Orwell would have admired; that is, we were combatting aggression by the Vietnamese against us in Vietnam, just as we had combatted aggression by the Mexicans against us in Mexico a century earlier. We had done the same in Greece in the late 1940s, Stevenson went on to explain, intervening to protect Greece from "the aggressors" who had "gained control of most of the country," these "aggressors" being the Greeks who had led the anti-Nazi resistance and who we succeeded in removing with an impressive display of massacre, torture, expulsion and general violence, in favour of the Nazi collaborators of our choice. The analogy was, in fact, more apt than Stevenson — apparently a very ignorant man — was likely to have known. As always, the American posture is defensive, even as we invade a country half way around the world after having failed to destroy the political opposition by large-scale violence and terror.

A closer look at the debate that did develop over the Vietnam war provides some lessons about the mechanisms of indoctrination. The debate pitted the hawks against the doves. The hawks were those, like journalist Joseph Alsop, who felt that with a sufficient exercise of violence we could succeed in our aims. The doves felt that this was unlikely, although, as Arthur Schlesinger explained, "We all pray that Mr. Alsop will be right," and "we may all be saluting the wisdom and statesmanship of the American government" if the U.S. succeeds (contrary to his expectations) in a war policy that was turning Vietnam into "a land of ruin and wreck." It was this book that established Schlesinger as a "leading war opponent," in the words of Leslie Gelb.

It is, of course, immediately evident that there is a possible position omitted from the fierce debate between the hawks and the doves, which allegedly tore the country apart during these trying years: namely, the position of the peace movement, a position in fact shared by the large majority of citizens as recently as 1982: the war was not merely a 'mistake,' as the official doves allege, but was "fundamentally wrong and immoral." To put it plainly: war crimes, including the crime of launching aggressive war, are wrong, even if they succeed in their 'noble' aims. This position does not enter the debate, even to be refuted; it is unthinkable, within the ideological mainstream.

It should be emphasized that departures from orthodoxy were very rare, among the articulate intelligentsia. Few journalists were more critical of the war than Anthony Lewis, who summed up his attitude in 1975 by explaining that the war began with "blundering efforts to do good," though by 1969 (1969!) it was clear that it was a "disastrous mistake." In mainstream academic circles, it would have been difficult to find a more committed critic of the war than John King Fairbank of Harvard, the dean of American Asian scholars who was considered so extreme as to be a 'Comsymp' or worse in McCarthyite terminology. Fairbank gave the presidential address to the American Historical Society in December 1968, a year after the Tet offensive had converted most of the corporate elite and other top planning circles to dovedom. He was predictably critical of the Vietnam war, in these terms: this is "an age when we get our power politics overextended into foreign disasters like Vietnam mainly through an excess of right-eousness and disinterested benevolence": "Our role in defending the South after 1965" was based on analytic errors, so that "we had great trouble in convincing ourselves that it had a purpose worthy of the effort." The doves felt that the war was "a hopeless cause," we learn from Anthony Lake, a leading dove who resigned from the government in protest against the Cambodia invasion. All agree that it was a "failed crusade," "noble" but "illusory" and undertaken with the "loftiest intentions," as Stanley Karnow puts it in his best-selling companion volume to the PBS TV series, highly regarded for its critical candour. Those who do not appreciate these self-evident truths, or who maintain the curious view that they should be supported by some evidence, simply demonstrate thereby that they are emotional and irresponsible ideologues, or perhaps outright Communists. Or more accurately, their odd views cannot be heard; they are outside the spectrum of thinkable thought. Few dictators can boast of such utter conformity to Higher Truths.

All of this illustrates very well the genius of democratic systems of thought control, which differ markedly from totalitarian practice. Those who rule by violence tend to be 'behaviourist' in their outlook. What people may think is not terribly important; what counts is what they do. They must obey, and this obedience is secured by force. The penalties for disobedience vary depending on the characteristics of the State. In the USSR today, the penalties may be psychiatric torture, or exile, or prison, under harsh and grim conditions. In a typical U.S. dependency such as El Salvador the dissident is likely to be found in a ditch, decapitated after hideous torture; and when a sufficient number are dispatched we can even have elections in which people march towards democracy by rejecting the Nazi-like D'Aubuisson in favour of Duarte, who presided over one of the great mass murders of the modern period (the necessary prerequisite to democratic elections, which obviously cannot proceed while popular organizations still function), and his minister of defence Vides Casanova, who explained in 1980 that the country had survived the massacre of 30,000 peasants in the 1932 *Matanza*, and "today, the armed forces are prepared to kill 200,000-300,000, if that's what it takes to stop a Communist takeover."

Democratic systems are quite different. It is necessary to control not only what people do, but also what they think. Since the State lacks the capacity to ensure obedience by force, thought can lead to action and therefore the threat to order must be excised at the source. It is necessary to establish a framework for possible thought that is constrained within the principles of the State religion. These need not be asserted; it is better that they be presupposed, as the unstated framework for thinkable thought. The critics reinforce this system by tacitly accepting these doctrines, and confining their critique to tactical questions that arise within them. To achieve respectability, to be admitted to the debate, they must accept without question or inquiry the fundamental doctrine that the State is benevolent, governed by the loftiest intentions, adopting a defensive stance, not an actor in world affairs but only reacting to the crimes of others, sometimes unwisely because of personal failures, naiveté, the complexity of history or an inability to comprehend the evil nature of our enemies. If even the harshest critics tacitly adopt these premises, then, the ordinary person may ask, who am I to disagree? The more intensely the debate rages between hawks and doves, the more firmly and effectively the doctrines of the State religion are established. It is because of their notable contribution to thought control that the critics are tolerated, indeed honoured — that is, those who play by the rules.

This is a system of thought control that was not perceived by Orwell, and is never understood by dictators who fail to comprehend the utility for indoctrination of a class of critics who denounce the errors and failings of the leadership while tacitly adopting the crucial premises of the State religion.

These distinctions between totalitarian and democratic systems of thought control are only rough first approximations. In fact, even a totalitarian State must be concerned about popular attitudes and understanding, and in a democracy, it is the politically active segments of the population, the more educated and privileged, who are of prime concern. This is obvious in the U.S. where the poor tend not even to vote, and more significant forms of political participation — the design and formulation of political programmes, candidate selection, the requisite material support, educational efforts or propaganda — are the domain of relatively narrow privileged élites. Three-quarters of the population may support a nuclear freeze, and some of them may even know that this is official Soviet policy as well, but that has no impact on the policy of massive government intervention to subsidize high technology industry through a State-guaranteed market for armaments, since no serious alternative is available in the system of political economy. Mass popular resistance to military aggression does serve as an impediment to the planners, as has been evident in the last few years with regard to Central America. Just last December the press reported a memorandum written by Secretary of Defense McNamara in May 1967, warning that escalation of the Vietnam war might "polarize opinion to the extent that 'doves' in the U.S. will get out of hand — massive refusals to serve, or to fight, or to cooperate, or worse?" The 'doves' that concerned him here are not the official 'doves' of the doctrinal system, few of whom were doves of any stripe at the time, but rather the general population. But such resistance, while sometimes effective in raising the costs of State violence, is of limited efficacy as long as it is not based on understanding of the forces at work and the reasons for their systematic behaviour, and it tends to dissipate as quickly as it arises. At the same time, a frightened and insecure populace, trained to believe that Russian demons and Third World hordes are poised to take everything they have, is susceptible to jingoist fanaticism. This was shown dramatically by the popular response to the Grenada invasion. The U.S. is again "standing tall," Reagan proclaimed, after 6000 élite troops managed to overcome the resistance of a handful of Cuban military men and a few Grenadan militiamen, winning 8700 medals for their valour, and eliciting a reaction here that cannot fail to awaken memories of other great powers that won cheap victories not too many years ago.

The more subtle methods of indoctrination just illustrated are considerably more significant than outright lying or suppression of unwanted fact, though the latter are also common enough. Examples are legion.

Consider, for example, the current debate as to whether there is a 'symmetry' between El Salvador and Nicaragua in that in each case rebels supported from abroad are attempting to overthrow the government. The Administration claims that in one case the rebels are 'freedom fighters' and the government is an illegitimate tyranny, while in the other case the rebels are terrorists and the government is a still somewhat flawed democracy. The critics question whether Nicaragua is really supporting the guerrillas in El Salvador or whether Nicaragua has already succumbed to totalitarianism.

Lost in the debate is a more striking symmetry. In each country, there is a terrorist military force that is massacring civilians, and in each country we support that force: the government of El Salvador, and the contras. That this has been true in El Salvador, particularly since the Carter administration undertook to destroy the popular organizations that had developed during the 1970s, is not in doubt. That the same is true in Nicaragua is also evident, though here we must turn to the foreign press, where we can read of "the contras' litany of destruction" as they murder, rape, mutilate, torture and brutalize the civilian population that falls within their clutches, primary targets being health and education workers and peasants in cooperatives (Jonathan Steele and Tony Jenkins, in the London *Guardian*; Marian Wilkinson, in the *National Times*, Australia; and many other sources where ample details are provided). The top commander of the 'Democratic Force,' Adolfo Calero, is quoted in the *New York Times* as saying that "There is no line at all, not even a fine line, between a civilian farm, owned by the Government and a Sandinista military outpost," and an occasional report indicates the consequences of these assumptions, but press coverage here is muted and sporadic, devoted to more significant matters such as opposition to the draft (in Nicaragua).

This is the real 'symmetry' between Nicaragua and El Salvador. Its significance is lost as we debate the accuracy of the government cases, meanwhile continuing to labour under the mysterious collective amnesia that prevents us from seeing that there is little here that is new, and from understanding why this should be so.

Or to turn to another part of the world, consider what is universally called 'the peace process' in the Middle East, referring to the Camp David agreements. Israeli-run polls reveal that the population of the territories under Israeli military occupation overwhelmingly oppose the 'peace process,' regarding it as detrimental to their interests. Why should this be so? Surely of all the people in the region, they are among those who must be yearning the most for peace. But no journalist seems to have inquired into this strange paradox.

The problem is easily solved. The 'peace progress', as was evident at the time and should be transparent in retrospect, was designed in such a way as to remove the major Arab military force, Egypt, from the conflict, so that Israel would then be free, with a huge and rapidly expanding U.S. subsidy, to intensify settlement and repression in the conquered territories and to attack its northern neighbour — exactly as it did, at once and unremittingly since. It is hardly a cause for wonder that the victims of the 'peace process' overwhelmingly condemn and reject it, though it is perhaps a little surprising that such elementary truths, obvious enough at the outset, cannot be seen even today. Meanwhile, we must continue to support the 'peace process.' Who can be opposed to peace?

In this case, too, it would be salutary to overcome our mysterious collective amnesia about the facts of recent history. There is no time here to review the diplomatic record, but anyone who troubles to do so will quickly learn that there have been possibilities for peace with a modicum of justice for about fifteen years, blocked in every instance by U.S.-Israeli rejectionism. In the early 1970s, this rejectionist stance was so extreme as to block even Arab initiatives (by Egypt and Jordan) to attain a general peace settlement that entirely ignored Palestinian national rights. Since the international consensus shifted to adherence to a two-State settlement a decade ago, any such possibility has consistently been barred by the U.S. and Israel, which persist in rejecting any claim by the indigenous population to the rights that are accorded without question to the Jewish settlers who largely displaced them, including the right to rational self-determination somewhere within their former home. Articulate American opinion lauds this stance, urging the Palestinians to accept the Labour Party programme that denies them any national rights and regards them as having "no role to play" in any settlement (Labour dove Abba Eban). There is no protest here, or even mere reporting of the facts, when the U.S. government blocks a U.N. peace initiative, stating that it will accept only negotiations "among the parties directly concerned with the Arab-Israeli dispute," crucially excluding the Palestinians, who are not one of these parties (January 1984). Analogous rejectionist attitudes on the part of Libya and the minority PLO Rejection Front are condemned here as racist and extremist; the quite comparable U.S.-Israeli stance, obviously racist in essence, is considered the soul of moderation.

The actual record has been obscured, denied, even inverted here in one of the most successful exercises in Agitprop in modern history. I reviewed the record up to mid-1983 in a recent book (*The Fateful Triangle*). It continues since, without change. To mention only one recent case, in April and May 1984 Yasser Arafat made a series of proposals in statements published in France and England in the mainstream press and in speeches in Greece and Asia. He called explicitly for direct negotiations with Israel under U.N. auspices and for "mutual recognition of two states," Israel and a Palestinian State; this has long been the basic form of the international consensus, though it is excluded by the rejectionist 'peace process.' Israel immediately rejected the offer, and the U.S. simply ignored it. Media coverage in the U.S. followed an interesting pattern. The national press — the *New York Times* and the *Washington Post* — did not report the facts at all. The local 'quality press' (the *Boston Globe, Los Angeles Times, Philadelphia Inquirer*) did report the basic facts, though they were obscured and quickly forgotten, to be replaced by familiar diatribes about Palestinian extremism. In the *San Francisco Examiner*, reputed to be one of the worst papers in any major city, a UPI story giving the basic facts appeared on the front page, under a full-page inch-high headline reading "Arafat to

Israel: Let's Talk." A rational conclusion would be that the less sophisticated press simply does not understand what facts must be suppressed as inconsistent with the Party Line.

This assessment is reinforced by an intriguing statement by Warren Hoge, foreign editor of the *New York Times*. A reader in Detroit sent a brief letter to the *Times* noting that Arafat's call for mutual recognition and negotiations had not been reported, though the *Times* "has chided Arafat over the years for his alleged refusal to recognize and negotiate with Israel." His letter was not published, but he did receive a response (which is rather unusual), written by Warren Hoge, which reads as follows:

> We saw the Arafat remarks you mention in the *Nouvel Observateur* and compared them to statements of his in the past. They did not represent any change of thinking on his part, and it would have been misleading for us to have published them as if they did.
>
> We have given ample coverage to Mr. Arafat and have published at some length both his public statements and stories about his sub rosa diplomacy with representatives of the United States and other Western governments. *When and if Mr. Arafat calls for mutual recognition and negotiations with Israel, you will read about it prominently displayed on the front page of* The New York Times. (Emphasis added)

This communication is quite revealing. The first paragraph is, in fact, close to true, though one could not know this from reading the *New York Times*, which regularly denies these facts. But the most interesting part is the last sentence. Arafat explicitly called for "mutual recognition and negotiations with Israel," but we did not read it on the front page — or anywhere — in the *New York Times*. Rather, the *Times* persisted with its astonishing record of suppression and falsification, reviewed for earlier years in my book, cited above. There could hardly be a clearer statement that none of this will be permitted to enter official history, of which the *Times* sees itself — with some accuracy — as the custodian. Future historians will turn to the archives of the *New York Times* to determine what is 'history,' not to the archives of the *San Francisco Examiner* (if they even exist).

I will not proceed with further examples. The crucial point is that the pattern is pervasive, persistent, and overwhelmingly effective in establishing a framework of thinkable thought.

Over sixty years ago, Walter Lippman discussed the concept of "manufacture of consent," an art that is "capable of great refinements" and that may lead to a "revolution" in "the practice of democracy." The idea was taken up with much enthusiasm in business circles — it is a main preoccupation of the public relations industry, whose leading figure, Edward Bernays, described "the engineering of consent" as the very essence of democracy. In fact, as Gabriel Kolko notes, "From the turn of the century until this day, [the public mind] was the object of a cultural and ideological industry that was as unrelenting as it was diverse: ranging from the school to the press to mass culture in its multitudinous dimensions." The reason, as an AT&T vice-president put it in 1909, is that "the public mind... is in my judgment the only serious danger confronting the company." The idea was also taken up with vigour in the social sciences. The leading political scientist Harold Lasswell wrote in 1933 that we must avoid "democratic dogmatisms," such as the belief that people are "the best judges of their own interests." Democracy permits the voice of the people to be heard, and it is the task of the intellectual to ensure that this voice endorses what far-sighted leaders know to be the right course. Propaganda is to democracy what violence is to totalitarianism. The techniques have been honed to a high art, far beyond anything that Orwell dreamt of. The device of feigned dissent, incorporating the doctrines of the State religion and eliminating rational critical discussion, is one of the more subtle means, though more crude techniques are also widely used and are highly effective in protecting us from seeing what we observe, from knowledge and understanding of the world in which we live.

It should be stressed again that what the Communists call 'Agitprop' is far more important in the democracies than in States that rule by violence, for reasons already discussed, and is therefore more refined, and possibly more effective. There are no Danchevs here, except at the remote margins of political debate.

For those who stubbornly seek freedom, there can be no more urgent task than to come to understand the mechanisms and practices of indoctrination. These are easy to perceive in the totalitarian societies, much less so in the system of 'brain-washing under freedom' to which we are subjected and which all too often we serve as willing or unwitting instruments.

# THE POVERTY OF AUTONOMY: THE FAILURE OF WOLFF'S DEFENCE OF ANARCHISM

*Graham Baugh*

Since its original publication in 1970, Robert Paul Wolff's *In Defense of Anarchism* has generated considerable controversy. Both advocates of State authority and anarchists have found his arguments unsatisfactory. Wolff himself has admitted that in formulating his argument he has "simply taken for granted an entire ethical theory."[1] It is only in his later work, *The Autonomy of Reason*, that Wolff sketches out the ethical theory upon which the arguments of *In Defense of Anarchism* ultimately depend.[2] A proper understanding of Wolff's anarchism and its inadequacies therefore requires an analysis of his arguments in relation to this ethical theory.

Through a formal analysis of rational agency tied to an instrumental view of reason Wolff seeks to demonstrate that insofar as people are rational and they are to act, they must be autonomous. By autonomy Wolff means acting only on one's self-chosen policies rationally connected to one's self-chosen ends. Autonomy therefore requires rational choice and deliberation and rational action. By rational action Wolff means action based on rational policies which consist of the most efficient means for achieving an individual's goals. Rational consistency requires that these policies be consistently applied or acted upon, and that they be consistent, taken together, with each other.

---

[1] Robert Paul Wolff, *In Defense of Anarchism: With a Reply to Jeffrey Reiman's "In Defense of Political Philosophy"* (New York: Harper & Row, 1976), p. viii.
[2] Wolff, *The Autonomy of Reason: A Commentary on Kant's "Groundwork of the Metaphysics of Morals"* (New York: Harper & Row, 1973), pp. 129, 223.

*Graham Baugh is a philosophy graduate doing research in moral and political theory.*

Two important consequences follow from Wolff's analysis of rational agency. The first is that ultimately the only obligation rational agents have is to be autonomous, for all obligations are a strict function of what is instrumentally rational for each person in relation to his or her goals. The second is that, because of Wolff's commitment to an instrumental view of reason, all choice of ends or goals is determined by neither reason nor desire, but is both nonrational and uncaused. "There are," Wolff argues, "in principle, no ends that reason requires and no ends that it rules out."[3]

It is on this basis that Wolff denies the validity of all claims to legitimate political authority, which Wolff defines as "the right to command, and correlatively, the right to be obeyed."[4] From a Wolffian perspective, the exercise of legitimate political authority is either unnecessary or positively immoral. Someone claiming a right to command and to be obeyed will either order other people to engage in activity which constitutes a rational means to their respective ends, which they are already obligated as rational agents to engage in, or that person will order people to engage in activity which is contrary to their own ends, which would be irrational and therefore immoral. To recognize in another person any right to command and to be obeyed would simply be an irrational policy, for there is no necessary connection between the commands such a person may make and the individual goals and policies of each agent. In fact, Wolff's analysis is subversive of the very concept of a right, for rights either entitle people to engage in activities they are obligated as rational agents to engage in, in which case they are superfluous, or they entitle people to engage in activities contrary to their own ends, which would be irrational.[5] All government claims to legitimate authority must therefore be rejected.

Wolff's argument also provides the basis for a rejection of all government claims to legitimate coercive power, conceived as the right to enforce one's commands. Not only is the concept of a right problematic,

[3] *Ibid.*, p. 223. For a more detailed analysis of Wolff's ethical theory, see my thesis: *Strange Anarchy: The Philosophical Anarchism of Robert Paul Wolff* (University of British Columbia, 1984).

[4] Wolff, *In Defense of Anarchism, op. cit.*, p. 4.

[5] In his "Reply to Reiman" Wolff states that he does not now believe that persons "have obligations and rights" in a state of nature, which is consistent with my analysis of his argument. See *In Defense of Anarchism, Ibid.*, p. 90.

but any form of coercion conflicts with rational agency or autonomy. For Wolff, an agent's actions are rational and autonomous only insofar as they are caused by the agent's own reason, "by one's conception of a rational connection between an end that one has posited for oneself and a bit of behaviour which either is an instance of or else will accomplish that end."[6] When someone does something out of fear of the application of a coercive sanction, rather than because he or she has decided that it is the rational thing for him or her to do, the rational connection between the agent's goals and policies is broken. To avoid the sanction the agent must act according to policies which are not rationally connected directly to his or her own goals, but which are instead intended to facilitate the achievement of State goals, forcing the agent to adopt the subsidiary goal of escaping punishment as well. In this case neither the agent's goals nor policies are freely chosen. To this extent the agent is no longer autonomous.

Because autonomy is the necessary precondition for all rational action, anything which inhibits or conflicts with it is illegitimate, or put another way, contrary to reason. The State, conceived as a group of persons claiming a right to make and enforce commands, and to be obeyed, is incompatible with autonomy and therefore illegitimate. Only a society without a State, 'anarchy,' provides the possibility of complete autonomy. Because autonomy is the necessary precondition for all rational action, anarchy is a rational, that is to say a moral necessity. Wolff concludes that "philosophical anarchism would seem to be the only reasonable belief for an enlightened man."[7]

Critics of Wolff have denied not only the validity of this argument, but the very anarchist status of the argument itself. For example, Jeffrey Reiman claims that Wolff's anarchism "is a personal, inner moral atitude — *and not the political doctrine of anarchism at all!*"[8] The anarchist theorist John P. Clark agrees with Reiman that "Wolff's argument that autonomy and moral authority are incompatible constitutes neither a defense of anarchism as a political theory nor a proof of the

---

[6] Wolff, *The Autonomy of Reason, op. cit.*, p. 216.
[7] Wolff, *In Defense of Anarchism, op. cit.*, p. 19.
[8] Jeffrey Reiman, *In Defense of Political Philosophy: A Reply to Robert Paul Wolff's "In Defense of Anarchism"* (New York: Harper & Row, 1972), p. xxii.

unjustifiable nature of the state and government."[9] Reiman argues
that a *political* anarchist, as opposed to a Wolffian *moral* anarchist,
"decries the state in the name of... freedom from coercion, not in the
name of any inner freedom or moral autonomy."[10] Alan Ritter provides
support for this claim when he notes that none of the four major
classical anarchist theorists — Godwin, Proudhon, Bakunin nor Kropotkin — "use Kantian autonomy as the normative basis for their
opposition to state coercion."[11]

These attempts to deny the anarchist status of Wolff's position fail,
however, for primarily two reasons. First, as I argued earlier, by
autonomy Wolff means both deciding for oneself what one ought to
do *and* acting on those decisions. Autonomy so conceived is incompatible
with any form of coercion, so Wolff's argument for autonomy is equally
an argument against the coercion of the State. Second, the classical
anarchist thinkers value autonomy very highly, in the sense of both
moral autonomy and rational agency, even if they do not assign either
kind of autonomy supreme normative value in their theories and arguments. As John P. Clark himself has argued, the concept of personal
autonomy, the "ability on the part of the individual to make meaningful,
critical, unprejudiced decisions," is central to the classical anarchist
conception of freedom itself.[12] Virtually all of the major anarchist
thinkers emphasize the need for individuals to act according to their
own reason rather than the dictates of authority. The supposed distinction
between Wolff's 'moral' anarchism and 'political' anarchism is then
not as clear-cut as Wolff's critics claim.

Nevertheless, I would like to argue that Wolff's argument fails as
a defence of anarchism, and further that his critics were right to
question its anarchist status, albeit for the wrong reasons. What Wolff
has really defended is a form of moral and political scepticism quite
distinct from the political theory of anarchism, and far less coherent
or convincing.

---

[9] John P. Clark, "What is Anarchism?" *The Anarchist Moment* (Montréal: Black Rose Books,
1984), p. 121.
[10] Reiman, *In Defense of Political Philosophy*, *op. cit.*, p. 48.
[11] Alan Ritter, *Anarchism: A Theoretical Analysis* (Cambridge: Cambridge University Press,
1980), p. 115.
[12] John P. Clark, *Max Stirner's Egoism* (London: Freedom Press, 1976), p. 61.

In a section of *In Defense of Anarchism* which has perplexed some of Wolff's critics, "Beyond the Legitimate State," he seems to have implicitly recognized some of the inadequacies of his approach. Completely contradicting his preceding anarchist argument, Wolff claims that the State "cannot be ineradicably *other*."[13] Wolff argues that "it *must* be possible" to create a State composed of rational agents who "determine to set private interest aside and pursue the general good... which accomplishes that end without depriving some of them of their autonomy."[14] I would now like to argue that Wolff is correct, that according to his own premises it is theoretically possible to reconcile individual autonomy with the State.

It is conceivable that a State authority could promulgate and enforce laws in such accordance with an individual agent's goals and policies that it would be rational for that agent to obey the commands of such an authority and to support the coercive apparatus necessary for their effective implementation. Moreover, if support of the State and obedience to its commands constitute the most effective means to the agent's ends, then he or she has a positive obligation as a rational agent to support and obey that State. To fail to do so would be irrational.

To expand on Wolff's own example, a group of agents committed to the pursuit of a common good, but who due to unavoidable limitations in knowledge lack the same competence as a State (perhaps with an extensive bureaucracy, expert social scientists, greater access to information, and so on) for determining which policies would most effectively realize the common good, and who lack the power to effectively implement these policies while the State does not, would be obligated as rational agents to obey the commands of that State and to support the coercive State apparatus needed to implement the required policies in an efficient and effective manner.

It should be noted that this is not a case of a mere coincidence between the individual agent's policies and the laws of the State; rather, the rationality of the agent's policies, and hence their obligatory character, follow from the antecedent rational efficacy of the law in providing for the effective achievement of the agent's goal. Neither does the agent independently evaluate each command, as the agent's

---

[13] Wolff, *In Defense of Anarchism, op. cit.*, p. 78.
[14] *Ibid.*, p. 78.

obedience to the command is based in part on his or her rationally based acknowledgement that he or she lacks the same competence as the State authority which issued the command to determine what would be the best policy for the achievement of the agent's goal. Here we have a case where the obligation to obey does not conflict with individual autonomy but in fact follows from the agent's own autonomous choice of ends. The State is *not* ineradicably other. Political philosophy, despite Wolff's premature obituary, would seem to be very alive and well. [15]

One might respond that this is hardly a crushing objection to Wolff's argument, for it is very unlikely that any State will ever be able to satisfy Wolff's criterion of legitimacy, and if the State and individual autonomy can be made at least theoretically compatible, so much the better. The problem is that not only can autonomy and the State be reconciled according to Wolff's own premises, but his moral theory can provide some persons with a rational justification for wielding coercive power, in the form of the State, over others.

It is important to remember that Wolff himself defines the State as "a group of persons who have supreme authority." [16] Clearly, a group of persons could adopt a goal, the exploitation of the working class, for example, which requires a coercive State apparatus for its achievement. To remain autonomous, this group of persons must adopt the most instrumentally efficacious means for the achievement of this end, which in this case includes the creation of a coercive State apparatus under its control to oppress the workers. Although the State, conceived as a "group of persons" may not have a *right* to command and to be obeyed, it is also the case according to Wolff's own analysis of rationality, morality and obligation, that from the perspective of this "group of persons" it may very well be rational and hence obligatory to command and to compel obedience to its commands. As Carole Pateman remarks, "no political ruler need quake at the implications of Wolff's 'anarchism.'" [17]

---

[15] In his "Reply to Reiman," Wolff proclaims that "[p]olitical philosophy... is dead." See *In Defense of Anarchism, Ibid.*, p. 110.

[16] *Ibid.*, p. 3.

[17] Carole Pateman, *The Problem of Political Obligation: A Critical Analysis of Liberal Theory* (London: John Wiley & Sons, 1979), p. 137.

Wolff's adoption of an instrumental view of reason is fatal to his entire enterprise. If all choice of ends is nonrational, then Wolff can offer no rational arguments for adopting either anarchy or autonomy as collective or individual goals. Neither can he provide rational arguments *against* adopting goals positively inimical to the ideals of anarchy and autonomy. Worse, given Wolff's moral theory, the sort of rational anarchist community he himself advocates is a conceptual impossibility.

In place of the nation-State Wolff proposes the creation of a rational community of autonomous persons who regulate their mutual affairs through a process of unanimous collective agreement. [18] Yet due to Wolff's instrumental view of reason, the members of such a community may not be able even to engage in meaningful moral discourse, let alone to rationally agree to the collective pursuit of various goals.

From the perspective of Wolff's moral theory, the meaning of moral concepts is strictly relative to each agent's subjective choices, for what is morally right and obligatory for an individual agent is whatever is the most rational and efficient means to his or her ends, and these ends are themselves subjective and nonrational. Wolff believes that if there is no rational ground for opposing something, there can be "no moral ground" for opposing it either. [19] There can therefore be no rational or moral ground for opposing any particular choice of ends, for all ends are equally nonrational. Because what is rational for one agent (in relation to his or her goals) is not rational for another agent with different goals, what is morally 'good' and 'obligatory' for the first agent will not be morally 'good' and 'obligatory' for the other. Indeed, if the other agent has adopted goals and policies positively incompatible with the first agent's, the two agents will have both conflicting conceptions of the good and conflicting obligations. Any

---

[18] This concept is discussed in the concluding chapter of *The Autonomy of Reason*, pp. 223-225. Wolff admits that it differs from the conception of unanimous direct democracy that he put forward in *In Defense of Anarchism* (pp. 22-27) as a solution to the conflict between authority and autonomy. In response to his critics, Wolff has concluded that this earlier formulation failed to resolve the conflict. "It may be that men are bound by the collective commitments they make," Wolff writes, "but such commitments do not create the sort of political authority I was attempting to analyse." See "Reply to Reiman," *In Defense of Anarchism. op. cit.*, p. 88.

[19] Wolff, *The Autonomy of Reason. op. cit.*, p. 225.

moral discourse between such agents will consist of competing but incommensurable and mutually unintelligible moral claims.

In Wolff's anarchist community there could be no meaningful debate or discussion of collective choice of ends. There could be limited rational discussion of policies but only in an instrumental sense: "given that x is your goal, adopt policy y, the most efficient means to that goal." Because policies are rational (and hence binding for autonomous agents) only in relation to goals, if one agent opposed the policy of another, or his or her autonomy was threatened by that policy, the only way he or she could convince that person to refrain from acting on that policy would be to convince him or her to abandon the goal which made adoption of the policy rationally binding (or 'obligatory' in Wolff's sense). But because choice of ends is nonrational, this cannot be done in a rational manner. The only way to get someone to change his or her goals and concomitant policies would be through threats, bribes, manipulation or some form of nonrational persuasion, but never through rational argument. So even if agreement among agents could somehow be obtained, one of the primary goals of Wolff's rational community, "that reciprocity of consciousness which is achieved and sustained by equals who discourse together publicly for the specific purpose of social decision and action," would be in essence defeated. [20]

Any agent whose choice of ends is determined by manipulation or some form of nonrational persuasion is not autonomous, according to Wolff's analysis, because the agent's action (of choosing) is not caused by his or her own reason. But to have any reasonable prospect for obtaining other agents' agreement to the pursuit of some goal, rather than merely hoping that everyone will miraculously share the same preferences, an agent will have to devise ways of manipulating and otherwise influencing other agents' nonrational preferences. Other agents will then agree to the pursuit of some goal, not because they were rationally convinced, but because they were successfully manipulated. Thus, the device of unanimous collective agreement will fail to preserve each agent's autonomy, because to get it to function effectively (rather than miraculously) each agent will have to treat all other members of the community as heteronomous agents incapable of rational choice or rational deliberation regarding their nonrational goals. Instead of

[20] Wolff, *The Poverty of Liberalism* (Boston: Beacon Press, 1968), p. 192.

a rational community of autonomous agents there will be a group of heteronomous agents mutually manipulating one another.

Although Wolffian autonomous agents cannot rationally agree among themselves to the pursuit of various ends, perhaps they can rationally agree to adopt a rational method for the resolution of conflict between their nonrational ends and corresponding policies which will either preserve or maximize their individual autonomy. However, it is impossible to derive from Wolff's purely formal analysis of rational agency any notion of justice or fairness which would limit the autonomy of each agent to a definite sphere of legitimate action, so that each agent would enjoy the maximum amount of autonomy consistent with the autonomy of others.

Any agent who acts according to self-chosen policies, which are internally consistent and rationally connected to his or her goals, is autonomous in a Wolffian sense. It is the formal structure of action, and not the actual content of the agent's goals and policies, which makes each agent's actions rational and autonomous, and hence for Wolff moral. That the agent may have adopted goals and policies which threaten the autonomy of others is not strictly relevant. Autonomous agents are not bound to respect the autonomy of others.

Even if agents did agree to a principle of equal respect, perhaps for prudential reasons, it is difficult to see how such a principle could be applied. Virtually any goal or policy may conflict, either directly or indirectly, with other goals and policies. Upon what basis can such conflict be resolved? Although it may be possible for individual agents to rank their goals on some sort of rational basis, Wolff cannot derive an interpersonal, objective standard or ranking of goals from his instrumental analysis of moral reason. For Wolff, all ends are equally nonrational, so to adopt one common standard or ranking of goals for the resolution of interpersonal conflict either would arbitrarily favour some agents over others, or it would implicitly assume that which Wolff explicitly denies — that some ends are rationally or morally superior to others.

Perhaps Wolff would endorse some sort of preference utilitarianism, but the maximization of the satisfaction of everyone's preferences, or autonomy, is a substantive principle which does not strictly follow from Wolff's formal analysis of rational agency, a goal no more rational than any other. Moreover, such a principle can justify the infringement of some people's autonomy, or the frustration of some people's preferences, in order to maximize the autonomy of others. As Keith Graham argues, it can also provide a possible justification for either unanimous or majoritarian direct democracy rather than anarchy, because in both unanimous and majoritarian direct democracy any conflict between goals and preferences can be resolved in favour of the greatest number.[21]

Ultimately, Wolff's concepts of autonomy and obligation are incoherent. One must question in what possible sense agents whose actions are ultimately determined by nonrational choice can be said to be free or responsible. To be autonomous, for Wolff, is to be "moved by reason", rather than by desire, impulse, and so on.[22] But it is to be moved by reason only in the sense of acting according to policies rationally connected to one's nonrational goals. These nonrational goals, which make the adoption of policies, and action in general, rational, can be said to be the *motor* of agency, for they provide the necessary impetus and rationale for action. As Wolff paraphrases Kant, "who wills the end wills the means."[23] For the autonomous agent, then, choice of ends and action are inextricably intertwined.

However, the act of choosing ends, which is uncaused by reason, is not an autonomous act but mere nonrational behaviour. But, Wolff argues, agents cannot be held responsible for their nonrational behaviour, as opposed to their rational actions.[24] In that case, agents cannot be held responsible for 'choosing' the ends they do choose, for such choice is not rational, or in the true sense of the word, autonomous. And if they cannot be held responsible for the ends they choose, how can they possibly be held responsible for adopting the policies which rationally follow from them? To be 'autonomous' they must follow these policies, but by doing so they make themselves slaves to their own nonrational choices. But to refuse to act according to these policies would also be irrational. Thus, either the agent's actions are ultimately determined by arbitrary choice or they are determined by some other nonrational cause (perhaps the arbitrary choice of another person), but

---

[21] Keith Graham, "Democracy and the Autonomous Moral Agent," in *Contemporary Political Philosophy: Radical Studies*, ed. Keith Graham (Cambrigde: Cambridge University Press, 1982), pp. 113-137.
[22] Wolff, *The Autonomy of Reason, op. cit.*, p. 216.
[23] *Ibid.*, p. 143.
[24] *Ibid.*, p. 136.

in neither case are they determined by reason. Yet even Wolff admits that to be free and responsible, which is what it means to be autonomous, one must be rational.[25]

Wolff cannot provide a coherent account of obligation either, for obligation arises from various social practices, such as promising, and Wolff's purely individualistic and abstract analysis of rational agency simply cannot provide a coherent account of *any* social practice, for social practices are constituted by intersubjective meanings and impersonal rules which transcend pure, subjective rational agency and arbitrary choice.

Wolffian agents lack a common moral vocabulary by which to constitute and sustain social practices. All moral concepts and values will be relative to each agent's subjective, nonrational goals and corresponding policies. Similarly, the 'rules' constituting a social practice will be different for each agent, being the most efficient and rational policies consistent with his or her goals and other policies, rather than impersonal standards. Even if agents can agree to abide by the same rules, despite their lack of a common moral vocabulary, these rules will always be subordinate to each agent's ends. Whenever it is rational to break the rules, the agent will be 'obligated' to do so. The rules constituting a social practice will then have no binding force — they won't really be rules at all. If the rules are binding and intersubjective, they will threaten individual autonomy just as much as any positive law, for the agent will be required to act in ways not always rationally consistent with a specific personal goal. Wolffian agents must always be superior to any obligations or commitments owed to others, whether an individual to whom one has made a promise or a political authority to whom one has promised obedience.

Wolff's moral contractarianism, his idea that the moral principles governing agents' interrelationships and interaction must (and *can*) be based on unanimous agreement, and that "all obligations are grounded in the collective commitments of a society of rational agents," is incompatible with his analysis of rational agency and his corresponding notion of individual 'obligation.'[26] According to Wolff's own analysis,

---

[25] *Ibid.*, p. 222. Indeed, Wolff defines autonomy itself as "the condition of taking full responsibility for one's actions." See *In Defense of Anarchism, op. cit.*, p. 14.

[26] Wolff, *The Autonomy of Reason, op. cit.*, p. 224.

the act of publicly committing oneself to a policy or a practice, of voluntarily assuming an obligation, adds nothing to the binding character of the policy or practice for the individual agent because any obligation to abide by a policy or practice ultimately depends on the individual agent's subjective commitment to the ends which make adoption of the policy or practice rational, and hence 'obligatory' insofar as the agent is to be autonomous. Any 'obligation' to adhere to a policy or practice is based on the efficacy of the policy or practice in realizing the agent's ends, not on any public act of agreement. Such agreements, if binding, may also threaten individual autonomy by requiring agents to abide by agreements even though it may no longer be rationally advantageous for each agent to do so. But if one's obligations are always subordinate to what is most rational for oneself, then obligations simply will have no real, interpersonal, binding force, in which case they really won't be obligations at all in the normal sense of the word.

Without any meaningful intersubjective moral notions and values, without even a concept of rationality which transcends subjective individual choice, in effect without the very notions which form the basis of social practices, Wolffian agents simply will have no meaningful notions of what a promise, a contract, an agreement or the corresponding obligations mean. Not only will they be unable to collectively and rationally agree to the pursuit of certain goals, they will lack the very conceptual apparatus by which to make any binding agreements whatsoever.

Bakunin captured the essential absurdity of such an abstract form of individualism long ago:

> How ridiculous then are the ideas of the individualists of the Jean-Jacques Rousseau school and the Proudhonian mutualists who conceive society as the result of the free contract of individuals absolutely independent of one another and entering mutual relations only because of the convention drawn up among them. As if these men had dropped from the skies, bringing with them speech, will, original thought, and as if they were alien to anything having social origin. Had society consisted of such absolutely independent individuals, there would have been no need, nor even the slightest possibility of them entering into an association; society itself would be non-existent, and those *free*

*individuals*, not being able to live and function upon the earth, would have to wing their way back to the heavenly abode.[27]

Ultimately, Wolff's 'autonomous' agents are left stranded in a nihilistic desert, unable to engage in any meaningful moral discourse or social practices, reduced to treating each other as morally 'mute' means to one another's arbitrary ends. It is a far cry from the 'rational community' Wolff originally envisaged. Not even the Categorical Imperative can help us here.

The sort of moral outlook which emphasizes efficiency in its account of rational (and moral) agency, and which treats ends as nonrational, precluding any intelligent debate over anything of moral importance, is typical of modern bureaucratic, technocratic society, socialist or capitalist, and exceedingly narrow and impoverished. It is not so much the mode of production in modern society, but its instrumental mode of reason which distinguishes it from other forms of society, and it is this particularly modern mode of reason which Wolff articulates.

This helps explain both why Wolff's concept of future society has a decidedly Marxist bent, and why he advocates a classically Marxist strategy for attaining it, for Marxism itself is irremediably tied to an instrumental view of reason which ultimately analyzes all social relationships in terms of their functional rationality.[28] Wolff's utopia is a society where politics is reduced to a problem of rational coordination, the administration of things, in which the State becomes the mere instrument of "rational men of good will" who eliminate the irrational domination of society by the market, subduing the market and society "to their wills" through the medium of the State, thereby moving "from the realm of necessity into the realm of freedom."[29] In such a society the individual and the general will are united and "a political order which harmonizes authority and autonomy" is finally attained.[30] The way to achieve such a society, of course, is to use the most instrumentally effective means possible, and, as Wolff has indicated

---

[27] Michael Bakunin, *The Political Philosophy of Bakunin*, ed. G. P. Maximoff (New York: Free Press, 1953), p. 167.
[28] See Marshall Sahlins, *Culture and Practical Reason* (Chicago: University of Chicago Press, 1976). For a defence of Marxism as a form of technological determinism, see G. A. Cohen, *Karl Marx's Theory of History: A Defence* (Princeton: Princeton University Press, 1978).
[29] Wolff, *In Defense of Anarchism, op. cit.*, p. 76.
[30] *Ibid.*, p. 78.

elsewhere, this means consists of nothing other than the State itself.[31] Only a very powerful and centralized State, Wolff claims, is capable of the massive restructuring of the economy and the redistribution of wealth which provide the necessary preconditions for the creation of a decentralized anarchist society in which each person enjoys full autonomy. In order to bring about anarchy one must first strengthen, not lessen, the power of the State.

Genuine anarchists have always strongly opposed this essentially Marxist idea that, in Bakunin's words, "anarchy or freedom is the aim, but the State or dictatorship is the means. Therefore in order to emancipate the masses they must first be enslaved."[32] Anarchists reject the instrumental view that the end justifies the means, insisting that ends and means are inseparable. Furthermore, they have increasingly come to reject the whole base/superstructure model and economic reductionism upon which the Marxist position is based.[33] Political power, anarchists argue, is not merely the 'excrescence' of the 'economic base,' nor will it necessarily disappear with the abolition of capitalism. The State is not, any more than technology, a morally neutral instrument which can be put to good uses, but by its very nature an instrument of class domination, whether of the capitalist class or a new class of Communist bureaucrats. Wolff's so-called 'philosophical anarchism' therefore is not only incoherent but contrary to anarchist ideals and in direct opposition to the mainstream of anarchist thought.

We see, then, that Wolff's critic, Jeffrey Reiman, was right to say that Wolff's "*moral* anarchism bears only the most superficial and largely misleading resemblance to *political* anarchism," if not for entirely correct reasons.[34] As Carole Pateman argues, Wolff's moral and political scepticism regarding the legitimacy of authority and the objectivity of substantive moral ends is a form of "scepticism which is inherent in abstractly individualist liberalism" but which "forms no part of a

---

[31] Wolff, interviewed in *The Black Flag of Anarchism*, Research Group One (Baltimore: Great Atlantic Radio Conspiracy, 1973), tape #43.

[32] Bakunin, *Selected Writings*, ed. Arthur Lehning (New York: Grove, 1974), p. 270.

[33] For recent anarchist critiques of Marxian analysis and politics, see Murray Bookchin, *The Ecology of Freedom* (Palo Alto: Cheshire Books, 1982) and *Toward an Ecological Society* (Montréal: Black Rose Books, 1980); and John P. Clark, *The Anarchist Moment: Reflections on Culture, Nature and Power* (Montréal: Black Rose Books, 1984).

[34] Reiman, *In Defense of Political Philosophy*, *op. cit.*, p. 52.

political theory of anarchism."[35] But from the failure of Wolff's particular argument neither the legitimacy of the State nor the falsity of anarchism in general follow. The State requires an independent justification. Whether such a justification has been successfully provided by any political philosopher is a question that cannot be answered here. Similarly, whether a successful defence of an alternative (and coherent) theory of anarchism is possible must also be left undecided. But at least this much is certain: Wolff has clearly demonstrated how *not* to defend anarchism.

---

[35] Pateman, *The Problem of Political Obligation, op. cit.*, p. 137.

# DEMOCRATIZING EUTOPIA: ENVIRONMENTALISM, ANARCHISM, FEMINISM

*Thomas W. Simon*

"Anthropologists tell us that blessed isles and paradise are part of a dreamworld of savages everywhere" (Manuel and Manuel, 1979, p. 1). In this age of doom-and-gloom the civilized pessimists far outnumber the cheery savages. Optimism, with a precarious hold on contemporary consciousness, is an endangered attitude. Few dare to advocate a radical transformation of society. At best we hear paeans to the continuation of the *status quo*. Seldom do we dare to dream, particularly in a utopian fashion.

The utopian literature fits very uncomfortably in this atmosphere of maintaining our present patterns, regardless of the costs. Even the word 'u-topia,' literally, 'no place,' biases us agaisnt it. Utopia was and is a term of derision, used by critics to dismiss the wild flights of fancy to never-land, to nowhere. 'Eu-topia,' meaning 'a good place,' serves as a more charitable label. Since this essay is, in part, a defence of this brand of dreaming, I will use the more positive term, 'eutopia.' This has the added advantage of more closely fitting the intents and desires of the writers who I will be discussing. Occasionally, however, I will revert to a convention of using 'utopia' to refer to the general class of literature and 'eutopia' to a particular subset of that literature, whose subject matter deals with environmentalism, feminism, anarchism, or some combination of these.

Many writers, including Manuel and Manuel in their monumental survey (1979), adamantly refuse to provide a definition of utopian literature. Luckily, we can avoid the definitional difficulties that beset any historical survey. For our purposes, eutopian writing is any form

*Thomas W. Simon teaches philosophy at the University of Florida in Gainesville.*

of social criticism through the literary depiction of a completely alternative future society with an aim to benefitting all. Within that genre, three works, all written around 1975, have been chosen: *Ecotopia* (1975) and, to some extent, its temporal predecessor, *Ecotopia Emerging* (1981), by Ernest Callenbach; *Woman On The Edge of Time* (1976) by Marge Piercy; and *The Dispossessed* (1974) by Ursula LeGuin.

These represent environmental, feminist, and anarchist eutopian visions, respectively. Risking charges of hasty generalization, I have peppered remarks throughout this essay, intended to show how the assets and liabilities of these novels are symptomatic of the assets and liabilities of the movements represented by each novel. For example, political drawbacks apparent in *Ecotopia* are readily seen in the environmental movement and its philosophies. While this type of analysis is not the major thrust of this essay, it does somewhat enhance our understanding of these politics.

Considering these three novels will also help us explore and understand some of the continuities and discontinuities between environmentalism, feminism, and anarchism — each closely associated, yet each quite different from the others. And if confessions are now in order, there is a hidden agenda on my part, namely, to find and develop a coherent philosophy and *praxis* among these three philosophies. This essay should take us a small step in that direction. My main aim, however, is to determine the status of eutopian writings. In order to assess the epistemological and political role of eutopia, I shall first evaluate these eutopian writings as a social science, then as a political theory, and finally as a particular brand of politics.

Despite some similarities, eutopia does not make a very good social science, particularly if it is the mainstream variety which places a high value on confirmable, experimental research. But that judgement says more about the status of social science than it does about eutopia. As we will see, a eutopian perspective offers a powerful vantage point to critique institutions like science. Unfortunately, this critique is seldom undertaken in utopian writings.

A political theory with little empirical content does not exactly qualify as a social science, but it does have a legitimate function in our culture. Perhaps eutopia fares better as a political theory than it does as a social science. In fact, when pitted against some academic fashions, such as the works by John Rawls and Robert Nozick, eutopian writings speed far ahead. The race is more complicated when eutopia and Marxism enter the field, since Marxists are ambivalent about utopian socialism. A case is made for integrating a political theory like Marxism with eutopian constructions.

Nevertheless, even though we will have then found a status for the eutopian mode, this interactive role between eutopian and political writings runs into other problems, particularly if participatory democracy is being advocated in the eutopian writings as it is in the case of LeGuin and Piercy. The problem, simply put, is that democracy is being advocated non-democratically, leaving the position open to the charge of being authoritarian and thereby inconsistent. The proposed solution is democratizing eutopia, a radical concept sometimes difficult to grasp — all of which will be duly explained. In the meantime, suffice it to say that not only does democratizing eutopia avoid the authoritarian charge, it also clarifies the status of eutopian proposals. In brief, I will argue that a politically informed democratized eutopia offers a powerful tool for evaluating our society and our institutional structures, especially influential ones like science.

Before making good on these promises, those who have not read the three novels may find a brief summary of each helpful.

Until the visit of crack U.S. investigator Will Weston in 1999, Ecotopia, in America's Northwest, has not been visited by a foreigner since it seceded from the U.S. in 1980. I'll let the book jacket describe the rest:

> Like a modern Gulliver, Will is sometimes horrified, sometimes over-whelmed by strange practices and sensual encounters. He discovers a nation which, in lucky circumstances, has taken charge of its own biological destiny. As Will becomes deeply involved with a sexually forthright Ecotopian woman, ritual war games, and a female-dominated 'stable-state' government, his confusion of values intensifies and reaches a startling climax.

Connie Ramos, a poor Chicana *Woman on the Edge of Time* 'future travels‘ from the horrors of a New York City insane asylum and finds Mattapoisett, Massachusetts, in 2137 in a state of ecological harmony, similar to but more advanced than Ecotopia. What also differentiates Mattapoisett from Ecotopia is the commitment of those in the former to anarcho-feminist non-hierarchical values.

> In it sex roles are unknown, biological relationships have given way to a broader concept of family, and the likenesses of her lost child and

lover live in a rare atmosphere of liberty and possibility. As the doctors close in, this poignant vision becomes a vivid counterpoint to the intensifying honor of Connie's reality. But gradually she comes to seize her own power to Act — not only for herself but also for the future.

Finally, a similar contrast between dystopia and utopia is found in *The Dispossessed*. Here, we find interplay between the authoritarian, propertarian (possessed) hell-planet Urras and its anarchist, dispossessed moon, Anarres, settled by refugees from Urras who are followers of Odo, a female revolutionary philosopher and activist. The contrast between the two becomes particularly vivid and pronounced when a famed physicist on Anarres, Shevek, who has discovered a revolutionary unified theory of time, visits Urras after the two worlds have had almost no contact for 160 years.

These three eutopias will be assessed within a framework provided by Barbara Goodwin and Keith Taylor in *The Politics of Utopia* (1982). If this essay is any indication, their aim of furthering research into utopian thought has been satisfied. While I am in basic agreement with their analysis, I do claim to offer a more radical and sounder defence of eutopian writing.

## Eutopia and Science

### Possibilities: Eutopian and Scientific Varieties

Do eutopian writings have any scientific status? Posing the question in these terms reflects the power of science in our age. Anointing an intellectual practice with the honorific title 'scientific' somehow automatically legitimizes the activity. Parapsychology, for example, attains respectability to the degree to which it can be considered scientific. On the surface, constructing eutopias ranks even below uncovering psi phenomena on the scientific respectability scale. At least, say the critics, parapsychologists attempt to conduct experiments, however flawed they might be.

Dismissing eutopian writings as non-scientific in this summary manner indicates an unjustifiably narrow conception of the scientific enterprise. Eutopian writers do not conduct controlled laboratory experiments, constructing miniature versions of ideal societies in the basements of sociology buildings, but neither do many 'legitimate' scientists such as astrophysicists and linguists. Even so, some utopian writers have tried to experimentally implement their visions, sometimes with disastrous results. Yet, unlike even these 'softer' sciences, eutopian writings all contain a strong normative element supposedly not found in science. The eutopianist not only describes what humans are but also prescribes what they should and could become.

If thinking about what might have been is a legitimate function of a social science like history, why not treat thinking about what might happen as equally legitimate? Goodwin and Taylor consider justifying eutopian writing as a "subspecies of the counterfactuals popular in philosophy and in historical studies" (1982, p. 210). Eutopias, then, "depict possible worlds" (1982, p. 212). The idea here seems to be that if we cannot find a room for eutopias in the more experimental buildings of science, perhaps a eutopian rental is available in the more formal projects of science. The use of counterfactuals ("If kangaroos had no tails, they would topple over") and possible worlds in philosophy have largely revolved around constructing particular kinds of logics. Whatever the merits of this might be, assimilating eutopias into this formalist mode strips them of their power.

To see this more clearly let us suppose that we are constructing a possible world differing from our own in only two respects. In this eutopia there is no private property (a common feature of utopias) and no centralized government. Presumably, any eutopia could be written in a more logically precise way. Allegedly, this does not detract from anything eutopians are saying; it just lends it some degree of precision.

The idea that formal procedures can only help and cannot hurt is misleading. It is no accident that most eutopias are presented in a fictional and therefore contextural mode. Eutopias are the *imaginative* constructing of an *entire* world, not the logical re-ordering of pieces of this world. In *The Dispossessed* the moon Anarres differs from the planet Urras and both of these differ from our own world not simply in that Anarres has neither private property nor centralized government. Rather, they all differ in ways that cannot be precisely specified. The context within which Anarres is portrayed makes it interestingly comparable to our own. To the degree that possible worlds modeling captures these context features is not only the degree to which it is like the depicted eutopia but also the degree to which it becomes itself a eutopian depiction. Eutopia is not simply a controlled thought experiment where only a few features of our world are altered; rather, it is a radical, contextural transformation of our world.

Perhaps eutopia and science, either in its experimental or in its formal varieties, will be forever at loggerheads. While Goodwin and Taylor try to edge eutopian writing closer to the scientific camp, Bauman wants to drive an immovable wedge between possibility, the exclusive domain of eutopia, and probability, the proper realm for science. Science deals with *facta*,

> ...to the realm of events which have already taken place, which can be relished or regretted, but cannot be changed; events in relation to which men [sic] have neither will nor liberty of action, neither power nor influence (Bauman, 1976, p. 33).

Oddly enough, Goodwin and Taylor accept this distinction:

> The empiricist chooses not to use this faculty [fantasy], confining himself [sic] to observations of what *is* (which all too often turn into justifications of the *staus quo*), while the utopian employs it in constructing alternative possibilities; in so doing he inevitably selects a theory-based method, since empiricism can carry him no further than the existent (Goodwin and Taylor, 1982, p. 99).

These distinctions underestimate the role of possibility in science and in logical empiricist philosophy. Science is not simply confined to the stale, old, dry facts; science continually goes beyond the data. Some philosophers of science take predictive novelty to be a crucial test for the viability of a scientific research programme. Elementary particle physicists search for possible particles. Science is replete with idealizations, another form of possibility.

This list, which undermines the eutopia-possibility/science-probability opposition, could go on. Yet, there is an important case, emphasized by Bauman, wherein the distinction holds. Bauman criticizes

> The scientific attitude, which would restrict the field of permitted knowledge to that part of the human world which has already been traversed and left behind (1976, p. 35).

This criticism is better directed at the social sciences, which do largely ignore a social/political sense of possibility whereby consideration is given to the future transformation of the entire society. Social scientists, so intent on attaining scientific responsibility, shun bold conjecture and speculation in favour of easily confirmed hypotheses, "which all too often turn into justifications of the *status quo*" (Goodwin and Taylor, 1982, p. 99).

Every research project in the social sciences involves some notion of possibility, either explicitly or implicitly. In order to study juvenile delinquency, for instance, researchers need some idea of other possible social arrangements, such as what non-delinquency among juveniles would be like. The problem is that more deeply rooted possibilities such as completely alternative social arrangements (the delinquency of the society itself) are seldom involved. This opting for a safe sense of possibility is reflected in the type of research chosen. Consider the following British example:

> It seems that the Social Science Research Council has opted for the politically safer sphere of managerial, administrative and organizational research of a kind which accepts the current institutional and political arrangements, and which acts more or less as a hand-maiden to government needs (on a 'customer-contract' basis) rather than opting for what might be termed 'deep structure' research (Leftwich, 1984, p. 9).

Considerations of possibility are thereby given free range only within a very limited set of restraints within the social sciences to the detriment of any 'deep' research. Of course, not all social scientists fall under this criticism, but the extent to which they do is the extent to which a strong rift exists between eutopian writings and social science.

So, although Bauman wrongly sees an unbridgeable gap between possibility and science, we can only find a limited sense of possibility evident in current social science practices. Eutopian writing utilizes a much more radical sense of possibility. If eutopian constructing was an integral part of social science, then you would have a very different sense of social science than you find today. It will not do to find a small niche for eutopian thinking within the social science edifice. At worst, this would create a new professional, the expert in charge of mapping out our future for us. Not finding a place for eutopian thinking in the social sciences says more about the status of the social sciences that it does about eutopias.

Trying to somehow accommodate eutopia to the sciences is further symptomatic of a failure on the part of both scientists (and eutopianists) to bring the institutional framework of science itself under question. We will take up this failure in the next section.

## Scientism in Eutopia

The failure to subject science itself to radical critiques infects some of the eutopian writings. An adoration of, or at the very minimum a refusal to question science in the same sweeping way in which the rest of society's institutions are questioned, is what I call scientism. We will see scientism at work, to varying degrees, in the works we are considering.

On the one hand, in *Ecotopia* the social sciences mysteriously disappear, for these are fit subjects for the citizens themselves. On the other hand, the natural sciences and philosophy are beyond the reach of the average Ecotopian. Science is pursued in roughly the same manner in 1999 Ecotopia as it is today except that smaller projects — solar energy and other appropriate technologies — are more readily funded by Ecotopian agencies than they are by the National Science Foundation.

In *The Dispossessed*, LeGuin is much more critical of science, although even here a contemporary version of scientific practice still prevails. Unlike their counterparts on Urras, the scientists on Anarres do not embark upon the scientific enterprise with the aim of domination, either of fellow humans or of nature. Even in this anarchist world, however, LeGuin sensitizes the reader to problems of scientists obtaining privileged status and science evolving into an hierarchical institution. Despite these valuable criticisms we are still left with a view of science as practised through the medium of the genius physicist, Shevek. Science is still great men like Shevek discovering truth. Shevek personifies the traits we have learned to falsely associate with the scientist:

> ...intellectual curiosity and a penchant for abstract thought, a fascination with the unknown and the problematical, a questioning mind, a love of free intellectual play, and a zest for knowledge for its own sake (Schwerkart, 1983, p. 207).

Piercy's *Woman On the Edge of Time* contains the most devastating indictment of science. Connie, about to undergo another scientific experiment as a mental patient, senses a connection between science and patriarchy:

> Suddenly, she thought that these men believed feeling itself a disease, something to be cut out like a rotten appendix. Cold, calculating, ambitious, believing themselves rational and superior, they chased the crouching female animal through the brain with a scalpel. From an

early age she had been told that what she felt was unreal and didn't matter. Now they were about to place in her something that would rule her feelings like a thermostat (1976, p. 282).

Science as practised in the future society, Mattapoisett, is very different from this caricature of beastly rationalism. Although we are given only a glimmer of how science operates on a day-to-day basis, we do know that this entire society determines the direction of science. For example, the people of Mattapoisett decided not to scientifically explore further means of prolonging life. Furthermore, the battle between the Shapers, who want to intervene genetically, and the Mixers, who regard genetic engineering as a "power surge," has so far been won by the Mixers. Simply because the society directly controls science does not mean Mattapoisett is anti-science. To the contrary, science is promoted, but only science that is truly for the people. Science helped wrest the only power women ever really had from them — the power to give birth.

> Cause as long as we were biologically enchained, we'd never be equal. And males would be humanized to be giving and tender (1976, p. 105).

So, reproduction takes place outside the womb, in brooders, so that all, male and female, can become 'mothers.' In addition, males are capable of breast-feeding.

Although it would take a lengthy discussion to fully show this, these three works are symptomatic of environmental, anarchist, and feminist, respectively, attitudes towards science. Environmentalists, like Ecotopians, rather than presenting a radical critique of science, work in alliance with a reformed but largely intact scientific institution. For the most part, environmentalists call for more scientific studies being directed towards environmental issues without a concomitant demand to change the way those studies are conducted. Anarchists, whether classical proponents like Peter Kropotkin or contemporary fellow travellers like Noam Chomsky, leave science relatively untouched by their radical critiques of societal institutions. It is feminists who are the most likely of the three to present radical critiques of science. Indeed, Piercy offers just such a critique.

In summary, eutopia and science have a much more complicated relationship than the question, "what is the scientific status, if any, of eutopia?" would lead us to believe. Ultimately, attempts to fuse eutopia into a scientific mould fail. Even many eutopian writers try unsuccessfully. But through that failure we have learned more about science and eutopia.


## Eutopia and Political Theory

As we have seen, there is little or no fit between eutopian writing and social science. Political theory is a better candidate for where we can place eutopian thought. Unlike the more empiricist versions of the social sciences, political theory is avowedly normative. In this section I shall try to evaluate the status of eutopian writing by comparing it to two very different styles of political theorizing: the liberal and libertarian tradition, represented by Rawls and Nozick, and Marxism. My aim will be to show the ways in which eutopian thought can be incorporated into political theories like Marxism, making it superior to the Rawls/Nozick variety.


### *Philosophical Fantasy vs. Eutopia*

Goodwin and Taylor correctly find eutopian elements in political writings throughout the ages. Ideals, hypotheticals, inversions are just a few of the devices used by political theorists, eutopian or otherwise. The similarities, however, can only be drawn out so far before the differences must be faced.

By devising a classification for distinguishing eutopian thought from other forms of political theorizing, Goodwin and Taylor unwittingly unleash a powerful criticism of much of what passes for political theory and unabashedly promote the virtues of eutopian thinking. This seemingly innocent classification is:

1.  idealization of the past and criticism of the present
2.  justification of the present by reference to a hypothetical past
3.  justification of the present by reference to a hypothetical present
4.  inversion of the present for critical purposes
5.  constructive criticism of the present via an ideal alternative (future or present)
6.  justification of the present by reference to a worse future (Goodwin and Taylor, 1982 pp. 23-27)

However exhaustive this list is in covering the range of hypothetical devices available to the political theorist, it should be noted that most writings in political philosophy fit snugly under categories (2) and (3). State-of-nature theorists Hobbes and Locke are placed in (2); contemporary theorists Rawls and Nozick are corralled under (3). Utopias, of almost any variety, occupy the high ground of category (5). Thus, according to this scheme, political philosophy tracts largely serve to justify the *status quo*, whereas eutopias offer one of the few vantage points for constructive criticisms of the here and now.

Philosophers would be quick to denounce Goodwin's and Taylor's abbreviated but allegedly outrageous attack. After all, philosophical works do not justify the present in the sense that they directly argue for the preservation of a particular political structure within a specific historical context. It would be difficult to find a Reagan-for-President philosophical article. Philosophers are, however, constantly making constructive criticisms. Followers of Rawls and of Nozick, for example, would readily point out that we do not live in either a Rawlsian or a Nozickian world. We do not live in a Rawlsian nation where social and economic inequalities are permitted only insofar as they benefit the least well off. Nor do we live in a Nozickian society with only voluntary exchanges and transfers and without any redistributional policies. According to these defenders, then, Rawls and Nozick do offer plausible standards for assessing our social/political institutions and policies and do not simply provide apologies for the *status quo*.

Nevertheless, the Goodwin and Taylor dismissal, however summary, of Rawls and Nozick is more defensible than it might first appear. Despite the differences between Rawls' welfare-State liberalism and Nozick's libertarian conservativism there is an important sense in which we do live in both a Rawlsian and a Nozickian world. In the end, Rawls' *Theory of Justice* and Nozick's *Anarchy, State, and Utopia* serve as justificatory tools for fundamental aspects of current political frameworks and as underpinnings for prevailing ideologies. A Rawlsian world does not differ all that much from the institutional framework of Western liberal democracies, and Nozick's philosophy helps bolster right-wing libertarian ideology. More importantly, an individualism underlies Rawls' and Nozick's theories. This individualism, invading and pervading our culture, places the individual above community.

> As a person's values and ends are always attributes and never constituents of the self, so a sense of community is only an attribute and never a constituent of a well-ordered society (Sandel, 1982, p. 64).

In contrast, the notion of community occupies centre stage within the pages of the eutopias. The constructive criticism offered by Rawls and Nozick is limited compared to the eutopianist, since the former avoids confronting the fundamental assumptions of our society, such as individualism. The works of Rawls and Nozick, then, do serve as justifications for the *status quo*.

There are even further difficulties with the Rawls-Nozick approach to political theory; these difficulties provide further justification for the Goodwin-Taylor classification. On the one hand, the works of Rawls and Nozick, like most of contemporary Anglo-American political philosophy, present a series of argued-for abstract principles. These principles are not situated in a specific time and place. Ironically, this way of political theorizing is quite literally a u-topia — no place.

On the other hand, eutopias provide us with a concrete picture of the present and future. They are situated in a specific time and place. In a word, they are topias — places. A concrete picture of the future sits before us to be analyzed, compared, mocked, debated, and embraced. Not only is the future set out in glowing detail so that we can compare it to the here-and-now, but a clear-cut picture of our present plight glares at us as well.

For example, the road to *Ecotopia* is laid out before us in soap-operatic detail in Callenbach's *Ecotopia Emerging* ("The astonishing novel that takes you back to the birth of your future"). Unfortunately, Callenbach's analysis of present society does not take us far beyond a contemporary journalist's report on Eugene, Oregon. Nevertheless, we are provided with a disturbing picture of current environmental degradation. Piercy's *Woman on the Edge of Time* paints a vivid picture of urban violence and the insanity of mental health institutions. "The personal is political" becomes more than a slogan. Only Le Guin's *The Dispossessed*, a fictional account of two planetary bodies in another solar system, does not present an explicit indictment of the here-and-now. Yet, the possessed planet of Urras is more similar to our own world than we care to admit.

Finally, these eutopian works cannot be dismissed as unworthy of philosophical attention because they lack philosophical argumentation. Serious political philosophy is at work in these present-to-future film frames. For in addition to the pictures themselves, philosophical argumentation abounds throughout the pages of these eutopian novels. Environmentalism, feminism, and anarchism are not simply described and pictured; they are forcefully argued. Weston does not merely report and describe ecotopia; ecotopians need to constantly counter his recurring skepticism. Luciente periodically allays Connie's fears about Mattapoisett. And Shevek challenges every propertarian that he meets on Urras to understand anarchism. The sophistication of argument will become even more apparent when we later examine some specific proposals coming from the eutopians.

This should be sufficient for elevating the status of eutopian writings to at least the level of Rawls and Nozick. At first blush, Goodwin's and Taylor's signalling out utopia for being the only theoretical mode through which present society can be fully critiqued seems too harsh and hasty. Yet when we compare works like that of Rawls and Nozick to eutopian writings we are minimally justified in treating eutopian writing as serious political theory. Now, we will further explore the ramifications of eutopian writing as political theory by looking at the actual and potential role of eutopian thinking in Marxism.

## *Marxism and Eutopia: An Interaction*

How do these eutopias fare when we compare them to a very different kind of political theory than the Rawls/Nozick variety — Marxism? An interesting approach to this is to imagine what Marx would say about eutopianism by examining what Marx did say about utopian socialism. Marx did not quarrel with the utopians' picture of social evils but with their lack of political, historical, and economic analyses. As Engels summarized the Marxist judgement:

> To the crude conditions of capitalistic production and the crude class conditions correspond crude theories. The solution of the social problems, which as yet lay hidden in undeveloped economic conditions, the Utopians [Saint-Simon, Fourier, Owen] attempted to evolve out of the human brain. Society presented nothing but wrongs; to remove these was the task of reason. It was necessary, then, to discover a new and more perfect system of social order and impose this upon society from without by propaganda, and, wherever it was possible, by the example of model experiments. These new social systems were foredoomed as

Utopian; the more completely they were worked out in detail, the more they could not avoid drifting off into pure phantasies (Engels, "Socialism: Utopian and Scientific").

As we will see, the eutopias must plead only partially guilty to this same charge. Of the three novels, *Ecotopia* is the most likely to be sentenced since it does not go far beyond extrapolating from a rather superficial understanding of the present. The polluting end-products of the production process are challenged frontally whereas the production process itself, including ownership, is left largely intact. For example, the one structural plank in the Survivalist Party's Bill of Rights — "No absentee ownership or control — one employee, one vote" (*Ecotopia Emerging*, 1981, p. 37) — is more of an afterthought than a frontal assault on structural evils of the system. Similarly, *The Dispossessed* conveniently by-passes our current predicament by leaping forward in time and space to two other worlds.

But this criticism is misleading. Certainly, these novels do not offer orthodox Marxist class analyses, applying dialectical materialism to history. Admitting that, however, does not mean that they are devoid of political, historical, and economic analysis. Like Marx we may disagree with their analysis, but that doesn't mean that they don't have one. The same applies to Marx's criticism of the utopian socialist, as Goodwin and Taylor argue (p. 74). It is unfair to saddle the eutopianists with the failure "to understand the workings of modern history, neither recognizing the restraints that history imposes nor appreciating the potentialities that history offers" (Meisner, 1982, p. 8). Even the furthest removed of the three, *The Dispossessed*, provides a plausible set of hypotheses about the historical development of the worlds Urras and Anarres. Odo, the philosopher-queen of anarchism, not only forged an inspiring theoretical framework, but she also led a movement on Urras (the possessed, propertarian world). All the eutopias evidence a recognition of the restraints and potentialities of history.

In fact, not only are there political/historical theories that can be inferred from these eutopian writings, but also there is a sense in which the political theory proposed by them is an improvement over classical Marxism or, for that matter, classical anarchism. For example, the fundamental unit of analysis for Marx is class; for the anarchist it is government. LeGuin and Piercy propose something more fundamental than either of these two — hierarchy. Accordingly, neither a classless nor a Stateless society can claim to have eradicated hierarchical power relations such as sexism. Admittedly, eutopian novels are not essential to making those kinds of emendations to Marxism or anarchism. Nevertheless, they do provide one means of developing and enhancing political theory in that direction.

Despite my enthusiasm, the case for eutopias as political theory needs to be tempered. To see both the political theoretic virtues and vices of these eutopias we need to concentrate on Piercy's *Woman on the Edge of Time*. Piercy's work is a more politically sensitive indictment of mental institutions than Ken Kesey's *One Flew Over the Cookoo's Nest*. Connie's class background, race, and gender make her particularly susceptible to harassment from the 'helping professionals.' Yet, we find little more than a glimmer of the historical/political preconditions of this kind of institution; nor do we come away from Piercy's novel with a better understanding of the structural foundations of this institution. Furthermore, Connie's political act, her rebellion, is largely a personal, individual one. Poisoning your oppressor's coffee hardly constitutes a full-fledged revolutionary act, even though its daring should not be underestimaed. Moreover, the political connections between the exposé of current mental institutions and the future eco-feminist society remain vague. To a certain extent, Piercy provides us with two unconnected political analyses, one focused on a current issue-oriented social injustice and the other outlining a future eco-feminist society. While juxtaposing the present microcosm to the future macrocosm is intentional on Piercy's part, it detracts from the political impact which a macrocosm to macrocosm juxtaposition would have had.

So the jury must remain out on the question of evaluating eutopia as a political theory. On the one hand, insightful fragments of political theory are readily found; on the other hand, important pieces to the political jigsaw are more often than not left out. Perhaps a higher reward can be conferred on the eutopias if we assess the role of utopia, or lack thereof, in Marx's own thinking.

The debate over whether Marx and Engels were utopian or anti-utopian can be easily resolved: they were both. Lukes cogently summarizes this ambivalence:

> Their anti-utopianism was a general critique of such fantasizing as premature and prescientific, that had become in their own time reactionary and dangerous; their utopianism a specific acceptance of the Utopian

Socialists' vision of the future which they synthesized and incorporated into their own vision of human emancipation (Lukes, 1984, p. 156).

The envisioned communist utopia is one

> ...where nobody has one exclusive sphere of activity but each can become accomplished in any branch he wishes. Society regulates the general production and thus makes it possible for me to do one thing to-day and another to-morrow, to hunt in the morning, fish in the afternoon, rear cattle in the evening, criticize after dinner, just as I have a mind, without ever becoming hunter, fisherman, shepherd or critic (Marx and Engels, *German Ideology*).

Yet, beyond pronouncements like these the number of utopian musings found in Marx are few and very far between. Marx and Engels are utopianists but only in the sense of presenting vague generalities about the future.

Lukes sees this watery form of utopianism as a serious defect in Marxism:

> ...Marxism has failed to clarify its ends and explore the institutional and political forms that could embody them (Lukes, 1984, p. 166).

Unlike the eutopias, in Marxism we do not get a very clear picture of what a communist society would actually look like. According to Lukes, Marxist anti-utopianism has systematically inhibited pursuing answers to such critical questions about the future state of high communism as:

1. What kind of morality does it embody?
2. How are resources to be allocated?
3. What forms of collective choice or decision making should be followed?

It will not do to respond that these questions will be answered by knowing and acting on the forces already at work within present social reality:

> But, one must ask, how can one have the one kind of knowledge (of the self-transforming present) without the other (of the shape of future society)? How can scientific observers know that 'what is happening before their eyes,' that the result of 'forces already at work within social reality' is the 'realisation of the ultimate objective,' the emancipatory transformation of capitalism into socialism, unless they also know, or at least have good reason to believe, that the 'new society,' latent in

the old, will take a form that *is* emancipatory, thus justifying their support for the proletariat's struggle? In other words, to assume that they do know the former is to assume that they know, or have good reason to believe, the latter (Lukes, 1984, pp. 158-159).

I have quoted Lukes at length because he is proposing a critical function for eutopian thought. Of course, certain principles of justice, etc., can be formulated by examining the here and now. But knowing about the future can and does inform our analysis about the present and *vice versa*. There needs to be an interaction between the two. Eutopianism should not be a model imposed on us without being rooted in the present. Neither should political theory completely shun eutopian thinking. The two need to mesh.

Irrespective of the importance of eutopian thinking and political theory to each other one obstacle remains in the path of making eutopian thinking part and parcel of political theory. Whether this obstacle exists depends on the political implications of the eutopia and/or the political theory. If the theorist advocates participatory democracy, where the people's control over critical policies of the society is continually maximized, then it is difficult to see how one could consistently bar the people from formulating and developing the future plan for the society. Granted by one person writing a eutopian novel, you are not thereby barring all others from this futures-planning. Nevertheless, given other institutional factors the vision of a single individual does lend itself to non-participatory practices.

Rather than try to determine whether a eutopianized Marxism is guilty of this charge, it would be more beneficial to determine whether there is anything about the politics of the various eutopias we are considering that would make them particularly vulnerable to this charge.

## Eutopia and Politics

### Uncovering Politics in Eutopia

What are the politics of the three eutopias we have been examining? What is their primary political agenda? Before answering these we need to clarify the concept of politics itself.

The word 'politics' has been bandied about without tying it down with definitional ropes. Intention lies behind the neglect. When pieced together, definitional fragments, sprinkled throughout this essay, help guide us towards an understanding of what politics means. Unravelling the interplay between politics and eutopia in this section will clarify the political neutral sense of politics. Fortunately, your sense of politics betrays your own politics.

The definitional problems aside, characterizing the role of politics in eutopian writing is complicated by the fact that utopias, in general, are regarded by proponent and opponent alike as non-political.

> Utopia seems to exclude politics because, simply, there is nothing left to argue about; also, because its insularity, or a convenient mountain range, eliminates the problem or external political relations (Goodwin and Taylor, 1982, p. 34).

Goodwin and Taylor quickly correct this misapprehension by pointing out that this judgement reflects a conflictional model of politics,

> indicative of our ideological conviction that politics equals argument, competition and the representation of rival interests, and that the successful politician is one who somehow gains power over the others and 'wins' (Goodwin and Taylor, 1982, p. 34).

Conflict, at the very heart of politics in our society, occupies a peripheral position in utopias. This does not mean that conflict is totally eliminated in eutopia. Absolute harmony, while found in some utopias, is not found in eutopia. Nevertheless, conflict need not be constitutive of the political.

Our commonly held narrow conception of politics comes further to the surface when we ask the person-on-the-street (or sidewalk) whether 'per' (to use Piercy's non-sexist pronoun) is political. Per will undoubtedly take this question to be on par with: 'Do you vote?' or, more daringly, 'Do you care about government?' If politics is equated with government, then eutopians have as little regard for it as our friend on the sidewalk is likely to have. Connie is told that Luciente, her guide into the future in Piercy's novel, "can show you government, but nobody's working there today" (p. 78). And LeGuin's Anarres represents the anarchist society *par excellence*, without government, ruled only by the laws of evolution.

The treatment of government within each eutopia reflects the stance taken by movements which these eutopias represent. In her teachings,

Odo, in keeping with anarchism, is quite explicit about government; she totally rejects it. The feminist practices in Mattapoisett are largely at one with Odo's teaching since Piercy's brand of feminism intricately intertwines with anarchism. Ecotopia, like its counterpart environmentalism, falls on the other side of the wire, keeping government relatively intact. There, even the two-party system (the Survivalists, led by a woman, Vera Allwen, and the Progressives) survives. The only real structural change from the present U.S. system found among Ecotopians is that their meetings are more participatory. Bean sprouts and tofu may prosper in Ecotopia, but so does government. Furthermore, the legal system operates with a vengeance. For example, polluters automatically receive a jail sentence. I want to leave this Ecotopian form of government aside and concentrate for a moment on the non-governmental politics proposed by LeGuin and Piercy. Aren't non-governmental politics the same as non-political politics?

Goodwin and Taylor are too quick to defend the non-political nature of utopias. Just because many eutopias like LeGuin's and Piercy's shun the institution of government, replacing it with administration, "so as to exclude the adversary element which we consider essential" to politics (Goodwin and Taylor, 1982, p. 111), does not mean that eutopia is defensibly apolitical or non-political. Politics, in the form of power and domination, will rear its head without governmental nurturing — even, or rather, especially within administration. Balbus, using the word 'utopia' pejoratively, complains at length about the non-political nature of Marx's utopia:

> Marx's vision of a completely consensual society that dispenses with politics is a hopelessly utopian vision (Balbus, 1982, p. 119).

Marx naively thought that there was no need for politics in the higher stages of communism, which is "bereft of politics but replete with administration" (Balbus, 1982, p. 12), since classes would be eliminated. To that Balbus replies:

> The absence of a theory of politics for the future society necessarily entails the absence of a critique of political domination in this society (Balbus, 1982, p. 120).

"Necessarily entails" is clearly too strong. Yet Balbus correctly chastises Marx for ignoring critical components of domination outside the scope of class.

Interestingly enough, because of their broader sense of politics in terms of power and domination the eutopias of LeGuin and Piercy avoid the pitfalls of thinking that politics will magically disappear in the hoped-for world of tomorrow. The consequences of power and domination disguised as administration and custom are admirably traced by LeGuin:

> 'government: the legal use of power to maintain and extend power' (LeGuin, 1975, p. 142).

Shevek wisely notes that all you need to do in this definition is to substitute 'customary' for 'legal' to see the abuses of domination-as-administration in the anarchist society of Anarres. Sabul, the administrator of the Syndicate of Instruction where Shevek teaches, becomes a force of domination through his administrative prowess.

Not only is administration treated as highly politicized but so is the personal realm, for in Piercy's eutopia the personal is indeed political. Questions of personal relations are political for they also involve power and domination. A simple change of semantics, where I have hand-friends and pillow-friends, instead of friends and lovers, reflects the political dynamics.

If there are politics in eutopia, how do the eutopianists propose to deal with it? For LeGuin and Piercy participatory democracy is a key way of handling political problems. A way to counter power and domination is to optimize the participation of all individuals in all aspects of community life. So, if we want to discover the politics of Anarres and Mattapoisett, we should look to the democratic practices of those peoples. Yet, as we shall see, finding participatory democracy in these eutopias also creates some problems.

## Authoritarianism on the Way to Eutopia

Curiously, the very attempt to found an ideal society is rejected by some on the grounds that the utopian project is totalitarian. Karl Popper leads this attack:

> Even with the best intentions of making heaven on earth [utopianism] only succeeds in making it a hell — that hell which man alone prepares for his fellow-men (Popper, 1963, p. 168).

For Popper, utopianism is another form of dogmatism, replete with authoritarian and exclusivist underpinnings. Our vision of the good for others will turn out to be in practice a nightmare for others. Jonestown is only the most recent example of the pursuit of a millennium turned into the attainment of horror.

Goodwin and Taylor offer ingenious but evasive replies to this Popperian challenge. They find the critics' main artillery, the concept of totalitarianism, elusive. Further, turning the tables on their critics, Popperian liberalism is accused of being as problematic as utopianism, if not more so. Finally, with a sleight of the semantic hand, utopianism is admitted to the authoritative but not authoritarian, and totalist (advocating expansion of the public sphere at the expense of the private) but not totalitarian.

Fortunately, these clever defences do not seem necessary to protect the eutopias. For these eutopian visions are a far cry from the ranks of totalitarianism. In none of the utopias do we find evidence of worldwide imperialist expansion. In fact, these eutopias expend most of their military energies defending their small piece of a good place. Ecotopia occupies only a portion of the United States; Mattapoisett employs high-technology to defend its tiny part of Massachusetts; and the people of Anarres are forbidden to travel to and from their moon haven. Moreover, within each eutopia democracy and diversity are encouraged. People are not forced to be a particular way because of someone's vision. It is, therefore, difficult to see how the totalitarian charge might stick against these eutopias.

Nevertheless, an aspect of Popper's charge remains. I take it that part of Popper's criticism is epistemological: How can a single individual *know* enough about all facets of human interaction to devise a perfect society? This challenge receives further force when placed in the context of those eutopias advocating participatory democracy. The charge then becomes: How can a single individual know enough and how can she or he (per) non-democratically advocate participatory democracy? To be consistent, the means for achieving participatory democracy need to be made democratic. A single vision set forth in a novel does not lend itself to these democratic means.

The charge receives further substantiation when we consider that devising utopia has largely been a quasi-professional activity. In fact, utopianizing has increasingly become professionalized. The job of imagining a better future has been taken over by trained élites in think-tanks and universities. Even the protest versions of some eutopias, *Blueprint for Survival*, for example, are developed by a committee of experts. Dramatically put, the act of dreaming has been robbed from us. With professionals conjuring up utopias for us, the educational system can ignore and stamp out any remnant of utopian proclivities in us. Teachers almost never help us sharpen our future focus by asking us to imagine a better world. To test this hypothesis just try to imagine your version of eutopia and see how blurred it is.

The eutopian novelist stands in an interesting but ambiguous position in this professionalization-of-utopia picture. The novel form as a vehicle for conveying eutopian ideas is more open-ended than the discursive blueprint. In that sense, it leaves us more latitude for interpretation, more room for our own imagination. Nevertheless, the eutopian novel remains a manufactured version of a single individual's vision. The word 'manufactured' is important in this context, for the eutopian novel, however reflective of other people's vision, is not the product of our own labours. To resort to popular protest rhetoric, it is not a people's product, not a people's eutopia. It is produced for a certain level of mass consumption. Hence, the eutopian novel, despite advocating participatory democracy, is largely non-democratic. From this it does not follow that eutopian novels should be banned or belittled. Rather, they should be taken in a political context. The eutopian novel is purely suggestive and should be pitted against our own visions; it should never be swallowed wholesale — or ever swallowed at all.

So, the only way around this charge is for the eutopian advocating democracy to further advocate democratizing eutopia. At the very least, that would make the democratic aspect of the eutopian project more consistent. Here, democratizing does not simply mean providing each individual with the opportunity for going into solitude and envisioning a better future, although that might well be involved. Rather, democratizing is an ongoing community process of each of us constructing a eutopian vision in political dialogue with others. Practically, this could take in small affinity groups or throughout the educational system — in fact, throughout our social interactions.

The eutopias of Callenbach, Piercy, and LeGuin adhere to this democratizing process to varying degress. In Ecotopia and Piercy's eutopia, democracy is taken as a static end-state, something to be protected after we have worked so hard to attain it. Only LeGuin treats democracy as a continuing process. The trouble with the Anarresti is that they, too, think they have achieved their final goal of an anti-authoritarian, democratic society. Shevek returns to Anarres from Urras "to shake up things, to stir up, to break some habits, to make people ask questions" (LeGuin, 1974, p. 317), that is, to continually democratize Anarres. Participatory democracy is not an end-state; it is a process.

This may all appear as idle fancy on my part. We have enough trouble getting people to agree to fight together for a specific cause. The reason, however, that consensus is difficult to reach about a future vision is not that consensus is impossible or impractical but rather that debate about future societal goals has been rare. Moreover, democratizing eutopia does not require consensus nor by itself does it constitute a full-blown political theory. Instead, democratizing eutopia involves debate and dialogue (not consensus and imposition) about how we envision the future.

If we take the idea of democratizing eutopia to its logical conclusion from the seeds sown by Callenbach, Piercy, and LeGuin, we begin to better understand the relationships of eutopia to science and to political theory. The gist of the matter is that the politics of eutopia is radically different from the politics of science and the politics of political theory. The relationship between eutopia and science is quite strained because the politics of each is so different. The politics of science is authoritarian and élitist; the politics of eutopia, democratic and participatory. I am not talking about some abstracted, ahistorical notion of scientific methodology, but rather about present-day institutionalized science. A science by and for the people is presently at best a delusion; a eutopia should depict a radically transformed vision of science — a democratized science. If eutopia represents a radically transformed society, how can it leave science intact?

Likewise, democratizing eutopia challenges the politics of political theorizing. By the politics of political theorizing I mean the institutional structure within which political theories are constructed, disseminated, etc. That institutional structure is largely composed of professional academics. Given that mutual interaction between constructing political theories and devising eutopias is critical to the healthy development of both. Also, given that I have already advocated democratizing the one, that is, eutopia. It follows that there is a need to democratize the other, political theorizing. If political theory is democratized, then the opportunity for constructing political theories is spread over a wider group of people. This would certainly challenge at least one form of academic monopoly.

All of this may sound extremely utopian, in the worst sense of the word. After all, doesn't science presuppose a certain level of expertise? And how can you expect the indoctrinated masses to understand the nuances of political theory, to say nothing of their ability to construct political theories? Replying to these types of questions would involve an even further lengthy discussion. Suffice it to say, these questions presupposed just the kind of non-democratic views of science and political theory that the idea of democratizing eutopia is meant to challenge.

## Conclusion

What is the status of eutopia? Clearly, it is not a social science, particularly in any positivist sense of science. On the contrary, eutopias do (although to a limited extent), could, and should challenge the prevailing conceptions and institutional practices of science. At the end of their mammoth survey of utopian literature, the Manuels have good reason to lament "the discrepancy between the piling up of technological and scientific instrumentalities for making all things possible, and the pitiable poverty of goals" (F. and F. Manuel, 1979, p. 811). At the very minimum, the eutopian mode provides an opportune vehicle for proposing and debating those goals.

Eutopia's relationship to political theory is somewhat more ambiguous. Of course, it does depend upon what kind of political theory we are comparing. If it is of Rawls/Nozick vintage, then there is a clear-cut clash between theoretical supports for the *status quo* and radical challenges to it. If the political theory is Marxist (or even anarchist), then a close intermingling between theory and eutopia is highly recommended. The resulting mixture, however, poses further problems, such as an authoritarian dilemma: If the political theorist proposes detailed blue-prints of the future society, then she or he (per) is open to the charge of trying to impose that vision on others. Now, this may seem like a benign sense of imposing. By my merely presenting a eutopian scheme, which others may adopt as they see fit, how am I being authoritarian? Admittedly, an important idle fancy or academic exercise can hardly be accused of being authoritarian, but a eutopian scheme which is part of a broader political theory, which, in turn, is meant to be implemented, can be accused of being authoritarian, particularly when it systematically excludes its followers from the formulating process.

Democratizing eutopia circumvents this authoritarian problem. Moreover, democratizing eutopia both dilutes and bolsters the status of eutopianizing. It dilutes the status in the sense that it takes the task of drawing up eutopian schemes out of the exclusive hands of academic-related professionals, who have been responsible for giving eutopia its status, however low that might be. The dilution is compensated for by the fact that eutopianizing, by becoming a more integral part of more people's lives, gains a new status. Eutopianizing becomes a vehicle for hope, for optimism.

Pessimism is characteristic of a current American age, and these eutopias stand as only small diversions against that current. Pessimism is a wonderfully self-serving prophecy. Allow me to explain this latter remark. Despite your own intellectual, theoretical predilictions, it is easy to become pessimistic about radical change since, among other things, radical change would also unseat your own, probably comfortable, position. Pessimism is the politics of impotence. Today, issues are largely approached from a non-eutopian perspective, as separate, isolated, unconnected problems. Nuclear power, nuclear weapons, sexism, racism, poverty — all are treated as separate issues with no underlying thread uniting them. A eutopian approach would help change that. For example, the debate about nuclear weapons would not be simply about those weapons. Rather, it is about what kind of future society we can have and that vision includes coming to grips with other related problems, such as feminism.

A peculiar quality of the eutopian novels considered in this essay are their non-eutopian quality. Eutopianism, the literature of hope and optimism, is riddled throughout with signs of doubt and pessimism. Early in *Woman on the Edge of Time*, Connie exclaims about the future society: "But you exist. So it all worked out" (p. 172), but later in the novel this same exclamation is followed by her guide Luciente's guarded reply: "Maybe, maybe not." Ecotopia, the anti-nuclear, solar power land, comes into being through the threat of using nuclear weapons. None of the three eutopias encompasses the entire spaceship earth. *Woman on the Edge of Time* and *Ecotopia* capture small eutopian enclaves, and for *The Dispossessed*, we need to go to the moon. The optimism in these eutopias is not overwhelming, to say the least.

The most important ingredient, the *sine qua non*, for any eutopia is hope. Eutopia is a world where our vision of the future and the future are ours.

> 'You would destroy us rather than admit our reality — rather than admit that there is hope.'
> 'I thought I knew what realism was,' King said.
> 'How can you if you don't know what hope is!' (LeGuin, 1974).

Eutopianizing is the process of recapturing that hope, that realism. Eutopia is the continuous, ongoing, never-ending process of eutopianizing.

### Bibliography

Isaac D. Balbus, *Marxism and Domination: A Neo-Hegelian, Feminist, Psychoanalytic Theory of Sexual, Political, and Technological Liberation* (Princeton, New Jersey: Princeton University Press, 1982).

Ernest Callenbach, *Ecotopia* (New York: Bantam Books, 1975).

Ernest Callenbach, *Ecotopia Emerging* (New York: Bantam Books, 1981).

Frederick Engels, "Socialism: Utopian and Scientific," Marx and Engels, *Selected Works*, Vol. 2.

Barbara Goodwin and Keith Taylor, *The Politics of Utopia: A Study in Theory and Practice* (London: Hutchinson, 1982).

Adrian Leftwich, "On the Politics of Politics," *What Is Politics*, Adrian Leftwich, editor (London: Basil Blackwell, 1984).

Ursula K. LeGuin, *The Dispossessed* (New York: Granada, 1974).

Steven Lukes, "Marxism and Utopianism," *Utopias*. Peter Alexander and Roger Gill, editors (London: Duckworth, 1984).

K. Marx and F. Engels, *German Ideology*.

Maurice Meisner, *Marxism, Maoism and Utopianism* (Madison, Wisconsin: The University of Wisconsin Press, 1982).

Marge Piercy, *Woman On the Edge of Time* (London: The Women's Press Limited, 1976).

K. R. Popper, *The Open Society and Its Enemies*, Vol. 1 (New York: Harper and Row Publishers, 1982).

Michael J. Sandel, *Liberation and the Limits of Justice* (New York: Cambridge University Press, 1982).

Patrocinio Schweickart, "What If... Science and Technology in Feminist Utopia," *Machina Ex Dea: Feminist Perspectives on Technology*, Joan Rothschild, editor (New York: Pergamon Press, 1983).

# EMMA GOLDMAN AND WOMEN
## Alice Ruth Wexler

Freedom. It isn't once, to walk out
under the Milky Way, feeling the rivers
of light, the fields of dark —
freedom is daily, prose-bound, routine
remembering. Putting together, inch by inch
the starry worlds. From all the lost collections.

Adrienne Rich

As he took the microphone in the main hall of the Architecture Faculty on the second day of last year's anarchist congress in Venice, I knew I had found him. He was tall and tanned, fine-featured, dressed in a white sports jacket, a handsome man in his eighties. He protested a statement by one of the speakers that Emma Goldman, in her later years, had grown bitter and hostile to men. He had known her well, he said, and this wasn't true.

Outside, over pasta and red wine at the Campo Santa Margherita, Arturo Bortolotti recalled the day he had seen Emma, at the age of sixty-five, holding hands with her 'boyfriend' (Frank Heiner), a beatific smile on her face. He told me how Emma had saved his life in Toronto back in 1939, when he was a young anti-fascist immigrant from Fruili, threatened with deportation to Mussolini's Italy. He told how she had hired a lawyer and raised money for his defence, how she had nursed him back to health after his illness in prison, and about her death a few months later. "What do you think is Emma's legacy today?" I asked. "To be human," he said, "to be gentle, to be amorous, the woman as partner..." Suddenly two comrades came rushing over to

*Alice Wexler is Visiting Scholar, University of California, Riverside. She recently published* Emma Goldman: An Intimate Life *(Pantheon) and gave the public lecture "Emma Goldman: Women and Freedom" at the Anarchos Institute conference of 1 June 1985.*

greet him in a flurry of smiles and embraces. The man who had been closest to Emma at the time of her death excused himself, and turned toward his friends.

As he rose to leave, I could not help thinking that Emma, a veteran of many anarchist congresses, would have relished this gathering in 1984, with some three thousand people crowding into Communist-run Venice — Spanish anarcho-syndicalists and Argentine psychoanalysts, French literary critics and Canadian peace activists, Italian sociologists and German 'punks' — filling the Campo Santa Margherita and the Campo San Polo with their dreams of a Stateless society. She would have welcomed the astute analysis of her legacy offered by speakers at the session on "Anarchism and Feminism": Marsha Hewitt, from Montréal, explaining Goldman's specifically female perspective on anarchism that challenged the division between the public and the private; Barbara Koster, from Frankfurt, stressing Emma's divided consciousness of herself as woman and anarchist heroine and the loneliness of her decision to remain childless in order to be an anarchist fighter;[1] Rosanna Ambroghetti, of Forli, pointing out Emma's strength in acting and fighting without waiting for others to join her. Today we do not need to make Emma's choice between children and militancy, said Ambroghetti. But in order to have both, we need great commitment from both male and female comrades.

For all these women, as for Bortolotti, Emma Goldman still speaks, still raises questions that engage us today. Though she belonged to a predominantly male movement, she pondered all her life the dilemmas of women. Women shaped Emma's early life in crucial ways, from her shrewd, imperious mother and her patient sister, to her dying teacher of German who encouraged her education, to the famous German-American socialist orator Johanna Greie, whose talk on the Haymarket affair, in Rochester, New York, first electrified Emma with the power of the spoken word. If Emma's intellectual mentors were men — Kropotkin, Stirner, Nietzsche, Most — her emotions were stirred more deeply by women, especially the women revolutionaries whom she took as her models — Louise Michel, Sophia Perovskaya,

---

[1] Candace Falk has persuasively suggested that Emma may have been infertile due to undiagnosed endometriosis. Thus her childlessness was not a conscious sacrifice but unavoidable. See Falk's *Love, Anarchy and Emma Goldman* (New York: Holt Rinehart Winston, 1984), p. 30.

Catherine Brehkovskaya. In a Missouri prison in the summer of 1917 for opposing the draft, she advised her niece not to worry. "Greater heroes and martyrs than I have paid for their ideals with prison and even death, so why not I? Babushka, L[ouise] M[ichel], Spiridonova and a galaxy of others will sustain me..."[2] Throughout her life Emma imagined herself in the company of these women, comparing herself anxiously with them, gaining reassurance from a sense of herself as part of a tradition of radical women. Lacking a support group of women in real life, she created one in her imagination, peopled with the heroines whose lives she tried to emulate.

Yet Emma's relations with women, real and imagined, were always problematical. She did not, of course, see herself as a feminist. Feminism to her meant the upper-middle-class movement in nineteenth century Russia, where women agitated for entry into the universities and for access to élite professions. It meant the heavily middle-class suffrage movement in America, which, by the turn of the century, had gone respectable. As an anarchist, she was indifferent — if not hostile — to the vote, although she also thought that men should not have privileges denied to women. She believed the vote was not important, "except as everything is important that helps a woman to think for herself and to act for herself."[3]

But Emma's argument with the American feminists went beyond the vote to issues of class. Most feminists, she insisted, saw "their slavery apart from the rest of the human family." Advocates of votes for women did not necessarily have progressive views about labour. She criticized them especially for their insensitivity to working-class women (though we must remember that by about 1910, many women workers were entering the suffrage ranks). While Emma agreed with feminists such as Charlotte Perkins Gilman that economic independence was vital for women, she pointed out the limited options actually available to most women, which often made that independence illusory. For the great mass of working girls and women, how much independence is gained if the "narrowness and lack of freedom of the home is exchanged for the narrowness and lack of freedom of the factory, sweat-shop, department store or office?" Moreover, Emma attacked the feminists

[2] Emma Goldman to Stella Ballantine, 15 July 1917, Emma Goldman Archive, International Institute of Social History, Amsterdam.
[3] *New York Sun*, 2 May 1909.

for allegedly believing that "having a man's role, or professions, makes them free." Invoking Ellen Key, the Swedish feminist whose popular books defended both economic equality and childbearing as woman's true destiny, Goldman worried that professional women would exhaust themselves trying to compete with men, depleting their 'feminine' gifts of intuition and empathy.[4]

Goldman also scolded the feminists for ignoring the psychological aspects of women's subordination. While American feminists had originally set out to "make it possible for woman to be human in the truest sense," to remove "all artifical barriers," clear the road of "centuries of submission and slavery," the movement had achieved merely "external" results, losing touch with its original radical aims. Woman must "begin with her inner regeneration," said Emma. She must free herself "from the weight of prejudices, traditions, and customs." She must learn how to assert herself "as a personality, and not as a sex commodity," and "refuse to be a servant to God, the State, society, husband, family, etc." True emancipation begins "neither at the polls nor in courts. It begins in woman's soul."[5]

Emma's charges were not entirely fair. While it was true that the radical exponents of justice for women in the 1840's had taken a broader view than the more conservative, expediency-oriented turn-of-the-century feminists, most Anglo-American feminists, from Mary Wollstonecraft to Elizabeth Cady Stanton, had taken some cognizance of 'woman's soul' in a psychological sense. Stanton, in her 1892 speech "Solitude of Self," had spoken a language much like Goldman's when she insisted on the necessity of freeing women "from all forms of bondage, of custom, dependence, superstition; from all the crippling influences of fear."[6] The socialist feminist attorney Crystal Eastman agreed that "women will never be great until they achieve a certain emotional freedom, a strong healthy egotism, and some un-personal sources of joy." She acknowledged that simply changing woman's economic status would not make her free "in this inner sense," though

---

[4] Emma Goldman, "The Tragedy of Woman's Emancipation," in *Anarchism and Other Essays* 1911; reprint ed. New York: Dover, 1969, p. 216; also *New York Sun*, 2 May 1909.
[5] Emma Goldman, "Tragedy," *Ibid.*, pp. 213-225.
[6] Elizabeth Cady Stanton, "Solitude of Self," in *Feminism: The Essential Historical Writings*, ed. Miriam Schneir (New York: Vintage, 1972), p. 158.

she thought feminists should work to "create conditions of outward freedom in which a free woman's soul can be born and grow."[7]

But if Goldman and the mainstream feminists agreed on the importance of psychological freedom for women, they disagreed about the part played by sexuality in creating this freedom. According to Goldman, modern feminists "thought all that was needed was independence from external tyrannies; the internal tyrants, far more harmful to life and growth — ethical and social conventions — were left to take care of themselves; and they have taken care of themselves." They existed as comfortably in the hearts of emancipated women as in "the heads and hearts of our grandmothers," preventing women from achieving their most vital right, the right to love and be loved. "The narrowness of the existing conception of woman's independence and emancipation; the dread of love for a man who is not her social equal; the fear that love will rob her of her freedom and independence; the horror that love or the joy of motherhood will only hinder her in the full exercise of her profession — all these together make of the emancipated modern woman a compulsory vestal, before whom life, with its great clarifying sorrows and its deep, entrancing joys, rolls on without touching or gripping her soul." "Now," she insisted, "woman is confronted with the necessity of emancipating herself from emancipation, if she really desires to be free."[8]

This is not as paradoxical as it sounds. Goldman was clearly arguing against the 'social purity' politics of most suffragists and progressive reformers — members of the American Woman Suffrage Association or the Women's Christian Temperance Union, for example — who insisted on women's moral superiority to men and claimed that political participation by women would help to 'purify' public life. These 'social purity' feminists upheld conservative sexual values. They defended traditional marriage and family life, arguing that upgrading women's status would strengthen these institutions. They urged that men conform to the same chaste sexual standards demanded of women. Emphasizing

---

[7] Crystal Eastman, "Now We Can Begin," in *Crystal Eastman on Women and Revolution*, ed. Blanche Wiesen Cook (New York: Oxford, 1978), p. 55.
[8] Emma Goldman, "Tragedy," *op. cit.*, pp. 221-224.

the dangers of sex, they also fought to legislate morality through the prohibition of prostitution and pornography.[9]

Goldman's position, on the other hand, reflected the far more marginal 'pro-sex' tradition within American feminist thought — associated with such people as Frances Wright, Victoria Woodhull and the 'free lovers.' These people stressed the pleasures of sex, romanticized sexual daring of all sorts, and fought all forms of censorship and prohibition. Like the earlier 'free lovers' whose inspiration she acknowledged, Emma sought to broaden the sexual options for women rather than narrowing those of men. She attacked the patriarchal family as an institution that exploited both women and children. Instead, she celebrated love outside of marriage (though not sex outside of love), denouncing the cult of virginity and the double standard as the morality of slaves.

Emma's boldness thrilled many young feminists and bohemians of the exhilarating years prior to World War I. Young women everywhere had begun to repudiate the old nineteenth century 'cult of true womanhood' with its stress on submissiveness and domesticity. In the 1890's they were already drawn to an image of the 'new woman' — independent and adventurous. They responded eagerly to Goldman's call for a revolution in morality. This was the great theme of all her lectures. To Emma, as to many of her comrades, anarchism was as much an ethical as a political movement. Though Emma liked to present herself as an enemy of all morality (as in "Victims of Morality," for example), in fact she was pre-eminently a radical moralist. She had a powerful vision of what women — and men — might achieve in a free society, and this vision illuminates much of her writing. For many people, moreover, Emma herself embodied that vision. Her text was less important than her presence. Her friend, the literary editor Margaret Anderson, once wrote, "She says it instead of putting it into books... she hurls it from the platform straight into the minds and hearts of the eager, bewildered, or unfriendly people..."[10] Emma offered women a new self-image, a new way of thinking about themselves, a new range of possibilities. She legitimized their discontent, assuring

---

[9] See Linda Gordon and Ellen DuBois, "Seeking Ecstasy on the Battlefield: Danger and Pleasure in Nineteenth Century Feminist Thought," *Feminist Studies* 9 (Spring 1983), pp. 7-25.
[10] Margaret Anderson, "The Challenge of Emma Goldman," *The Little Review*, 1 (May 1914, pp. 5-9).

them that their stirrings toward independence were not signs of selfishness. Echoing Nora in Ibsen's *Doll's House*, Emma would ask, "How can any woman give herself to the fullest extent to the race, to the country, to her children, unless she stands for something in her own life and is no longer a mere echo or a slave? She must be an individual before she can do anything for anybody else." [11]

Moreover, Emma offered practical advice. She urged women to join unions or anarchist groups. She told them to come out from behind their leaflets and literature tables and learn to speak in public. Organize meetings. Sell *Mother Earth*. Demonstrate for free speech, campaign for birth control, raise money for the striking textile workers at Lawrence or Paterson. Read, attend lectures, go to the theatre. If they fell in love, she advised them to follow their impulses, and even occasionally offered her 'farm' retreat up the Hudson River at Ossining, New York, as a place to *rendez-vous*. Emma did not, for most of her life, support the idea of separate women's organizations — indeed, she became less enthusiastic about a separate women's politics after her deportation. "The Tragedy of the Modern Woman" (an unpublished revised version of the earlier essay), a talk given in Canada in the 1920's, warned that women will become free only when men are free. "The main task in the world today," she wrote, is the emancipation of society, economically, politically, socially and ethically." In her autobiography, published in 1931, she boasts of persuading an allmale club that "there is nothing duller in all the world than exclusive gatherings of men or of women..." [12] Though she did attempt to organize some birth control meetings for women students in 1916, Emma did not always work well with women. Unless, that is, they were distinctly her subordinates, like the *Mother Earth* secretary, Eleanor Fitzgerald (who was also Berkman's lover), or her beloved niece, Stella Ballantine. With prominent women in the anarchist movement, such as Voltairine de Cleyre and Lucy Parsons, her relations were tense and competitive. (Emma's closest comrades in America were always men: Max Baginski, Alexander Berkman, Hippolyte Havel, Ben Reitman.) Still, when she went to Spain in 1936, she enthusiastically championed the Mujeres Libres (Free Women), a separate anarchist organization

[11] *New York Sun*, 6 May 1909.
[12] Goldman, *Living My Life* (1931; reprint ed. New York: Dover Press, 397).

of women which worked to upgrade the status of women while aiding in the war effort. [13]

Emma always insisted that anarchism meant openness to change, yet her own varying statements often reflected confusion rather than flexibility. Her lectures on women, especially when revised for publication, are riddled with contradictions, flawed by the carelessness of a polemicist more concerned with rhetorical effect than with accuracy. "The Tragedy of Woman's Emancipation," for example, claims (in 1904) that "emancipation has brought woman economic equality with man" (in the sense of being able to choose her profession) while "The Traffic in Women" (circa 1911) explains prostitution largely as a result of women's social and economic inferiority to men. "Nowhere," she writes, "is woman treated according to the merit of her work, but rather as a sex." Yet elsewhere Goldman breezily claims that "the revolutionary process of changing her external conditions is comparatively easy; what is difficult and necessary is the inner change of thought and desire." [14]

In 1910, the eight million women in the U.S. workforce were concentrated in the least-skilled, lowest paying, most vulnerable jobs. The largest number were domestic servants. Farm labour, laundry work, teaching, the garment trades, saleswork and stenography were also important female occupations. While one in every five male industrial workers belonged to a union, only one in fifteen women industrial workers were unionized — some eight per cent of women workers. The tremendous obstacles to unionizing women alone suggest the difficulty of changing woman's 'external conditions.'

Emma's point, of course, was that women had succeeded in gaining entry to many formerly male professions, such as medicine and architecture. Yet they remained inhibited by traditional moral values that prevented them from seeking love and motherhood outside conventional marriage. Clinging to respectability, they had not become independent in spirit or free in their personal lives. Yet instead of sympathizing with their dilemmas, Emma scolds them for their conservatism and fear of censure, coming close to blaming the victims rather than explaining their victimization.

[13] See David Porter, ed., *Vision on Fire: Emma Goldman on the Spanish Revolution* (New Paltz, New York: Commonground Press, 1983).
[14] *New York Sun*, 2 May 1909.

In addition, the examples Goldman cites in her lectures on women were often historically inaccurate or distorted. In her lecture on "Woman Suffrage," for instance, she claims that in "Russia, with her absolute despotism, woman has become man's equal, not through the ballot, but by her will to be and to do. Not only has she conquered for herself every avenue of learning and vocation, but she has won man's esteem, his respect, his comradeship..." along with the admiration of the entire world.[15] It may have been true that among the Narodniks of the 1860's and 1870's, women achieved an impressive equality with men, although even then some felt compelled to form their own separate circles (the "Fritschi" in Zurich, for example) to achieve their goals. It was not true, in 1910, that women in Russia were in any sense equal to men, in education, employment, in law or political rights. (Indeed, Emma herself admitted this years later when she wrote "...it was really the Russian Revolution which raised the status of all women in Russia."[16])

Nor was it true that suffrage for women in certain countries (Australia, New Zealand) and states (Wyoming, Utah, Idaho, Colorado) accomplished nothing. (These were among the earliest to grant women the vote.) Emma's insistence that women in power had failed to 'purify' politics was beside the point, proving only that women were more bound to class and ethnic loyalties than to their identity as women, and they were not so puritannical as she claimed. Her attack on the vote as woman's latest 'fetish' also missed the point, since quite a few suffragists saw the vote not as an end but a means to more substantial change. Equal suffrage had a powerful symbolic meaning, at the very least, in recognizing women as legitimate members of society. As Emma herself later admitted, even if the vote had no intrinsic value, in a society where men voted the denial of the vote to women impeded their development as human beings.[17]

Goldman never claimed to be more than a propagandist; certainly she never regarded herself as a theorist, so it is perhaps not fair to scrutinize her thought too closely. Yet at the heart of all her writings about women is an assumption — erroneous in my view — that

[15] Emma Goldman, "Woman Suffrage," pp. 209-210.
[16] Emma Goldman to Ethel Mannin, 16 July 1937, Goldman Archive, IISH.
[17] See *New York Sun*, 2 May 1909.

incorrect ideas were the fundamental source of women's inequality. Her insistence that woman was enslaved "not so much by man as by her own silly notions and traditions"; her dismissal of the "ridiculous notion that to be loved, to be sweetheart and mother, is synonymous with being slave or subordinate"; her allusion to "the absurd notion of the dualism of the sexes" suggests that, if only women can change these 'notions' we can achieve emancipation. Such conceptions and notions are not simply bad habits that we can change at will, but entrenched cultural arrangements in which some elements in society have a vested interest. The question is how such 'notions' can be changed. Lectures and pamphlets do not make a revolution.

In theory, Emma believed in changing ideas through the direct action of 'intelligent minorities': "direct action against the authority in the shop, direct action against the authority of the law, direct action against the invasive, meddlesome authority of our moral code." She urged "the conscious, intelligent, organized, economic protest of the masses through direct action and the general strike." She looked forward to an anarchist society "based on voluntary cooperation of productive groups, communities and societies, loosely federated together, eventually developing into free communism..." [18] But although she was a communist anarchist in theory, in practice she behaved like an extreme individualist, eschewing any identification with groups, even her own *Mother Earth* group. Her direct action most often took the form of speaking and engaging in free speech fights, at least until 1915, when she engaged in her first act of civil disobedience since 1892 by giving out illegal birth control information (and that was after the arrests of Margaret and William Sanger). Moreover, Emma put a high premium on publicity, which at times seemed almost the goal of her politics. For example, having given out contraceptive information, having gone to jail for two weeks, having lectured around the country for two years on the subject, she felt satisfied that the publicity she had gained for birth control had advanced the cause by ten years. She had achieved her goal and was ready to go on to something new.

The disparities between Emma's theory and practice emerged most sharply in her sexual life. Her letters express passions contradicting

---

[18] Emma Goldman, "What I Believe," in *Red Emma Speaks: Selected Writings and Speeches by Emma Goldman* (New York: Vintage, 1972), p. 36, 46.

the most cherished of her theories. Insisting on freedom and equality in love, Emma discovered when she fell in love with her hobo-physician Ben Reitman that she was far more inclined both to domination and dependence. This advocate of free love longed to possess her lover, and gloried in the dependence which she publicly denounced. She compared herself to Mary Wollstonecraft, reassured by the thought of their shared erotic bondage, as if this were an emblem of their heroic sisterhood. "Mary Wollstonecraft, the most daring woman of her time, the slave of her passion for [Gilbert] Imlay. How could anyone forgive such weakness?" But now "EG, the Wollstonecraft of the 20th century, even like her great sister, is weak and dependent, clinging to the man no matter how worthless and faithless he is. What an irony of fate." [19] With Reitman, Emma lived a see-saw relationship, in which power shifted back and forth, with Ben controlling Emma with his absences and his unfaithfulness, Emma manipulating Ben with her pose as the martyred mother. Instead of harmony, she found constant conflict, moments of rapture, long periods of despair.

In subsequent relationships as well — an on-and-off affair from 1926 to 1928 with Leon Malmed, an anarchist delicatessen owner from Albany, New York, a married man and long-time Goldman admirer; a two-week idyll, in the summer of 1934, with the much younger Frank Heiner, a sociologist from Chicago, blind, also married — Emma found herself involved with men who were essentially unavailable to her. Love plunged her into "a desperate state of mind," she told Heiner. "Some days I am furious with myself for ever having permitted you to get hold of my imagination, my every thought, my every nerve. Other days I bless the force that has brought you to me and has rekindled my youth long dead and buried. I am in constant conflict with myself, with you, with our love." [20] Far away from Heiner with no possibility of seeing him, Emma concluded that she preferred the certainty of solitude to the anguish of longing. She wrote him, after deciding to end their amorous correspondence, that "I have not felt so much at peace in a long while. Just to be on the firing line again, to plead for our ideal, to make people see its justice and beauty,

---

[19] Emma Goldman to Ben Reitman, 26 July 1911, Ben Reitman Papers, Supplement II, University of Illinois, Chicago Circle.
[20] Emma Goldman to Frank Heiner, 7 July 1935, Goldman Archive, IISH.

has put new energy into me."[21] Love caused extreme pain, and in the final analysis, she preferred to do without it. "I am so constituted that I can't bear being at the beck and call of what is commonly called love."[22] (Curiously, Emma once told a friend that she knew what it meant "to have to be on guard all the time against the invasive tendency of one another, usually more invasive and possessive the more one is loved. I could never submit to such claims and infringement, that is why I am now so terribly alone, inwardly so anyhow."[23]) In reality, Emma suffered in her love affairs far more from distance and absence than from invasions on her privacy; if anything, she was the more possessive partner in her relationships.

In any event, it is clear that Emma's experience was far more complex than the simple advice she dispensed from the lecture platform. Indeed, she even admitted as much to Stella Ballantine, when she wrote that "sex is like a double edged sword, it releases our spirit and it binds it with a thousand threads, it raises us to sublime heights and thrusts us into the lowest depths. What people will do to each other in their intimate relations they never could or would do to their friends."[24] Yet she never attempted to reconcile her life with her ideas. Acknowledging the disparity, she resolved to keep them separate; she would do without 'reality' if it muddied her ideal. Celebrating love as liberating and inspiring, "the harbinger of hope, of joy, of ecstasy," she kept her darker knowledge to herself.

This I think is the deepest limitation of Goldman's sexual politics: that despite the anguished richness of her own erotic life, she was unable to reflect on it in any fruitful way. Though she certainly did not deny her contradictory feelings, for Reitman particularly, she could not allow herself to think about them, to analyze them, or integrate her conclusions into her lectures. She brooded endlessly over her obsession with the man, but never achieved any real insight. The superficiality of her lectures reflects not so much a failure of candour as of thought: she simply could not allow herself to think deeply about her own

---

[21] Emma Goldman to Frank Heiner, 2 March 1936, Goldman Archive, IISH.
[22] Emma Goldman to Ethel Mannin, 15 May 1933, Goldman Papers, New York Public Library.
[23] Emma Goldman to Ethel Mannin, 15 August 1937, Goldman Papers, New York Public Library.
[24] Emma Goldman to Stella Ballantine, 18 July 1931, Goldman Archive, IISH.

erotic life. If she had, she would have been forced to admit that the equation of love with slavery and submission was not such a 'ridiculous notion' after all, that woman's "fear that love will rob her of her freedom and independence" had a basis in reality. It corresponded to her own experience in love. Emma's scorn for the realities of erotic domination, in fact and in fantasy, expressed her inability to come to terms with this most dramatic dilemma in her life. Instead of using her life to illuminate her theory, she used her theories to deny and defend herself against the realities of her life.

I do not agree with Candace Falk that had Emma scaled down her expectations, had she been less idealistic, admitted human weakness and frailties, she would have achieved greater personal happiness. Emma's expectations of harmony in love do not seem to me so unrealistic. Certainly she did not believe that sorrow and unhappiness come only from the outside, as Falk suggests.[25] Rather, "they are conditioned in our very being," and no one "at all capable of an intense conscious inner life need ever hope to escape mental anguish and suffering."[26] Emma's problem seems to me to lie in an altogether different direction: at least partly in a conviction of herself as unloved and unlovable which led her to seek love where she could not find it, from men who could not give it to her. As she herself wrote, "The tragedy of it all is that my soul is frozen and I cannot enjoy the kindness and thoughtfulness of the people who would lie [sic] down their lives for me. Instead I crave the impossible, the one thing that will *never never* be."[27] But instead of analyzing this 'tragedy,' she chalked it up to fate. "Oh Ben, my lover, I love you too much, ever to be really happy. I will always want more than you will be able to give, therefore I shall always be bitterly disappointed, it is inevitable and I must bow to the Inevitable."[28] Perhaps this sense of private failure was part of her motivation to achieve public recognition: audiences could offer what lovers did not.

Emma also suffered a failure of imagination, for, ironically, she seemed unable to conceive of personal happiness apart from romantic

---

[25] Falk, *Emma Goldman, op. cit.*, pp. 522-3.
[26] Emma Goldman, "Jealousy: Causes and a Possible Cure," in *Red Emma Speaks, op. cit.*, p. 168.
[27] Emma Goldman to Reitman, 23 June 1910, Supplement II, Reitman Papers.
[28] Emma Goldman to Reitman, 30 December 1909, Supplement II, Reitman Papers.

love for a man. Even though she herself lived in a bohemian (if hard-working) manner, she clung in her mind to a surprisingly conventional image of happiness. She could not really imagine that single childless women, or homosexual couples, could actually live fulfilling lives. She seemed determined to see the 'modern' woman as 'tragic'; single professional women as unfulfilled; childless women as empty and un-satisfied. Admittedly, the pressures of convention weighed heavily on such dissidents; many single women did suffer from loneliness and longing for children. Yet had Emma reflected more deeply on her own experience, or observed more carefully that of other single women — some of whom, we know, had deeply gratifying lives — she might have found cause for greater optimism. [29] Given to bemoaning her 'failures' — at least in a personal sense — she overlooked the alternative view that her own history demonstrated the fruitful possibilities of living outside the conventions of monogamy and motherhood. She herself showed that a celibate life, which she mostly lived in her fifties and sixties, could also be a good life, and that friendships with women and with men might yield enduring rewards.

The one personal success Emma did recognize was her friendship with Alexander Berkman, which grew closer, more trusting, and more affectionate in the years before Berkman's death in 1936. Despite the tensions and quarrels between them — especially with respect to Berkman's young companion, Emmy Eckstein, toward whom Emma was inordinately jealous and sometimes cruel — their relationship served as Emma's one anchor in a turbulent world.

As poignant testimony to the depth of their feeling for each other, Emma carried with her until her death a letter scrawled in pencil by Berkman in 1917, from the Tombs prison in New York, as he awaited extradition to California on charges of conspiring in a San Francisco bombing — false charges he felt certain would lead to conviction. (Her strenuous campaign blocked his extradition and he was released.) That letter, preserved in a packet of identity papers, passports, wills and visas that Emma had with her when she died, contained Berkman's

---

[29] See, for example, Blanche Wiesen Cook, "Female Support Networks and Political Activism: Lillian Wald, Crystal Eastman, Emma Goldman," in *A Heritage of Her Own*, ed. and with an introduction by Nancy F. Cott and Elizabeth H. Pleck (New York: Simon and Shuster, 1979) pp. 412-444.

most moving statement of his feeling for Emma and for their lives together.

"Dearest Sailor girl," he began, "Our friendship and comradeship of a lifetime has been to me the most beautiful and inspiring factor in my whole life. And after all, it is given to but few mortals to live as you and I have lived. Notwithstanding all our hardships and sorrows, all persecution and imprisonment — perhaps because of it all — we have lived the lives of our choice. What more can one expect of Life... I don't know when I shall be able to write to you in this mood again. So let me bid you farewell now, my dear, beloved friend and comrade. You have been my mate and my comrade in arms — my life's mate in the biggest sense, and your wonderful spirit and devotion have always been an inspiration to me, as I'm sure your life will prove an inspiration to others long after both you and I have gone to everlasting rest. Let me take you once more by your hands, my dear Sailor Girl. I know that whatever happens you will remain the Immutable in the strength of your spirit, in your passionate love of liberty and human welfare... I take you in my arms, my beloved Sonya."[30] Almost twenty years later, Emma and Sasha expressed similar sentiments to each other, in almost the same language.

Perhaps her lasting friendship with Berkman gave her a greater sense of security, or perhaps the loneliness of her later years deepened her dependence on her women friends. Whatever the reasons, Emma did grow more sympathetic toward other women. From a harsh, judgemental, somewhat haughty young woman ready to dismiss contemporaries who appeared less independent than she was, she grew more tolerant, more understanding, less arrogant. She accepted more readily her own responsibility for the tensions in her relations with others. From one who identified principally with men, she came gradually to accept her identity with women, to see herself as part of a community of women, "still rooted in the old soil, though our desire is to be free and independent..."[31]

---

[30] Alexander Berkman to Emma Goldman, 1 October 1917, zerox copy in possession of author.
[31] Emma Goldman to Alexander Berkman, 4 September 1925, in *Nowhere at Home: Letters From Exile of Emma Goldman and Alexander Berkman*, ed. Richard Drinnon and Anna Maria Drinnon (New York: Schocken, 1975), p. 133.

Emma never found a solution to this problem, but it is just that struggle which engages us today. Her divided soul, "woven of many skeins, conflicting in shade and texture," still pleads for wholeness. Even now as I write about her years in exile, I hear her insistent arguments and complaints, her questions to which we still have no answers: "the modern woman cannot be the wife and mother in the old sense, and the new medium has not yet been devised, I mean the way of being wife, mother, friend and yet retain one's complete freedom. Will it ever?"[32]

---

[32] Emma Goldman to Alexander Berkman, 4 September 1925, *Ibid.*, p. 133.

# EMMA GOLDMAN: THE CASE FOR ANARCHO-FEMINISM
*Marsha Hewitt*

Feminists are still divided on the question of separatism, which, simply put, is the dilemma of whether to forge links with other emancipatory movements for social change.

Many feminists insist that the struggle for the liberation of women will be compromised if women participate in organizations and movements in which men are involved. As one libertarian feminist of my acquaintance recently put it: "Feminists have little to gain directly from the anarchists... in fact... anarchism has much to learn from the feminist movement... it is crucial that women work together alone and that men form their own all-men's groups."

This is a point of view with which I have some sympathy. My own experience in working with men on various political projects has been that no matter how understanding of feminist issues and arguments they may be, most men do harbour some degree of sexism. Not even women can entirely escape a sexist culture. Women, like men, are socialized by the same historical and cultural process, although women experience a specific form and sometimes a greater degree of social injustice. It would be both foolish and erroneous to say that women have not themselves internalized various exist attitudes toward both other women and men. There is a strain in feminist thinking, for example, that tends to identify the male with nature and thus sees the world in terms of the false dichotomies of 'phallocentricity' as opposed to 'gynocentricity.'

---

*Marsha Hewitt is a writer and teaches Humanities and Religious Studies at Vanier College in Montréal. She is co-author of* Their Town *and* One Proud Summer. *An active trade unionist and feminist, she is co-ordinator of the administrative committee of Anarchos Institute.*

We must recognize that women are and always have been active participants in history, whether or not this fact has been acknowledged; women have been *at the centre* of the historical process and culture. Our consciousness has been shaped in ways similar to that of males, so that we too live and experience alienation; we too think in terms of antagonistic duality. This does not mean to say, however, that women or men are devoid of the capacity for critical self-consciousness or the ability to recognize alienation and oppression, and that they cannot attempt to overcome this existential situation.

It is not a pleasant experience to run up against sexism in the attitudes and behaviour of one's comrades. The frustration and disappointment that result can well lead women to the conclusion that their only option is to get out of groups which include men and form their own separatist organizations. But although it is tempting as a short-term solution to anger and frustration, the separatist option is a mistake, on the level of both theory and praxis. A sectarian politics based on gender, or on *anything else*, can too easily become a politics of paranoia, and as such stands in danger of being marginalized and irrelevant. Instead, I must agree with the point of view expressed in the Anarcho-Feminist Manifesto of *ANORG* (the Anarchist Federation of Norway) which reads, in part: "A serious anarchism must also be feminist, otherwise it is a question of patriarchal half-anarchism, and not real anarchism. It is the task of the anarcho-feminists to secure the feminist feature in anarchism. There will be no anarchism without feminism."

I would add to this statement by asserting that there will be no real, effective feminism without anarchism. Emma Goldman would agree. It was her conviction that feminism could not develop an adequate theory and praxis of liberation in isolation from the larger struggle for human liberation. Alice Wexler, in her biography, *Emma Goldman: An Intimate Life*, quotes Goldman: "My quarrel with the feminists... was that most of them see their slavery apart from the rest of the human family."[1] Goldman believed that "regardless of all artificial boundary lines between woman's rights and man's rights... there is a point where these differentiations may meet and grow into

---

[1] Alice Wexler, *Emma Goldman: An Intimate Life* (New York: Pantheon Books, 1984), p. 197.

one perfect whole."[2] The danger of feminism as a single-issue politics oriented strictly to the emancipation of women, is, of course, social and political reformism; as Goldman herself saw in her critique of the women's suffrage movement, women achieving the vote does nothing to challenge the prevailing political system — it merely strengthens it. Liberation presupposes the radical transformation of the entire political, economic and social order. And while this ultimate goal may be impossible, we must think and act according to this *necessarily* utopian ideal. It is a question of living creatively, of creative fictions, necessary fictions that are not divorced from the realm of rational possibility.

According to Alice Wexler, Goldman "gave a feminist dimension to anarchism and a libertarian dimension to the concept of women's emancipation."[3] She did so by insisting that anarchists acknowledge the political nature of sex, by recognizing that women's complete sexual and reproductive freedom is absolutely central to women's emancipation. This is an insight which cannot be over-emphasized in any discussion of feminism *or* anarchism, because an analysis of the politics of sexuality will further reveal the interconnected complexity of human experience, in terms of thought, feeling and action: we are now required to think feelingly. This forces us to re-think the nature of revolution as *process*, as transformative praxis of thought, feeling and collective social activity.

In making the link between sexual liberation and human liberation, Goldman saw power through hierarchy and domination as extending beyond economic structures and social institutions. It is the task of contemporary anarcho-feminists to develop this analysis. An awareness of domination as an internal, mental construct that reflects the structures of consciousness is crucial to contemporary anarchist thought. According to Murray Bookchin, "Hierarchy is not merely a social condition; it is also a state of consciousness, a sensibility toward phenomena at every level of personal and social experience."[4] Anarchism is and must be much more than a critical analysis of social structures and organizations of domination; its challenge goes far beyond opposition to the State.

---

[2] Emma Goldman, *Anarchism and Other Essays* (New York: Dover Publications, 1969), p. 213.
[3] Wexler, *op. cit.*, p. 277.
[4] Murray Bookchin, *The Ecology of Freedom* (Palo Alto, Calif.: Cheshire Books, 1982), p. 4.

Anarchist theory recognizes the power of ideas to change material conditions, and the "primacy of consciousness in shaping the conditions of life."[5] As such, thought and language — the means by which we interpret and communicate our experience of the world — is praxis as much as it is social activity. Goldman rejected the determinant nature of the role of economics in social structures and personal relations. According to Wexler, she went even farther than her anarchist contemporaries in her insistence that "The key to the anarchist revolution was a revolution in morality, the 'transvaluation of all values,' a conquest of the 'phantoms' that have held people captive."[6] This, of course, explains Goldman's interest in culture, art and literature, as well as her regard for the power and influence of the individual, however problematic at times her views on this latter point may have been.

What Goldman understood as well was the necessity of transforming the very manner in which we think, although she confined herself mostly to discussions of social mores and attitudes. But her insistence on the centrality of sexuality, and its potentially creative energy as a positive force in the process of individual and social transformation, helped break new ground for later developments in anarchism and feminism which have in turn helped foster a deeper understanding of the relationship between theory and praxis. This is an area which is in need of further exploration: that theory (by which I mean critical thinking) *is* praxis, and praxis *is* theory. Thus the revolutionary process must by necessity take place within the mind as well as in society, or no liberatory, transformative change is possible. It cannot be over-emphasized that I am not referring simply to 'correct' ideas or 'right' ideology, because a fixed ideology is a closed system, and is thus inherently authoritarian. Critical thinking must always be open and changing within the historical process. At this point I want to make it perfectly clear that feminism is as much a critical theory, a theory of knowledge — a rationality critique, but *not* an alternative rationality, as some feminists would argue — as it is a practical, social movement.

If we restrict our theory/praxis dialectic to the social and economic sphere, we fall into the trap of reification, where 'the revolution' is

[5] Wexler, *op. cit.*
[6] *Ibid.*, p. 98.

understood to take place at a specific point in history, after which heaven is established on earth in the form of concrete/concretized bureaucracies and institutions of the post-revolutionary order. This results in an 'October Revolution' that produces reified socialism; a process is replaced with dead institutional forms and new hierarchies of domination. Critical self-consciousness disappears, it becomes anathema, and thus with it comes the obliteration of the historical subject — human beings. The locus of change, of praxis, of the dialectic itself* which is human beings as historical agents, dissolves into new (old) mechanisms of control and authoritarianism, inevitably.

This is Emma Goldman's most important contribution to anarcho-feminism, which contemporary anarcho-feminists must further develop, and that is the importance of the transformative power of ideas, and the necessity to live the revolution in our daily lives, including our most intimate personal relationships. What I wish to explore a little further here is the concept of thought as revolutionary praxis. Here it is appropriate to quote Gajo Petrović, a Yugoslav Marxist who was a member of the journal *Praxis*: "An interpretation of the world that does not change the world is both logically and empirically impossible. When man [sic] interprets the world, by this very fact he changes at least his conception of the world. In changing his conception of the world he cannot help changing his relationship to the world as well. And in changing his conception and his behaviour, he influences the conception and actions of other people with whom he is in different relationships... Is he... outside the world when he thinks and interprets the world?"[7]

Thought is not just passive reflection on completed action; what Petrović says about thought as praxis and the relationship between consciousness and action is important to both feminism and anarchism, because in challenging the rigid dislocations of private and public, subject and object, thought and action, male and female, humanity and nature, this critique attempts to address the nature of epistemological

---

* What I mean here by 'dialectic' is the dialectic of negativity; that is, negation and transcendence in which we engage as beings of praxis. The structure of praxis is that of human negativity and creativity, or alienation and its transcendence. This is the essential nature of a critical and revolutionary dialectic, the locus of which is the human being.

[7] Gerson S. Sher, *Praxis: Marxist Criticism and Dissent in Socialist Yugoslavia* (Bloomington, Ind.: Indiana University Press, 1977), p. 104.

alienation. How we live and experience our most intimate relationships with others, how we live out our daily lives and how we *think* our lives and about our lives is in itself part of the ongoing revolutionary process.

To return to the theme of sexual liberation and its role in the revolutionary process, Goldman very clearly saw the destructive and oppressive impact of the institutionalization of female sexuality in the structure of marriage, and its implications for the social restriction of women: "As always, [Goldman] especially stressed the repressiveness of marriage, both as an 'economic arrangement, an insurance pact,' and as 'a safety valve against the pernicious sex-awakening of woman.' Was anything more outrageous, she would ask, 'than the idea that the healthy, grown woman, full of life and passion, must deny nature's demand, must subdue her most intense craving, undermine her health and break her spirit, must stunt her vision, abstain from the depth and glory of sex experience until a 'good' man comes along to take her unto himself as a wife? This is precisely what marriage means.'"[8]

Here I want to say a brief word on the question of marriage and monogamy. I do not wish to argue that marriage and monogamy are synonymous, although they are often so identified. The left must re-think the values which it used to denounce as 'traditional' — values of family, monogamy, and committed relationships. The sexual rev-olution did its share to reduce sexuality to technical experimentation for its own sake, and so contributed to the concept of sexuality not as a shared, meaningful experience between people, but as a commodity exchange. And women suffered a great deal of exploitation during the 'sexual revolution' of the 1960's and early '70's, partly because they, too, bought into this particular ideology. The left must begin to see that 'traditional' values such as monogamy can be oppressive or be emancipatory. It is vital that a new analysis be constructed of sexual ethics and values, because today the 'New Right' has stepped into the breach and is dominating the discourse on 'traditional' values with a popular positive response. Certainly, Emma Goldman understood very well the contradictions of interpersonal relationships, the contradiction and tension between the principle of 'varietism' and the agonizing experience of sexual jealousy and the deep desire to form exclusive

[8] Wexler, *op. cit.*, p. 193.

sexual relationships, as her correspondence with Ben Reitman clearly shows. However, we cannot afford to dismiss these contradictions. We must begin to analyze them with dignity and humanity.

In the traditional marriage arrangement, with all its legal and social sanctions and its sexual division of labour, women are deprived of autonomy and the opportunity for growth. But the most insidious form of oppression of women was the internalization of those restrictions imposed by society and marriage which undermined women's capacity to think about real alternatives to their condition. Goldman saw, and rightly so, that women's liberation was not to be realized in external, material improvements, although these are obviously important; the key to the liberation of women must begin with their 'inner regeneration,' with their willingness to "cut loose from the weight of prejudices, traditions and customs. True emancipation, [Goldman] argued, began not at the polls or in court, but in woman's soul."[9]

Goldman's feminist insights deepened and enriched anarchist thought because she tried to show interdependence of collective social transformation and the inner psychological, mental and spiritual liberation of individuals. It is this legacy that anarcho-feminists must develop further and build upon.

The feminist vision *is* a libertarian vision, as Peggy Kornegger has written: "Feminists have been unconscious anarchists in both theory and practice for years."[10] The most important link between feminism and anarchism is a common recognition of the need to transform the power structures and social relations of hierarchy and domination. Anarchism helps feminism to address the problem of power, to understand its destructive dynamics, and to pose alternative forms of organization. The feminist practice of 'networking,' for example, has much in common with anarchist forms of organization, particularly affinity groups and federated organizations. Perhaps eco-feminist thinking has begun to develop anarcho-feminism in ways that attempt to show the integral connections between ecology and feminism. The eco-feminist perspective views life "on earth as an interconnected web, not a hierarchy. There *is* no natural hierarchy; human hierarchy is projected onto nature and

[9] *Ibid.*, p. 195.
[10] Carol Ehrlich, "The Unhappy Marriage of Marxism and Feminism: Can It Be Saved?" in *Women and Revolution*, ed. Lydia Sargent (Montréal: Black Rose Books, 1981), p. 114.

then used to justify social domination."[11] The abuse of power through hierarchy and domination is a human construct which we are socialized to accept and reproduce in all aspects of social life, from personal relations to social institutions. Anarcho-feminism understands very well the interconnectedness of oppressive social institutions and personal relations, as is reflected in the paradigm of traditional marriage. Goldman saw the relationship between *enforced* monogamy and the "domestication and ownership" of women, which created a male monopoly of women's sexuality.

It seems to me that insights such as those which I have mentioned reveal the natural (in terms of inherent logical necessity) affinity between anarchism and feminism, on the level of both theory and practice. Feminists cannot operate in isolation either from men or from other emancipatory social movements; we simply cannot afford to do so. "A feminist movement which is confined to the specific oppression of women cannot, in isolation, end exploitation. We have to keep struggling to go beyond our own situation."[12] It is also the special task of anarcho-feminism to draw out and reflect upon the interrelatedness of all forms of oppression, whose common root is domination. There is no liberation for anyone without the liberation of all. An anarcho-feminist analysis is able to show the interconnected roots of misogyny, imperialism, militarism, the arms race, and the attempt to obliterate nature, and therefore insists that the revolutionary project/process is a comprehensive, multidimensional project/process that is taking place now, in all areas of human experience. Domination is the source, focus and rationale of all hierarchy, be it rank, class, family, the State, or sex/gender.

Thus whatever our negative experiences may be in working with men in a common movement for a better society, it is important not only that we remain in that movement, but that we confront sexist behaviour and attitudes in our comrades at each point of encounter. As women, we are specially placed to do it, since our life experience

[11] Ynestra King, "The Ecology of Feminism and the Feminism of Ecology," *Harbinger*, Vol. 1, No. 2, Fall 1983, p. 17.
[12] Sheila Rowbotham, *Woman's Consciousness, Man's World* (Harmondsworth: Penguin, 1973), p. 123-24.

as women has taught us an intimate lesson about the dynamics of power. In confronting our male comrades with this knowledge, we can only strengthen the movement, and with it, hopefully, but more problematically, our personal relationships.

# SHOWDOWN IN SEATTLE
*A Renewal?*

# DEMOCRACY IN SEATTLE'S STREETS
*Chris Ney*

It was in Chile as an international observer of the 1988 plebiscite that voted Augusto Pinochet out of office, that I first saw the dramatic transformative power of nonviolence. I saw it the second time in Seattle during the protests of the meeting of the World Trade Organization.

The Seattle protests relied, not on State power, but on the strength of well-organized people's power. On November 30 and the following days, decentralized nonviolent direct action won the day, transforming a city (and changing the perceptions of the world) by defeating one of the most powerful bureaucratic financial institutions ever created.

### Simple Intent, Complex Design

The direct action plan was as simple in its intent as it was complex in its logistics and design. The plan was to surround the WTO meeting sites with a human blockade, preventing delegates from entering and forcing the cancellation of the meeting. Protesters gathered at 7:00 a.m. on both sides of the convention center where the WTO meetings were to take place. In a cold and driving rain, my group marched from Pike Place Market on Seattle's waterfront toward the city center. We passed streets blocked with dumpsters, garbage cans, and yellow plastic strips that looked like police crime scene tape but read, "Unseen Crimes." Affinity groups peeled off to construct high- and low-tech barricades at downtown intersections. (High-tech barricades included tripods — tall, three-pole structures with someone sitting at the top, which can't be dismantled without harming the person — and lock boxes, pipes made of plastic or steel in which protesters lock their hands, making it difficult for police to separate people standing in a line.) My group marched to the Paramount Theater, where U.S. Trade Representative Charlene Barshefsky was to hold the WTO's opening press conference at 9:30 a.m.

*Chris Ney is War Resisters League's Disarmament Coordinator. He conducted nonviolence training for protestors in Seattle.*

We found a line of buses blocking the street, with a small opening guarded by Seattle police in modest riot gear. Strictly low-tech, using nothing but our bodies, we locked arms at the only opening in the bus line, in front of the police, and prepared to hold that ground all day. From high on a hill with a wonderful view we watched the city as the rain slowed. The King County Sheriffs guarding the nearby bus depot were friendly and talkative, in contrast to Seattle police. They joked that they had the easiest job, and we commiserated about our common inability to leave our posts for bathroom breaks.

When a stymied delegate looked as if he might try to break the barricade violently, the sheriffs quickly moved in to protect the protesters.

At 8:00 a.m. our tactical coordinator heard via walkie-talkie that the blockade was in place, securely surrounding the meeting site and preventing delegates from entering. At 9:30 a.m., Barshefsky canceled the press conference because no one could enter the Paramount Theater. The opening plenary was also canceled. We, the people, had stopped the WTO!

### Gas, Spray and Bullets

No one could believe the police weren't arresting the blockaders. But around 10:30 a.m. we smelled and felt the presence of tear gas or pepper spray. Cloth soaked in a solution of water and baking soda helped block the mild but noticeable effects on my nose and lungs. A little later, we heard that police had used rubber bullets in addition to tear gas and pepper spray (and also that the police were jamming the tactical teams' walkie-talkies with repeated sexual obscenities). As the day wore on, we smelled and felt the chemical presence more intensely. We walked to the other side of the convention center, where students from two different campuses were in lock boxes. They told us that the cops had been good to them all day, "except in the morning when they pepper-sprayed and tear-gassed us!" Although the chemicals inflicted real pain, the barricades held. Back at our site near the Paramount Theater, sometime around 2:00 p.m., we saw "hard shell" riot police in SWAT uniforms and body armor approaching. Later in the day, we would see more hard shells and mounted police break through human barricades to escort delegates inside — but the first hard shell group had a different mission. I tried to get close to find out what they were doing. They were very edgy, intently focused on their task, which (as we learned a little later)was to monitor the movements of a group of anarchist youth. The group arrived about ten minutes after the police. They approached our line, then turned and left; the hard shells disappeared with them. Later, I wondered how it was possible that at two in the afternoon, police could track this group so effectively that they arrived ten minutes before the anarchists, yet only a few hours later could not deter them from breaking windows and setting fires. Did the police actually want violence to occur?

### Honeycomb of Activism

The Direct Action Network, which planned the blockade and other protests, is a loose-knit coalition of West Coast-based nonviolent direct action groups. It organized the actions out of an old warehouse turned-dance-club in the residential neighborhood of Capital Hill, now known as the Convergence Center. During the two weeks that preceded the WTO protests the building was a honeycomb of protest activity.

When I arrived November 27, I saw as many as 100 people at a time learning about nonviolence through discussion and role play in one room. In another, activists used the same techniques to plan legal strategy. In the alley outside, others learned about blockades and constructing tripods. In the far corner of the largest room, artists and activists worked day and night to make props, signs, banners and puppets. A medical clinic took care of the sick and distributed free condoms, information about sexually transmitted diseases and tips for dealing with tear gas and pepper spray. Volunteers prepared nutritious vegan meals, feeding up to 1,000 people a day. A large sign in the dining area read, "We got bugs in the wall, bugs on our phones, bugs at our actions, we don't need bugs in our food. Please wash your hands." At the front orientation table people answered questions, gave out direct action information packets, asked for donations, kept a sign-in sheet, recruited volunteers and sold T-shirts. Organizers maintained security and kept one room locked for luggage.

War Resisters League representative to War Resisters' International Vivien Sharples and I participated in a training on high- and low-tech blockades — from human knots to steel-pipe lock boxes — and in a legal training to prepare for arrest and jail. Organizers prepared clear "jail solidarity" guidelines: Carry no identification and do not give your name; refuse to allow the group to be separated; demand equal treatment for all; demand that all arrestees be issued citations (not felony or misdemeanor charges). Protesters were advised to plead not guilty to all charges and demand court-appointed attorneys and jury trials if those conditions were not met.

All that activity happened without an office, without staff, without funding, without an executive director. The Direct Action Network (DAN) paid $4,000 to rent the Convergence Center, but the benefit of sharing and developing skills with all those young activists was priceless. It was anarchism at its best, a decentralized effort that happened below the radar screens of both the more mainstream protesters and the police — even though DAN's media savvy had brought far more press attention than usual to the preparations. The day before the action, the *Seattle Times'* list of upcoming events included the "Nonviolent Blockade to Shut Down the WTO" — and the information that a prior training was encouraged and could be gotten at the headquarters of the Direct Action Network. One of Seattle's two mainstream newspapers was telling its readers to get nonviolence training if they wanted to participate in civil disobedience!

The Convergence Center and DAN represented a remarkable coming together of movements and efforts, some of which, like the Ruckus Society (which held a special training camp to prepare for WTO), Rainforest Action Network, Global Exchange, Center for Campus Organizing and War Resister League, had been working on these issues for years. DAN also gained from recent campus-based activism including animal rights, environment and anti-sweatshop campaigns.

### Speaking Truth

Much of the post-action press coverage focused on the Protesters' alleged lack of information about the WTO. Apparently, the reporters who wrote the stories hadn't heard exchanges like the one I witnessed between a demonstrator and a delegate from the European Union who claimed that he wanted to break the barricade and enter the Convention Center "to convince your government [the United States] to accept protections for European farmers."

The protester asked how the WTO could be beneficial when it overturned labor and environmental standards. While the delegate tried to explain that he thought the WTO could be reformed, the protestor asked about one of the WTO's controversial rulings, which overturned local laws requiring shrimp trawlers to have equipment protecting dolphins from the trawling nets.

"Perhaps [the protections are] a burden to industry," replied the delegate.

"Do you know how much such devices cost?" asked the protester.

The delegate admitted he didn't.

The protester did: "Fifty dollars," he said.

The conversation went on for thirty minutes, during which the protester offered well-reasoned and well-informed arguments supported by statistics and analysis. And that was only one of hundreds that took place that day, as delegates, blocked from entering the convention hall, were met by protesters with questions and comments. The nonviolent blockade afforded protesters the kind of access that corporations and lobbyists pay thousands of dollars for; it was the best kind of lobbying, not in the marble halls of power, but in the streets — streets that were like a carnival.

Or a liberation zone. There were dancers, puppets, clowns, street theater, radical cheerleaders, people dressed like turtles and cows and butterflies, people on stilts and lots of music. There was a young man in a Boy Scout uniform who claimed some of his merit badges were for civil disobedience and blockade-making.

It may have been the closest I will ever come to a general strike, and I saw it in the only U.S. city that has actually ever had a one-day general strike. At the end of the day, as we walked, tired but satisfied, through downtown Seattle streets still filled with the stench of pepper spray and tear gas, we chanted again the words that captured the spirit of the day: "This is what democracy looks like!"

# THERE'S A MOVEMENT OUT THERE: INTERVIEW WITH CHOMSKY

## David Barsamian

*David Barsamian: Let's talk about what occurred in Seattle in late November/early December around the World Trade Organization ministerial meeting. What meaning do you derive from what happened there, and what are the lessons to be drawn?*

*Noam Chomsky*: I think it was a very significant event. It reflected a very broad opposition to the corporate-led globalization that's been imposed under primarily U.S. leadership, but by the other major industrial countries, too. The participation was extremely broad and varied, including constituencies from the United States and internationally that have rarely interconnected in the past. That's the same kind of coalition of forces that blocked the Multilateral Agreement on Investment a year earlier and that strongly opposed other so-called agreements like NAFTA and the WTO.

One lesson from Seattle is that education and organizing over a long term, carefully done, can really pay off. Another is that a substantial part of the domestic and global population, I would guess probably a majority of those thinking about the issues, ranges from being disturbed by contemporary developments to being strongly opposed to them, primarily to the sharp attack on democratic rights, on the freedom to make your own decisions and on the general subordination of all concerns to the specific interests, to the primacy of maximizing profit and domination by a very small sector of the world's population.

*Thomas Friedman, writing in The New York Times, called the demonstrators at Seattle "a Noah's ark of flat-earth advocates."*

From his point of view that's probably correct. From the point of view of slave owners, people opposed to slavery probably looked that way. For the one percent of the population that he's thinking about and

---

*David Barsamian is director of* Alternative Radio *in Boulder, Colorado. What is printed here is an edited version of that interview.*

representing, the people who are opposing this are flat-earthers. Why should anyone oppose the developments that we've been describing?

*Would it be fair to say that in the actions in the streets in Seattle, mixed in with the tear gas was also a whiff of democracy?*

I would take it to be. A functioning democracy is not supposed to happen in the streets. It's supposed to happen in decision-making. This is a reflection of the undermining of democracy and the popular reaction to it, not for the first time. There's been a long struggle, over centuries, in fact, to try to extend the realm of democratic freedoms, and it's won plenty of victories. A lot of them have been won exactly this way, not by gifts but by confrontation and struggle. If the popular reaction in this case takes a really organized, constructive form, it can undermine and reverse the highly undemocratic thrust of the international economic arrangements that are being foisted on the world. And they are very undemocratic. Naturally one thinks about the attack on domestic sovereignty, but most of the world is much worse. Over half the population of the world literally does not have even theoretical control over their own national economic policies. They're in receivership. Their economic policies are run by bureaucrats in Washington as a result of the so-called debt crisis, which is an ideological construction, not an economic one. That's over half the population of the world lacking even minimal sovereignty.

*Why do you say the debt crisis is an ideological construction?*

There is a debt, but who owes it and who's responsible for it is an ideological question, not an economic question. For example, there's a capitalist principle that nobody wants to pay any attention to, of course, which says that if I borrow money from you, it's my responsibility to pay it back, and if you're the lender, it's your risk if I don't pay it back. But nobody even conceives of that possibility. Suppose we were to follow that. Take, say, Indonesia, for example. Right now its economy is crushed by the fact that the debt is something like 140 percent of GDP. You trace that debt back, it turns out that the borrowers were something like 100 to 200 people around the military dictatorship that we supported, and their cronies. The lenders were international banks. A lot of that debt has been by now socialized through the IMF, which means Northern taxpayers are responsible. What happened to the money? They enriched themselves. There was some capital export and some development. But the people who borrowed the money aren't held responsible for it. It's the people of Indonesia who have to pay it off. And that means living under crushing austerity programs, severe poverty and suffering. In fact, it's a hopeless task to pay off the debt that they didn't borrow. What about the lenders? The lenders are protected from risk. That's one of the main functions of the IMF, to provide free risk insurance to people who lend and invest in risky loans. That's why they get high yields, because there's a lot of risk. They don't have to take the risk, because it's socialized. It's transferred in various ways to Northern taxpayers through the IMF and other devices, like Brady bonds. The whole system is one in which the borrowers are released from the responsibility. That's transferred to the impoverished mass of the population in their own countries. And the lenders are protected from risk. These are ideological choices, not economic ones.

In fact, it even goes beyond that. There's a principle of international law that was devised by the United States over a hundred years ago when it "liberated" Cuba, which means it conquered Cuba to prevent it from liberating itself from Spain in 1898. At that time, when the United States took over, it canceled Cuba's debt to Spain on the quite reasonable grounds that the debt was invalid since it had been imposed on the people of Cuba without their consent, by force, under a power relationship. That principle was later recognized in international law, again under U.S. initiative, as the principle of what's called "odious debt." Debt is not valid if it's essentially imposed by force. The Third World debt is odious debt. That's even been recognized by the U.S. representative at the IMF, Karen Lissaker, an international economist, who pointed out a couple of years ago that if we were to apply the principles of odious debt, most of the Third World debt would simply disappear.

*Newsweek had a cover story on December 13 called "The Battle of Seattle." It devoted some pages to the anti-WTO protests. There was a sidebar in one of the articles called "The New Anarchism." The five figures the sidebar mentioned as being somehow representative of this new anarchism included Rage Against the Machine and Chumbawamba. I don't suppose you know who they are.*

I know. I'm not that far out of it.

*They're rock bands. The list continues with the writer John Zerzan and Theodore Kaczynski, the notorious Unabomber, and then MIT professor Noam Chomsky. How did you figure into that constellation? Did Newsweek contact you?*

Sure. We had a long interview [chuckles].

*You're pulling my leg.*

You'd have to ask them. I can sort of conjure up something that might have been going on in their editorial offices, but your guess is as good as mine. The term "anarchist" has always had a very weird meaning in elite circles. For example, there was a headline in the Boston Globe today on a small article saying something like "Anarchists Plan Protests at IMF Meeting in April." Who are the anarchists who are planning the protest? Ralph Nader's Public Citizen, labor organizations and others. There will be some people around who will call themselves anarchists, whatever that means. But from the elite point of view, you want to focus on something that you can denounce in some fashion as irrational. That's the analogue to Thomas Friedman calling them flat-earthers.

*Vivian Stromberg of Madre, the New York-based NGO, says there are lots of motions in the country but no movement.*

I don't agree. What happened in Seattle was certainly movement. Students have been arrested in protests over failure of universities to adopt strong anti-sweatshop conditions many student organizations are proposing. There are lots of things going on that look like movement to me. In many ways what happened in Montreal a few weeks ago [at the Biosafety Protocol meeting] is even more dramatic than Seattle.

It wasn't much discussed here, because the main protesters were European. The United States was joined by a couple of other countries that would also expect to profit from biotechnology exports. But primarily it was the United States against most of the world over the issue that's called the "precautionary principle." That means, is there a right for a country, for people, to say, I don't want to be a subject in some experiment you're carrying out? The United States is insisting on exactly that, internationally. In the negotiations in Montreal, the United States, which is the center of the big biotech industries, genetic engineering and so on, was demanding that the issue be determined under WTO rules. According to those rules, the experimental subjects have to provide scientific evidence that it's going to harm them, or else the transcendent value of corporate rights prevails. Europe and most of the rest of the world insisted [successfully] on the precautionary principle. That's a very clear indication of what's at stake: an attack on the rights of people to make their own decisions over things even as simple as whether you're going to be an experimental subject, let alone controlling your own resources or setting conditions on foreign investment or transferring your economy into the hands of foreign investment firms and banks. It's a major assault against popular sovereignty in favor of concentration of power in the hands of a kind of state-corporate nexus, a few mega-corporations and the few states that primarily cater to their interests. The issue in Montreal in many ways was sharper and clearer than it was in Seattle.

# BLACK BLOCK INTERVIEW

*The following is an interview with an anarchist participant in the Seattle shutdown of the World Trade Organization demonstrations. For obvious reasons the interview subject is anonymous.*

*Active Transformation: First off what made you decide to go to Seattle?*

*Black Block*: I had a feeling it would be important. I remember reading about the WTO in an anarchist newspaper from Minneapolis called the Blast, probably four years ago...and it stuck with me as a pretty evil entity. I had not heard much of it since, until about a year before the Seattle demo. The various People's Global Action events, especially the J18 demos against the G8, had been very inspiring. I always felt like protests in the U.S. have always been disappointing, but the preparation for N30 seemed interesting. There was a sense from the beginning that it would be a mass event, even if not extremely militant. On the chance that it might be a massive protest against global capitalism, me and a few others decided to go. I had no reason to believe it would be so successful at disrupting the WTO's ability to function or even exist, at this point.

*Why do you think the protests were so successful?*

I think this was probably the most important event for the American Left in the last twenty-years. There have been large events, like the Gulf War protests, etc., but nothing that has been so diverse and interested in disrupting business as usual, and then been successful.

There were three main reasons the protests were so successful. The first reason was that there were hundreds of different organizations: labor, environmental, anarchist, students, women, anti-sweatshop — the whole spectrum. This alone didn't do it though. What made it powerful was that it was pretty much understood this was not going to be a passive, stand in the street and give speeches, appeal to the masters, kinda demo. It was well understood by all that it was going to be about disrupting the conference — and that is a big step for the American movement.

The second reason it was so successful was that the strategy developed through the Direct Action Network meetings the entire week was anarchism in action. The plan developed was based on affinity groups, which are small clusters of people who know each other, who have similar political goals or desires, etc. What we did was divide the downtown area into pie slices, with the convention center as ground zero. Then different affinity groups would take responsibility for different slices, and plan however they saw fit to cause disruption that would hinder the operation of the conference. This made police disruption utterly impossible. The cops could foresee very little since the strategy was so decentralized among closely knit groups.

The third, and most controversial reason, was that of the Black Block elevating the protest to a different extreme level. I am not saying that the Black Block was more radical or more politically advanced, but that the key to the success of the protest was the diversity of tactics, interrelating in a number of ways to cause disruption that was not policable.

*Could you talk a little bit about the anarchist Black Block?*

Before I do that I would like to mention that anarchists were not isolated in the Black Block. There were anarchists involved in every possible way. There were anarchist labor activists, puppeteers, non-violent lockdown blockaders, marching musicians, medics, communication people, media people, whatever — as well as a group of about two hundred in black masks who had prepared, also in affinity groups, to do as much symbolic physical damage to multi-national capitalism as possible.

I have seen Black Blocks used in protests in the U.S. a lot but never so successfully. It is important to note that the Black Block was not the result of some conspiracy. It too happened quite spontaneously, with people who came from all over the country with similar desires.

The day started with Black Block people in small groups making impromptu blockades with whatever was handy in the streets — dumpsters, newspaper boxes, warning tape, planters, among other things. In addition to this the black-clad anarchists supplemented attempts to make human blockades at the Sheraton Hotel, where there were many delegates, and across the street at the convention center. Where the pacifist lines were weak, the Black Block would fill in and create a second line, further away from the police. They would also surround delegates in the street and force them, non-violently, to alter course away from the hotels or the convention center. At one point a delegate pulled a handgun on protesters, at which point the protesters hit the deck, and the delegate was escorted through the police line, gun still in hand.

One false line that is being pushed by the mainstream media, as well as a lot of underground media, was that the violent police response was somehow caused by the property destruction. I would like to state that the police violence had begun by 9:00 a.m., in response to very successful street and door-way blockades, way before the window breaking began shortly after "Reclaim the Streets" at 11:00 a.m. They began with tear gas, rubber bullets, etc. The first window broken actually was when a tear gas grenade was shot through a store window.

There had been minor property "transformation" throughout the morning, and even the day before. It was mostly graffitti — on buses, cop cars, the Sheraton, etc. The day before N30 a protest at McDonalds, sponsored by French farmers, caused minor destruction to windows. It should have been a sign of what was to come.

When the large scale window breaking began it was quite awe-inspiring. All of a sudden people we were walking with pulled out all sorts of tools: nail pullers, hammers, crow bars. They then proceeded to very quickly knock windows out of every bank, upper-class or multi-national clothing store. I even saw a woman smashing an ATM machine with a sledge hammer. I was afraid at any moment a police tactical team would break through the crowd and violently assault the Black Block.

*On 60* Minutes *they put most of the emphasis on the anarchists from Eugene, OR. Do you think they are responsible for what happened?*

While I know they were there, the Black Block had a few hundred people in it. I know there were people there from all over the country. The Eugene people have just been very open about violent demo tactics. The 60 Minutes episode really does disfavor to revolutionary anarchism, in that it portrays all anarchists through the eyes and mouths of the primitivists — who in my mind make up a small minority of anarchist activists.

The primitivists put anti-technology and environmentalism at the forefront of their politics, and downplay, in my opinion, the real social and class struggle that has to take place. While the primitivist critique is useful, it ignores the liberatory aspects of technology. Without computers Seattle would not have happened the way it did. Also, drawing a line between the Unabomber and anarchism has serious marginalizing consequences.

*Could you talk a little bit about the police response to the events in Seattle?*

I would say that they messed up big time, way to our advantage. The first day they thought they would be effective by undermining what they thought to be our strategy of filling up the jails. They planned to make no arrests and just use plenty of non-lethal force. That non-lethal force just strengthened people's resolve to disrupt the conference. It also led a lot of people to move away from strict pacifism. It is easier to remain a pacifist if you've never felt the force of the State. When their [the police] strategy failed all they could do was try and maintain the police lines, which they had a lot of trouble with.

By the end of the first day a state of Civil Emergency had been declared and there was a lot of criticism of the more destructive activists. The police and the city had an opportunity to turn things around for themselves and they blew it. The cops went on a rampage for twenty-four hours indiscriminately attacking people all over the city. While they arrested a lot of activists for civil disobedience, the brunt of the force was directed against non-activist civilians. The police were already under a lot of heat for mishandling the day before. With the ensuing day of police rioting they had turned our struggle into a much more popular struggle, and the cops lost all respect.

*How do you view the other groups that were out there, like the environmental and labor groups?*

They were all critical to the success of the demonstration. It was the barrage from all sides that led to the all-consuming critique that has spread out across the country. Before N30 next to no one had heard of the WTO. And now almost everyone has heard of it and has a bad taste in their mouth about it. The coalition that shut down the WTO ministerial was extremely diverse and that is what made it powerful.

Even within the categories of labor and environmental groups there is a huge diversity. You go from Earth First! to the Sierra Club, and from the AFL-CIO to the Longshoremen. While the more liberal groups made it a mass event, the more radical groups transformed the day into a celebration of anti-capitalist disruption. The Longshoremen and Sheetmetal workers both broke with the labor marshalls' plan to divert the demos away from the action downtown. The Sheetmetal workers came and stood against the police lines and faced tear gas with the rest of us. Other unions did the same the next day.

*What meaning does Seattle have for the larger movement?*

I can only begin to answer this in a brief context. First off it provides evidence of at least two really important things: that there is a movement and that we can win. The graffitti on walls all over the city stated clearly

"We Are Winning!" By that evening when the state of civil emergency was declared the downtown had been completely altered — it felt like a revolution was underway — it was really powerful. I know that people came back to their cities totally energized to carry on the struggle.

We need these boosts. So often it feels like there is no hope for a better future. That has changed drastically for me. Another thing was that in talking with people over the next couple of days I got the impression that a good majority of the people who came out were new, young activists. That for me is really exciting. I am sure they have been totally empowered by the experience and will make our movement entirely more vibrant.

I think it is important that we build on the foundation of Seattle. We need to take advantage of this chance to dialogue between different groups. The chance for communication between labor, anarchist, and environmental groups is open to us all to learn and develop stronger ties. We must continue to push for strategies that challenge the power of business and State, not appeal to it.

We also need to root our struggles in the communities we live in and around issues of oppression and injustice that are everyday issues to people all around us. There has been a large critique among people of color that the largely white anti-WTO protesters mobilize against injustice around the world, but fail to connect with, prioritize, or even attempt to understand important struggles going on right here. That is one of the critical lessons we need to take to heart.

*So what can we look forward to next?*

Besides the plethora of local issues and projects we can get involved in there are a few potentially interesting things on the near horizon. In April the International Money Fund is having an international conference in D.C. It is questionably the WTO's bigger, eviller brother. People's Global Action has also called for the next big international day of action against global capitalism to be on May Day, May 1st this year. There are already plans in the works for events in Seattle, Detroit, Edmonton, Phoenix, London, and 'Shutdown Wall Street' in New York City, as well as a number of other cities around the world.

One critical thing to remember is that there are a number of people facing charges from the Seattle events, some of which are very serious. It is critical to the growth of a healthy radical movement that we do the necessary legal support to free these folks and get them back out in the streets with us.

# OPEN LETTER TO THE SEATTLE TRASHERS, THE UNIONS, THE PEACEFUL PROTESTERS, AND THE NON-VIOLENT RESISTERS

*Jim Campbell, Philippe Duhamel, Scott Weinstein, Bob Walter*

This critique will not deal with the moral or ethical questions of "peaceful protest" vs. destroying property. So far the major critiques of the trashing, and the defenses ("Black Block" and "Activists Show Support For Anarchists" by Ward Churchill, *et. al.*), have been political in nature. This will focus on tactics, strategy and consequences. It is written by older movement veterans who warn against repeating our past mistakes.

In so many ways, the carnival of resistance against the World Trade Organization scored an historic and amazing victory. First, tens of thousands of people were mobilized to participate in the direct actions and the marches despite the pro free trade propaganda from the media. The youth made us proud, and served notice to the ruling class. Secondly, there has been a broad-based unity of multiple sectors from Philippine indigenous peoples, to Canadian health care consumers, healthy food lovers, French farmers, environmentalists, the AFL-CIO, punks, grannies, students, etc. Historically, this unity between the unions and the broad based progressive movement in the U.S. is a needed break with the recent past of reactionary cold-war unionism. Thirdly, we have been

*Jim Campbell is editor of* The Bulldozer *and the* Prisoner News Service *(now defunct), and a former member of the Vancouver Five defense committee. Philippe Duhamel is an activist and trainer in civil disobedience who organizes for civil resistance against corporate globalization with Operation SalAMI. Scott Weinstein is a former member of* The Anarchist Black Dragon *prisoner newsletter,* The Vancouver Five defense committee, *and CISPES — The Committee In Solidarity with the People of El Salvador. Bob Walter is an activist.*

rapidly increasing consciousness about capitalism, globalism and free trade, while proposing alternatives towards a civil society that values global solidarity, eco-sustainability, and justice. Many of the forums leading up to Seattle, and the counter-summit in Seattle, were excellent and well attended. Fourth, the days of protests in Seattle proved that victory is possible with ordinary people who are creative and inspired; and that we can face our fears of State repression while doing ongoing direct action.

However, the actions of the few property destroyers, and the reactions from the majority protesters has emerged as our major controversy. (Strangely, there has been silence about the overwhelming whiteness of the direct-action participants, and little discussion about organizing strategies to move us forward.)

### Were the property trashers committing violence?

Violence is an act against living beings and the earth. Destruction and vandalism against corporations is simply that. Poverty is also violence as the victims are people, but corporations are not living beings.

The overwhelming violence during the protests came from the State sending the police to attack us with tear gas, pepper spray, concussion grenades and rubber bullets which incited a number of regular protesters and non-involved Seattle residents to throw bottles at the police, burn dumpsters and smash windows.

### Were the property trashers raising consciousness?

Not very much, and arguably some of the actions might have shut out good opportunities at consciousness raising. A net assessment of some of the window breaking and destruction at Gap, Nike, or Starbucks outlets has to take into account how some of these actions might have contributed to turn off average people from the crucial central message that these corporations are the real vandals and violators.

Also, the credibility of some of the actionists was destroyed by their own apparent lack of prior consciousness, such as the man wearing Nike shoes destroying a Nike sign, a fact the corporate media highlighted. Other types of action, such as creative redecoration or theater along with an invitation to boycott, could have done a lot more to sensitize the public to the crimes being committed by these corporations.

### Did the property destruction raise the profile of resistance against the WTO?

Yes, but probably only a small amount. The large and successful street blockades and union organized march, combined with the dramatic police response raised the resistance's profile way over the threshold. The trashing allowed media to replace coverage of mass mobilization with fringe vandalism.

### Did the property destruction raise the costs to free traders?

Not nearly as much as their fear from tens of thousands of ordinary people from various walks of uniting in a coherent and effective opposition.

### Are the unions and non-violent protestors hypocritical by complaining about the property trashers?

Some union leaders and peaceful demonstrators failed to differentiate between systemic and massive corporate/state violence, and retail property damage in the streets. Violence as defined by ruling elites (i.e., any attack on their privileges and property) has to be questioned. It is naive at best, and hypocritical at worst, to publicly denounce a few window smashers while ignoring the very real death and destruction rained on our sisters, brothers, and the earth's creatures by the corporations represented in downtown Seattle, and the nearby war lovers at Boeing, McDonald-Douglas, etc. Let's put some vandalism in perspective.

### Were the trashers exhibiting bravery in the face of police violence?

No. It was the street blockaders who were on the front lines, absorbing most of the police violence. Not only did they hold the blockades and prevent the WTO meetings on the first day, but their numbers increased ten fold. Their actions hark back to the civil-rights days of the brave SNCC (Student Non-Violent Coordinating Committee) resistance against lethal State brutality that so inspired broad public solidarity.

The property destroyers took advantage of the police's preoccupation with the direct-action blocking the WTO. They piggybacked their agenda, against the common agreed tactics and goals, onto the well organized day of resistance. This was done without consultation or agreement with the organizers. If the trashers had more courage, they could have done their action at a distant time afterwards.

### Are the property smashers advancing the revolutionary cause?

We must conclude the opposite. While they claim to be attacking corporate capitalism, what's a few broken windows now and then? It was a symbolic act at a time when symbolic action only showed our weakness. The complete blockade and marches proved we can act as a powerful mass movement — so let's take ourselves seriously.

The trashers have no possibility of toppling the powerful system by themselves. Revolutionary change will only come through massive public participation.

The smashers strategy refused tactical collaboration with the unions and the popular protesters. It is a thoughtless strategic blunder to anger and turn off potential allies in the unions, who are now becoming a major resource and force for social change, and it is even more thoughtless to alienate natural allies in the popular movement.

All successful revolutionary movements use a unified strategy, even if their tactics differ. The various elements are responsive to each other, and the dialectical needs at the time. A minority element that sabotages the struggle in the eyes of the majority, sabotages progress.

### Are the trashers police agents out to divide and discredit the movement?

It is an irresponsible charge by many unionists and veteran organizers to claim that the trashers are police agents. While we should not put it beyond police tactics to plant provocateurs (ample historic examples can be found, including COINTELPRO-like programs against various movements in the last few decades), there is yet no proof that any of them were under the control of the police. However, by confusing and pissing-off many in the movement, grabbing the lion's share of publicity, and sabotaging the organizers' message for the day of resistance, the smashers' actions could be considered consistent with some goals of agent provocateurs. We need to think and organize in ways that do not make us vulnerable to undercover tactics, while avoiding any kind of witch-hunts and speculations that can be very destructive for our organizations and mobilizations.

The ruling elite's goal is to divide and weaken us, while scaring away our supporters. The State treated the unions with kid gloves. Despite ample opportunity during the live-televised gassing and trashing during the evening, the police didn't arrest the trashers. Some maintain the police were purposefully stimulating and prolonging the trashing and gassing so the corporate media could show about how "dangerous" the protests were. Then they went after their real threat — the non-violent activists — arresting over five hundred during the next few days.

## Conclusion

We understand the rage and frustrations leading to the trashing. Our message is that strategy calls for much more than mere release of pent up emotions. Being political means going beyond symbolism and a personal need for catharsis. Self righteousness by both the non-violent and property trashing activists prevents clarity. It is vital that we in the popular resistance examine ours' and others' actions critically. What tactics and strategies are mobilizing people, and which ones are de-mobilizing?

In the Battle of Seattle, the organized trashing was tactically wrong. So was the union leadership's attempt to separate their marchers from the direct-action blockade. Fortunately the beauty and strength of the movement won the battle in spite of these blunders. To work together, we must respect each other. Keep your eyes on the prize.

*complied and edited by DIMITRIOS ROUSSOPOULOS*

# THE ANARCHIST PAPERS 2

The question of the individual and his/her freedom is looked at through the feminist-infused existentialism of L. Susan Brown, and then, by Janet Biehl, through a critical examination of the relationship between ecofeminism and deep ecology. Ron Sakolsky analyses the continuing relationship between production and consumption — "toiling to live that we may live to toil" —and where, in the scheme of things, this leaves cultural creativity.

The fundamental assumption of anarchist theory that political representation is neither possible nor desirable is addressed by William R. McKercher, by Thomas S. Martin, by Karl Hess, and by Marie Fleming. Most theorists would, however, allow for some form of representation, and by far the most mature statement of principles and programmatic objectives is that of the Vermont and New Hampshire Greens. *Toward a* New *Politics* offers a sound beginning and represents a continuity with the best of the 1960s new Left.

> *Some of the more interesting aspects of contemporary anarchism...useful to the social and political debate.* —Choice
>
> 192 pages
> Paperback ISBN:0-921689-36-5    $12.99
> Hardcover ISBN:0-921689-37-3    $41.99

# THE ANARCHIST PAPERS 3

George Woodcock's introduction to Kropotkin's monumental work on the French Revolution is followed by a piece by Brian Morris who raises the idea that the French Revolution was essentially not a permanent revolution but an unfinished one. Bruce Allen looks at Poland's new generation of oppositionists, Frank Harrison at the crisis of Soviet Statism, Raymond Wrabley at the conflicts inherent in neo-conservatism and social ecology, L. Susan Brown at the connection between feminism, anarchism and human freedom, and finally, the ideological position of a community disillusioned with a dictatorship is revealed through a selection of documents from witnesses to the Tiananmen Square massacre.

> *This collection further defines anarchist thought and practice in a modern environment...a stimulating compendium.* —Ottawa Citizen
>
> 211 pages
> Paperback ISBN: 0-921689-52-7    $12.99
> Hardcover ISBN: 0-921689-53-5    $41.99

DIMITRIOS ROUSSOPOULOS, editor, writer and economist, has written widely on international politics, democracy, social change and ecology. His most recent books are *Dissidence: Essays Against the Mainstream, Political Ecology,* and *The Public Place: Citizen Participation in the Neighbourhood and the City.*

*The history of anarchism in Portugal.*

# FREEDOM FIGHTERS
## Anarchist Intellectuals, Workers, and Soldiers in Portugal's History
### João Freire

*translated by Maria Fernanda Noronha da Costa e Sousa*

Some eighty years ago, Portugese libertarians were organized under the banner of syndicalism. This movement deeply marked the history of Portugal.

*Freedom Fighters* examines anarchist ideas and how these arrived in Portugal, and how the anarchist programme gained popularity with both the working class and intellectuals, people who believed in the slogan 'with neither God nor master.'

This fascinating history is traced from the beginning of the 20th century through the Spanish Civil War and the Second World War. The role of the anarchists during Salazer's dictatorship is examined with much previously unknown documentation. Of particular interest is the history of the anarchists during the 1974 'Carnation Revolution' and during Portugal's emergence as a contemporary liberal democracy.

> Freedom Fighters *is now, and will remain for a long time, a necessary book to any who look to do new research on the subject of anarchism.*
> —Miguel Serras Pereira, *Público*, Lisbon

*Freedom Fighters* fills a large gap in the history and sociology of Portugal. Much of the analysis and documentation presented in this important work will help the contemporary reader to understand Portugal today.

João Freire is a professor of Sociology at the University of Lisbon.

216 pages, photographs
Paperback ISBN:1-55164-138-0     $24.99
Hardcover ISBN:1-55164-139-9     $53.99

*complied and edited by DIMITRIOS ROUSSOPOULOS*

# RADICAL PAPERS

In this volume, Murray Bookchin, in a forty page critical, but affirmative review, focuses on the anarcho-syndicalist role during the fascist revolt in Spain. Other essays include a discussion on the limits of the peace movement; a detailed examination of the life and influence of Gustav Landauer killed during suppression of the 1919 Bavarian Soviet Republic; a refutation of alleged anarchist 'elitism'; a study of the relationship of Proudhon and Bakunin; a memorial to Lucy Parsons, widow of the man hanged in 1887 as one outcome of the Haymarket Affair that recalls her as one of the founders of the IWW who continued radically active into her eighties; and finally, an essay by Noam Chomsky wherein he shows that the only connection between socialism and the Soviet Union is that of contradiction.

> *Very good introductions...highly recommended. An interesting, and stimulating collection.* —Canadian Book Review Annual
>
> *A good read...pieces of our lives we would otherwise lose in the dust-heaps of history.* —Humanist in Canada

Contributors include: Murray Bookchin, Noam Chomsky, Russell Berman, Juan Gomez Casas, Tim Luke, Brian Martin, Arlene Meyers, Gary Prevost, William Reichert and Daniel Guérin.

> 160 pages
> Paperback ISBN: 0-920057-86-1     $12.99
> Hardcover ISBN: 0-920057-87-X     $41.99

# RADICAL PAPERS 2

Contains an essay by Noam Chomsky on the Reagan administration, describing the underpinnings of American foreign policy in Central America, that illustrate the contradictions within the U.S. doctrinal system; the theory of the ecological movement by Murray Bookchin; an examination of Canada-U.S. free trade by Gary Temple; a retrospective look at Edward Carpenter's socialism by William Reichert; the Barcelona women's bread riots of 1918 by Martha Ackelsberg; and a painstakingly argued contribution to feminist theory on the origins of male domination by Rosella Di Leo.

> *...attempts to make up the ground the left has lost...the essays...reflect a post-Reagan urgency in left-wing debates. Chomsky's excellent essay succeeds in underlining the paradoxes surrounding Reagan's vision of democracy in Central America.* —Kingston Whig-Standard

> 168 pages
> Paperback ISBN: 0-921689-12-8     $12.99
> Hardcover ISBN: 0-921689-13-6     $41.99

*Pays tribute to an anarchist tradition that continued in Weil, Camus and Sartre.*

# THE ANARCHISM OF JEAN GRAVE
## Editor, Journalist and Militant
Louis Patsouras

Jean Grave (1854-1939) was a leading French anarchist whose theoretical works and activity place him alongside such luminaries as William Godwin, Pierre-Joseph Proudhon, Michael Bakunin, and Peter Kropotkin. Drawing on various archival and library sources, Louis Patsouras traces the controversies and convictions that shaped the life and career of this extraordinary radical thinker, set within the fascinating socioeconomic context of Grave's time.

As editor of two newspapers, *Le Révolté* and *Les Temps Nouveaux*, Grave was able to pioneer the fusion of revolutionary politics and art: to effectively combine the cultural struggle with the social one, and to advocate his own anarchist ideal of a democratic society of self-managed worker collectives. This work covers many of the doctrinal controversies that characterized the various anarchist factions of Grave's day but it also extends into the broader realms of proletarian revolution, class struggle, and the vison of a new society.

*A classic piece of historical writing, easy to read and excellently researched.*
—William Fishman, University of London, UK

*A conscientious study of the history of French anarchism in general, and of Jean Grave, in particular.* —Dr. Jean Maitron, *Le Mouvement Social*

Louis Patsouras is Professor of History at Kent State University. His other published works include *Simone Weil and the Socialist Tradition*, *The Crucible of Socialism*, and *Debating Marx*.

204 pages
Paperback ISBN: 1-55164-184-4    $19.99
Hardcover ISBN: 1-55164-185-2    $48.99

BOOKS OF RELATED INTEREST BY

Anarchism and Ecology, *by Graham Purchase*
Bakunin: The Philosophy o f Freedom, *by Brian Morris*
Bakunin on Anarchism, *Sam Dolgoff, editor*
Canada and Radical Social Change, *Dimitrios Roussopoulos, editor*
Dissidence: Essays Against the Mainstream, *by Dimitrios Roussopoulos*
Ecology of Everyday Life, *by Chaia Heller*
Europe's Green Alternative, *by Penny Kemp, editor*
Fugitive Writings, *by Peter Kropotkin*
Legacy of the New Left, *by Dimitrios Roussopoulos*
Perspectives on Power, *by Noam Chomsky*
Politics of Social Ecology, *by Janet Biehl, Murray Bookchin*
Political Ecology, *by Dimitrios Roussopoulos*
Post-Scarcity Anarchism, *by Murray Bookchin*
Public Place, *by Dimitrios Roussopoulos*
Rethinking Camelot, *by Noam Chomsky*
Words of A Rebel, *by Peter Kropotkin*
Writers and Politics, *by George Woodcock*

send for a free catalogue of all our titles
BLACK ROSE BOOKS
C.P. 1258, Succ. Place du Parc
Montréal, Québec
H3W 2R3 Canada
or visit our web site at: http://www.web.net/blackrosebooks

To order books:
In Canada: (phone) 1-800-565-9523 (fax) 1-800-221-9985
email: utpbooks@utpress.utoronto.ca

In United States: (phone) 1-800-283-3572 (fax) 1-651-917-6406

In UK & Europe: (phone) London 44 (0)20 8986-4854 (fax) 44 (0)20 8533-5821
email: order@centralbooks.com

Printed by the workers of
MARC VEILLEUX IMPRIMEUR INC.
Boucherville, Québec
for Black Rose Books Ltd.